DATE DUE

State Names,
Seals, Flags,
and
Symbols

State Names, Seals, Flags, and Symbols

A HISTORICAL GUIDE

Benjamin F. Shearer and
Barbara S. Shearer

ILLUSTRATIONS BY

Jerrie Yehling Smith

Greenwood Press

NEW YORK
WESTPORT, CONNECTICUT
LONDON

Library of Congress Cataloging-in-Publication Data

Shearer, Benjamin F.
    State names, seals, flags, and symbols.

    Bibliography: p.
    Includes index.
    1. Names, Geographical—United States—States.
    2. Seals (Numismatics)—United States—States.
    3. Flags—United States—States.   4. Capitols.
    5. Mottoes.   6. State flowers—United States.
    7. State birds.   8. State songs—United States.
    9. United States—History, Local—Bibliography.
    I. Shearer, Barbara Smith.   II. Title.
    E155.S44   1987   973   86-27135
    ISBN 0-313-24559-2 (lib. bdg. : alk. paper)

Library of Congress Catalog Card Number: 86-27135
ISBN: 0-313-24559-2

First published in 1987

Greenwood Press, Inc.
88 Post Road West, Westport, Connecticut 06881

Printed in the United States of America

The paper used in this book complies with the
Permanent Paper Standard issued by the National
Information Standards Organization (Z39.48-1984).

10 9 8 7 6 5 4 3 2 1

Copyright Acknowledgments

    The authors and the publisher gratefully acknowledge permission to use excerpts from
the following copyright materials:
    Code Sections 50-3-1, 50-3-2, and 50-3-30 from State Seals-Georgia and State Flags-
Georgia. Copyright © 1985 by the State of Georgia. Reprinted with permission of the Code
Revision Commission.
    State Statutes in the annotated codes published by the West Publishing Company, St.
Paul, Minnesota.
    Statutory material from the Alaska Statutes publication.
    Permission for the publication of certain sections of Tennessee Code Annotated was
granted by the State of Tennessee.
    Permission to use portions of certain state codes was granted by The Michie Company,
Charlottesville, Virginia.
    To all 50 states, we express our gratitude for the use of their flag and seal illustrations.
The flags and seals of certain states are provided courtesy of: the Alabama Bureau of
Tourism and Travel, the Michigan Travel Bureau, Montana Travel Promotion, New Jersey
Travel and Tourism, New Mexico Department of Tourism, and the Oklahoma Department
of Libraries. The flags for Alaska and Maryland were provided courtesy of the Alaska
Division of Tourism and Maryland Tourism, respectively.

Contents

Introduction

This work presents a single, up-to-date, documented source for state names and officially designated symbols. Not since George Shankle's pioneering effort, *State Names, Flags, Seals, Songs, Birds, Flowers, and Other Symbols,* revised in 1938, has a new reference source with current information been available.

Much, of course, has changed since 1938. Alaska and Hawaii have since joined the Union, new statehouses have been built, and new symbols have been designated. Some old symbols of statehood have fallen by the wayside; still others have been refurbished and redesigned to give them a modern look. In 1938, no state could boast a state insect, fish, dog, or cat; however, today such special state symbols have become quite common.

State Names, Seals, Flags, and Symbols brings together current information on the origin of state names, officially designated state symbols, and a selected bibliography of general state histories. Chapter 1 discusses the naming of the states as well as the origin of some more popular state nicknames. The origin of state mottoes and a description of state seals are presented in Chapters 2 and 3. The state flags are described in Chapter 4. Chapter 5 presents descriptive information on state capitols. State flowers, trees, and birds are the subjects of Chapters 6 through 8. Chapter 9 lists the officially designated state songs, marches, and folk songs. Chapter 10 lists the myriad, miscellaneous symbols designated by the states and the Bibliography, the state histories that have stood the test of time or represent solid new research. The states are listed alphabetically in each chapter of this book.

State publications and state codes have provided much of the documentation for state symbols and other official designations. State libraries and secretary of state offices throughout the country were extremely cooperative and helpful in supplying state publications as well as unpublished sources.

The Michie Company, West Publishing Company, Banks-Baldwin Publishing Company, and Equity Publishing Corporation graciously granted permission to quote the text of flag and seal descriptions from the state codes they publish. States holding copyright of their own codes were likewise gracious in granting their permissions. Permission for the publication of certain sections of Tennessee Code Annotated was granted by the State of Tennessee.

United States government publications also provided rich sources of descriptive material. John P. Harrington's extensive scholarship on the origin of state names, found in the *Annual Report of the Smithsonian Institution, 1954*, summarizes years of debate on many names and convincingly discards some long-held misinformation. *The Yearbook of Agriculture, 1949* provided descriptive information on state trees. *Bulletins of the United States Museum*, numbers 50, 107, 113, 121, 162, 174, 176, 179, 191, 195, 196, 211, and 237 provided behavioral and descriptive information on state birds.

Full information concerning state songs, marches, and folk songs was beyond the scope of the present volume. However, work is under way on a volume which will provide lyrics, melodies, and other information about these pieces.

State Names,
Seals, Flags,
and
Symbols

1 | State Names and Nicknames

The names of the states taken all together honor the important players in the early exploration and history of the nation. Georgia, the Virginias, the Carolinas, New Jersey, New Hampshire, and Maryland, among others, were named by the English. Maine, Vermont, and Louisiana were named by the French. The Spanish left their names to Florida, Colorado, California, Nevada, and Texas. The Dutch were responsible for naming Rhode Island. The United States honored the first president when it created the state of Washington and the Native Americans displaced by the country's westward expansion when it named Indiana. In fact, the majority of state names are derived from Indian names. From the Choctaw in Alabama, to the Aleuts in Alaska, to the Massachusetts on the East Coast, Indian tribes left their mark on the naming of the states.

Nicknames for the states have come out of particular incidents and events or in an effort to promote state industries, businesses, and tourism. The nicknames listed below are those that have stood the test of time and illustrate some historical or economic fact. Not included here are the many slogans devised by the states to promote a particular industry or image.

Alabama

The Alabama River was named after the Indian tribe that was settled in central Alabama when early European explorers first arrived there. The state received its name from the river. The name Alabama first occurs in chronicles of DeSoto's 1540 expedition, spelled variously Alibamu, Limamu, and Alibamo. Numerous other variant spellings were set down by English, French, and Spanish explorers.[1]

The origin of the name Alabama is probably in two Choctaw words. "Alba" in Choctaw means vegetation, herbs, plants, or weeds. "Amo" means a gatherer, picker, or shearer. It was not unusual that a tribe would accept a descriptive name from a contiguous tribe. The description "vegetation gatherers" was appropriate for the Alabama Indians, who cleared land for agricultural purposes.[2]

While the state of Alabama has no officially adopted nickname, Alabamians proudly display the nickname "The Heart of Dixie" on their license plates. Alabama is also known as the Yellowhammer State. The state bird is the yellowhammer, chosen because of the color of the uniforms of a company of Alabama confederate soldiers. The NASA-Marshall Space Flight Center in Huntsville has provided Alabama with another nickname—The Pioneer Space Capital of the World.

Alaska

Alaska is taken directly from the Aleut "aláxsxaq," meaning "the object toward which the action of the sea is directed," or the mainland.[3] Alaska was known as Russian America until its purchase by the United States in 1867. The Russians had used the term Alaska to refer only to the Alaskan peninsula. The name was appropriated by the United States to refer first to the Territory of Alaska and then to the state.[4]

The American purchase of Alaska, negotiated by Secretary of State William Seward, gave Alaska two of its first American nicknames—Seward's Folly and Seward's Ice Box. While obviously meant to be derisive, Seward's purchase of Alaska for $7,200,000 has proved a fine investment. Alaska has also been spoken of more fondly as the Land of Midnight Sun and America's Last Frontier.

Arizona

The name Arizona is derived from two words in the Papago Indian dialect of the Pima language—"Aleh-zon," which means "little spring." Spaniards used the term as early as 1736. The springs, now located in Mexican territory, are near a large silver find made in 1735 in the Arizona Creek. Arizona was chosen as the territorial name, in part owing to Charles D. Poston. Poston was a mining speculator who claimed to have first suggested the name Arizona in a petition to Congress to make Arizona a territory.[5]

Arizona is known as the Copper State because of its large copper production and as the Apache State because of the large number of Apache Indians who once lived there. Arizona's most familiar nickname today is the Grand Canyon State.

Arkansas

The pronunciation of the word Arkansas is actually prescribed by an 1881 state statute. Although Arkansas is actually another form of Kansas, the Arkansas legislature declared that the correct pronunciation of the three-syllable word should have the final "s" silent, all "a's" with the Italian sound, and the accent on the first and third syllables. This pronunciation follows from the fact that Arkansas was first written in French, as Frenchmen tried to record the sounds they heard from native American Indians.[6] The Kansas Indians are a tribe of the Sioux. Fr. Marquette first used the word Arkansas in a 1673 map.[7]

Arkansas has many nicknames, including the Bowie State and the Toothpick State, which refer to Bowie knives and to the handles for them. The Hot Water State is a nickname that refers to the hot springs in the state.[8] Arkansas also has an officially designated nickname: The Land of Opportunity.[9] The slogan "Arkansas Is a Natural" is also used to promote recreation and tourism.[10]

California

California was an island filled with gold in an early sixteenth century novel, *Las Sergas de Esplandian* by Garcia Ordonez de Montalvo. Although the eleventh century *Song of Roland* mentions a capital city called Califerne, it is most probable that Spanish explorers Ortuno Ximenez and Hernando Cortez were familiar with the contemporary Spanish novel and drew their inspiration for naming California, which they thought to be an island, from Montalvo's book. By 1541, California had become an established place name and location on the maps.[11]

Although several slogans have been used by the state of California over the years to promote business and tourism, the only official nickname, designated by the California legislature in 1968, is The Golden State.[12] This nickname was chosen not only in reference to the discovery of gold in 1848, but also to the fields of yellow poppies that bloom in California in the spring.[13]

Colorado

The Pike's Peak Region, land attained originally from the Louisiana Purchase, Mexican cession, and Texas, became the Colorado Territory soon after gold was discovered near Denver. A number of names were suggested for the territory, including Osage, Idaho, Jefferson, and Colona; however, the name Colorado, Spanish for red, referring to the color of the Colorado River whose headwaters lie within the boundaries of the state, was chosen over the others. Local native Indians from a number of tribes had referred to the river's color in naming it even before the Spanish arrived.[14]

Colorado is known as the Centennial State because it attained statehood in 1876, the one-hundred-year anniversary of the signing of the Declaration of Independence. It is also known as the Highest State and the Switzerland of America for its elevation and mountainous terrain. Many slogans have also been used over the years to promote skiing and tourism in Colorado.

Connecticut

The name Connecticut was clearly established in the early seventeenth century as applied to the Connecticut River.[15] The native Indian word "Quinnehtukqut" was translated into the current English spelling and means "beside the long tidal river."[16]

In 1959, the Connecticut legislature officially adopted the nickname The Constitution State[17] because Connecticut was the first of all the states to have a written constitution. Connecticut is also known unofficially as the Nutmeg State, not because the state produces the spice in large quantities, but because its early citizens were so skilled and industrious that they could make and sell wooden nutmegs.[18]

Delaware

The state of Delaware and the Delaware Indians are both named after the Delaware River. The Delaware River was named by the English after Sir Thomas West, Lord de la Warr, who was the Virginia Company's first governor.[19]

Delaware was the first state to ratify the United States Constitution, thus earning it the nickname the First State. Delaware is also known as the Diamond State, a sobriquet originated by Thomas Jefferson, who referred to Delaware as like a diamond—small but of great value.[20]

Florida

Florida was named for the day on which it was discovered by Spanish explorer Ponce de Leon. On Easter Sunday in 1513, de Leon named the new land La Florida in honor of Pascua Florida, the Spanish Feast of the Flowers at Eastertime.[21]

Florida has a number of nicknames owing to its geographical location and the importance of tourism. Florida is commonly known as the Sunshine State. It is also called the Alligator State, the Everglades State, and the Southernmost State for obvious reasons. The Orange State is still another nickname that acknowledges the importance of the citrus industry to Florida's economy.

Georgia

Georgia was founded in 1733 by James Oglethorpe, who had been granted a charter by King George II in 1732 to found a colony named after the king. Oglethorpe carried out the terms of the charter by naming the last of the thirteen British colonies in America Georgia.[22]

The state of Georgia has no officially designated nickname, although it recognizes the use of several unofficial nicknames. Georgia is known as the Peach State and the Goober State for the importance of peaches and peanuts in the state's agricultural economy. Two nicknames refer to the determination and will of Georgia's citizens to lead the South in industrial and economic development—the Empire State of the South and the Yankee-land of the South. Georgia is also known as the Cracker State and the Buzzard State. Crackers, originally a derogatory term meaning braggarts, was the term used to describe immigrants into Georgia who came from the mountains of Virginia and North Carolina. The Buzzard State refers to the fact that buzzards were once protected by law in Georgia.[23]

Hawaii

Captain James Cook named the islands he discovered in 1778 the Sandwich Islands in honor of his patron, the Earl of Sandwich. By 1819, however, King Kamehameha I had united the formerly independent islands under his rule in the Kingdom of Hawaii. In 1893, Hawaii became a republic and a territory in 1898 when the islands were annexed by the United States. Statehood came in 1959.

The name Hawaii itself is said to have come from the traditional discoverer of the islands, Hawaii Loa. Another explanation is that Hawaii means a small or new homeland. "Hawa" means a traditional homeland, and "-ii" means both small and raging. The latter meaning may refer to Hawaii's volcanoes.[24]

The state of Hawaii recognized the Aloha State as its official popular name in a 1959 legislative act.[25] Hawaii is also known unofficially as the Pineapple State for its extensive pineapple industry, the Paradise of the Pacific for its natural beauty, and the Youngest State because it is the last state to join the Union.

Idaho

Contrary to long-held common belief, Idaho is not a Shoshone word meaning "gem of the mountains." In fact, the name Idaho was invented by George M. Willing, who unsuccessfully sought to become a delegate from what would become the territory of Colorado. The more traditional name of Colorado was maintained when Colorado became a territory, partly because the name Idaho was discovered to have been a coined term. Nevertheless, the name Idaho took hold in settlements such as Idaho Springs and gold discoveries on the Salmon and Clearwater Rivers known as the Idaho mines. Even a Columbia River steamship was christened *The Idaho*. In 1863,

Congress designated the Idaho Territory with the erroneous understanding that Idaho meant "gem of the mountains," while Montana, another name proposed for the territory, was said to mean nothing.[26] In spite of the misunderstanding concerning the origin of the name Idaho, the state of Idaho continues to be known as the Gem State and the Gem of the Mountains.

Illinois

When La Salle traveled up the Illinois River in 1679, he named it after the native Americans he found living along its banks. Illinois is a French spelling for the Illinois and Peoria Indian word " 'ilini," the plural of which is " 'iliniwok," meaning a man or a warrior and also possibly a member of the Illinois tribe.[27]

The Illinois legislature officially adopted "Land of Lincoln" as its slogan in 1955, referring to Illinois as the state where Abraham Lincoln began his political career.[28] Illinois is also known unofficially as the Prairie State, a fitting sobriquet for a state that sets aside the third full week of September each year as Illinois Prairie Week "to demonstrate the value of preserving and reestablishing native Illinois prairies."[29] The Corn State is another fitting nickname for Illinois, owing to the importance of that crop to the state's agricultural economy.

Indiana

The United States Congress created the name Indiana, meaning "Land of the Indians," when it created the Indiana Territory out of the Northwest Territory in 1800.[30]

"Crossroads of America" was designated by the Indiana legislature as the state's official motto or slogan.[31] Indiana is popularly known, however, as the Hoosier State. The origin of the term Hoosier is unclear. It may be a corruption of the terse pioneer question "Who's here?" Another explanation has it that the men who worked for an Indiana contractor, Sam Hoosier, became known as Hoosiers. Still another explanation is that the term Hoosier is a corruption of "husher," a term applied to early riverboat workers who could hush anyone with brute force.[32]

Iowa

The Iowa District was the name of the territory of Wisconsin west of the Mississippi. The district became first a territory and then, in 1846, a state. The Iowa River was named for the Iowa Indians who inhabited the area, and the name of the state was derived from the river. The tribal name

" 'Ayuxwa" means "one who puts to sleep." The French spelled Iowa as Ayoua and the English, as Ioway.[33]

Iowa's most enduring but unofficial nickname, the Hawkeye State, was first suggested in an 1838 newspaper article by James G. Edwards as a tribute to Chief Black Hawk. Black Hawk had come back to Iowa to die after his release from prison, where he had served a sentence for fighting the encroachment of white settlers on Indian land.[34]

Kansas

Kansas is the French spelling of the Kansas, Omaha, Kaw, Osage, and Dakota Sioux Indian word "KaNze." In the language of the Kansas, the word Kansas means the "south wind." The tribal name was applied to the Kansas River and also to the territory occupied by the tribe.[35]

Kansas has several nicknames that describe its history, resources, and weather. Kansas was known at one time as "Bleeding Kansas," an apt appellation for pre-Civil War Kansas and the carnage that occurred there at the time. In a sense, Kansas was a precursor of things to come as the United States was about to embark on civil war. Kansas is also called the Squatter State for the squatters who settled the new territory. The Cyclone State is a nickname that calls to mind the worst of Kansas weather; the Sunflower State calls to mind the wild sunflowers of the plains, the official flower of the state. Finally, Kansas is called the Jayhawk State for the unruly irregulars and pillagers who first occupied the Kansas borders. Kansas soldiers came to be known as a result as Jayhawkers.[36]

Kentucky

The name Kentucky, the Wyandot word for "plain," referring to the central plains of the state, was first recorded in 1753. Kentucky, which had been a province of Virginia, became a territory in 1790, a state in 1792.[37]

Kentucky is commonly nicknamed the Bluegrass State, in spite of the fact that it is officially a commonwealth. Bluegrass is actually green, but its bluish-purple buds, when seen from afar, give a field of bluegrass a bluish tint.[38] Kentucky is also nicknamed for two crops that have figured in its economic history—the Hemp State and the Tobacco State. Finally, Kentucky has been called the Dark and Bloody Ground, a nickname passed down by Daniel Boone from an Indian chief to describe the battles Indians and whites fought in Kentucky.[39]

Louisiana

In 1682, explorer Sieur de La Salle was the first European to descend the Mississippi River all the way to its delta. He named the area he discovered

La Louisianne after Louis XIV of France. The state of Louisiana was carved out of the New Orleans Territory, which was only a portion of the Louisiana Purchase.[40]

Nicknames for Louisiana are plentiful and descriptive. Louisiana is known as the Bayou State for its numerous bayous and the Fisherman's Paradise for the variety of excellent fishing available in the state. The Child of the Mississippi is a nickname that describes the state's geological origin. The Sugar State is a tribute to Louisiana's sugar industry, and the Pelican State is a tribute to the state bird, the brown pelican, which is native to Louisiana.[41]

Maine

The origin of the name Maine is uncertain. French colonists may have named the area after the French province of Mayne. "Main" was also a common term among early explorers to describe a mainland.[42]

The state of Maine recognizes the nickname the Pine Tree State. The white pine is the state tree and Maine possesses 17 million acres of forest.[43] Maine is also known as the Lumber State for its lumber industry and as the Border State for its geographical position below Canada. The Old Dirigo State refers to the state's motto "Dirigo," which means "I lead" or "I direct."[44]

Maryland

When Lord Baltimore received the charter for the colony from Charles I of England, it contained the proviso that the colony be named Maryland in honor of Charles I's wife, Queen Henrietta Maria, who was popularly known as Queen Mary.[45]

Maryland is known as the Free State and the Old Line State. The first of these nicknames originated in 1923. Hamilton Owens, editor of the *Baltimore Star*, coined the term after Maryland refused to pass an enforcement act for Prohibition. He continued to use the nickname in his editorials. The second nickname, by some accounts, was created by George Washington in praise of Maryland's regular line troops who served well in many Revolutionary War skirmishes.[46]

Massachusetts

Massachusetts was named after the Massachusetts Indian tribe, which populated the Massachusetts Bay region before Columbus first arrived in the New World. Massachusetts means "large hill place." The tribe was named after Great Blue Hill, which lies south of Milton.[47]

Massachusetts Bay lends the state two common nicknames—the Bay State and the Old Bay State. Massachusetts' early settlers were responsible for two more nicknames—the Pilgrim State and the Puritan State. The Old Colony State is a nickname that refers to the original Plymouth Colony. Finally, the Puritan practice of serving baked beans for Sunday meals gives Massachusetts the nickname the Baked Bean State.[48]

Michigan

The name Michigan first appeared in written form in 1672 in connection with a clearing on the west side of the lower peninsula. In Chippewa, the word "majigan" means "clearing." European explorers named Lake Michigan after the clearing. The attribution of Michigan's name to the Chippewa word "micigami," meaning "large water," is not accurate.[49]

Michigan has long been known as the Wolverine State for the large numbers of wolverines that once roamed the peninsula. The Great Lakes that surround Michigan lend it the nicknames the Lake State and the Lady of the Lake. Michigan's extensive auto industry, centered in Detroit, also gives Michigan another nickname, the Auto State.[50]

Minnesota

The state of Minnesota received its name from the Minnesota River in southern Minnesota. The Dakota word "mnishota" means "cloudy" or "milky water."[51]

Minnesota is known as the North Star State; its motto is translated from the French as the "Star of the North." Although having many more lakes than the nickname suggests, Minnesota is also called the Land of 10,000 Lakes. Minnesota is nicknamed the Gopher State for the many gophers that roamed its prairies and also the Bread and Butter State for its extensive production of wheat and dairy products.[52]

Mississippi

The state of Mississippi is named after the Mississippi River, although the river itself has had a number of names throughout history. Indians on the Gulf Coast called the river Malabouchia. Spaniards called it Rio del Espiritu Santo and Rio Grande del Florida during the sixteenth and seventeenth centuries. The French called it the Colbert River after La Salle explored it and then, after the founding of the colony at Fort Maurepas in 1699, the St. Louis River. Mississippi, the name given the river by Northwest Indians visited by La Salle and Marquette, is the name that finally won out. La Salle's map of 1695 actually uses the name Mississippi. Mississippi, contrary to common opinion, means "large river" in Chippewa, not "the father of waters."[53]

Mississippi is nicknamed the Magnolia State for the state flower and tree and the abundance of magnolias in the state. The state coat-of-arms, which depicts an American eagle, lends the nicknames the Eagle State and the Border-Eagle State to Mississippi. The numerous bayous in Mississippi, like Louisiana, lend the nickname the Bayou State to Mississippi. Finally, Mississippi is known as the Mud-cat State for the catfish that are abundant throughout the state's streams and swamps.[54]

Missouri

The Missouri Territory was named for the Missouri River, which, in turn, was named for the Missouri Indians. The earliest use of the word in writing occurs on the Marquette map of 1673. The Missouri, a small tribe, lived along the Missouri River with the Illinois to the east and the Little Osage to the west. The name means "canoe haver."[55]

The state of Missouri is commonly known as the Show Me State, a nickname attributed to Representative Willard Vandiver of Missouri. It connotes a certain self-deprecating stubbornness and devotion to simple common sense. Another politician, Thomas Hart Benton, gave Missouri the nickname the Bullion State for his advocacy of hard money, that is, gold and silver. Missouri is also called the Cave State for its numerous caves and caverns open to the public, the Lead State for its lead production, and the Ozark State for the Ozark Mountains in southern Missouri.[56]

Montana

Montana's name is derived from the Latin word *montaanus* meaning "mountainous." Montana Territory was created in 1864 out of Idaho Territory.[57]

Montana is popularly known as the Big Sky Country, an allusion to its immense area of mountains and valleys. The Stub Toe State, another nickname, refers to the state's mountainous terrain. The Bonanza State and the Treasure State refer to the importance of mining in Montana. "Naturally Inviting Montana" is a slogan used to promote Montana tourism.[58]

Nebraska

The state of Nebraska is actually named after the Platte River, a French name meaning "broad river." The Omaha Indians called the river Nibôápka, or "broad river." When Fremont was in Nebraska in 1842, he first used the word Nebraska in reference to the Platte River, and this name was applied to the territory created in 1854.[59]

Nebraska has had two official nicknames. In 1895, the legislature designated Nebraska as the Tree Planters' State because it is "preeminently a tree planting state."[60] In 1945, the legislature changed Nebraska's official nickname to the Cornhusker State in recognition of Nebraska football.[61] Nebraska is also unofficially nicknamed the Antelope State for the herds of antelope that once roamed its territory and the Bug-eating State for its numerous bull bats, which eat insects.[62]

Nevada

Seventeenth and eighteenth century Spanish sailors traveling between the Philippines and Mexico saw mountain ranges in California from out at sea. They named these mountains Sierra Nevada or "snowy range." When a new territory was designated out of Utah, it was decided to name it Sierra Nevada, but the territory was named simply Nevada in 1859.[63]

Nevada is nicknamed the Sage State and the Sagebrush State for the wild sage that grows there prolifically. It is also known as the Silver State and the Mining State for its silver mines. Because Nevada was admitted to the Union in 1864 while the Civil War was raging, it has the additional nickname of the Battle Born State.[64]

New Hampshire

Captain John Mason of the Royal Navy received a grant in 1629 for the part of the land that became the state of New Hampshire. He named the area New Hampshire after the central English county of Hampshire, where he had spent a number of years of his youth.[65]

New Hampshire is nicknamed the Granite State for its extensive granite formations and quarries and the White Mountain State for the range of that name in northern New Hampshire. New Hampshire's mountains also lend it the nickname of the Switzerland of America. The mountains, which spawn five of New England's rivers, lend New Hampshire still another name, The Mother of Rivers.[66]

New Jersey

New Jersey was named after the island of Jersey in the English Channel by Sir John Berkeley and Sir George Carteret. Berkeley and Carteret obtained a royal charter for this colony. Carteret was born on the island of Jersey and had been its lieutenant governor.[67]

New Jersey is known as the Garden State for its truck farms which provide produce to nearby cities and as the Clam State for the clams taken in off its coast. The Camden and Amboy State is an old nickname that recalls the influence of the Camden and Amboy Railroad in New Jersey. Two other nicknames are derived from an even earlier period: the Jersey Blue State recalls the blue uniforms of the New Jersey soldiers in the Revolutionary

War,[68] and the Pathway of the Revolution recalls the many battles fought on New Jersey soil in the American Revolution.[69]

New Mexico

The upper region of the Rio Grande was called "Nuevo Mexico" as early as 1561 by Fray Jacinto de San Francisco in the hope that this area would hold the riches of Mexico. Mexico, which is the Aztec spelling, means "place of Mexìtli," one of the Aztec gods. When New Mexico came under American control, the Spanish name was anglicized.[70]

New Mexico is nicknamed the Cactus State for the numerous cacti that grow there and the Spanish State in honor of its history as a Spanish-speaking state.[71] While New Mexico has an official slogan for business, commerce, and industry—"Everybody Is Somebody in New Mexico"—the sobriquet the Land of Enchantment adorns automobile license plates and is used frequently in the state publications that promote tourism.[72]

New York

When the British took over New Amsterdam from the Dutch in 1664, the city's new name was proclaimed to be New York in honor of the brother of England's Charles II, the Duke of York and Albany. The Dutch Colony was called New Netherlands, but New York became the name of both the city and the state.[73]

New York is commonly nicknamed the Empire State for its wealth and variety of resources. It is also known as the Excelsior State because the state motto is *Excelsior*. New York is also called the Knickerbocker State in reference to the breeches worn by early Dutch settlers.[74]

North Carolina

North Carolina and South Carolina were one colony until they were divided in 1729. Carolina was originally named in honor of France's Charles IX and then in honor of England's Charles I and Charles II, both of whom made grants of Carolina. Carolina is the feminine form of the Latin word *Caroliinus*, an adjective derived from the name *Carolus*, or Charles.[75]

North Carolina is known as the Old North State in reference to its separation from South Carolina in 1729. It has also been called the Turpentine State for its large production of turpentine. Possibly the most familiar nickname of North Carolina, however, is the Tarheel State. Originally a derisive term, "tarheels" is said to have been a name given to North Carolina Civil War soldiers by soldiers from Mississippi when the Carolina soldiers were routed from a position on a hill. They had forgotten to "tar their heels" and could not maintain their position.[76] Today the term has lost its derogatory inference.

North Dakota

The Dakotas were divided into North and South Dakota by an omnibus bill passed in 1889.[77] Dakota is a Sioux word meaning "friends" or "allies." When Dakota Territory was created in 1861, it was named for the Dakota tribe which inhabited the region.[78]

North Dakota recognizes two nicknames. The Sioux State is a nickname that recognizes the Dakota tribe, also called the Sioux. The Flickertail State is a nickname referring to the flickertail squirrel which inhabits North Dakota. North Dakota is also sometimes called the Land of the Dakotas.[79]

Ohio

The state of Ohio is named after the Ohio River. The French explorer La Salle noted as early as 1680 that the Iroquois called the river "Ohio," meaning "large" or "beautiful river."[80]

Ohio is commonly called the Buckeye State for the buckeye trees that grow abundantly in the state and for an incident that occurred in 1788 when a very tall Colonel Sproat led a procession to a fort and the onlooking Indians, impressed by his stature, referred to him as "Big Buckeye." Ohio is also sometimes referred to as the Mother of Modern Presidents, having spawned seven American presidents.[81]

Oklahoma

The word Oklahoma first appears in the 1866 Choctaw-Chickasaw Treaty. Allen Wright, a native American missionary who spoke Choctaw, made up the word by combining two Choctaw words: " 'ukla" or person and "humá" or red. Oklahoma therefore means "red person."[82]

Oklahoma is known as the Sooner State and as the Boomer's Paradise. Both of these nicknames derive from the opening of the Oklahoma Territory for settlement in 1889. Boomers were those who came in hordes to settle the new land and sooners were those who illegally entered the territory to stake claims before the designated date and time.[83]

Oregon

The origin of the name Oregon is unclear. There are at least three possibilities, each quite different. Oregon may come from the French Canadian word "ouragan" meaning "storm" or "hurricane." The Columbia River was probably at one time called "the river of storms" by Canadian fur traders. Another possibility is that the name Oregon comes from the Spanish word "orejon" or "big-ear." This term was applied to a number of tribes of the region. Still another possibility is that the name of Oregon comes from the Spanish word "orégano" or wild sage, which was corrupted to Oregon. Sage grows abundantly in eastern Oregon.[84]

Oregon is known as the Beaver State because the beaver has been declared the state animal and is depicted on the state flag and as the Web-foot State in reference to its abundant rainfall. The Hard-case State is a nickname that was given to Oregon because of the difficulties encountered by early settlers.[85]

Pennsylvania

When William Penn was granted a charter in 1680 by England's Charles II, the king gave the name Pennsylvania to the land. *Sylvania* is Latin for woods or woodland and, thus, Pennsylvania means "Penn's woods."[86]

Pennsylvania is sometimes called the Quaker State in reference to William Penn's religious affiliation and the Quakers who settled the state.[87] More commonly, Pennsylvania is nicknamed the Keystone State. Although the origin of this nickname has been lost, it was used and accepted by the turn of the eighteenth century. The term probably refers to Pennsylvania's geographical location in the original thirteen colonies that straddled the Atlantic Ocean.[88]

Rhode Island

When Dutch explorer Adrian Block came upon an island with red clay shores, he named it in his native tongue "Roodt Eylandt," meaning "red island." Under English rule, the name was anglicized in the then current spelling.[89]

Rhode Island's status as the smallest state lends it the nicknames Little Rhody and the Smallest State. Roger Williams, who founded Providence Plantation in 1636, is honored by the sobriquet the Land of Roger Williams. Rhode Island, whose full name is actually The State of Rhode Island and Providence Plantations, is also known as the Plantation State. Finally, Rhode Island uses the nickname the Ocean State to promote tourism.[90]

South Carolina

The Carolinas were originally named in honor of Charles IX of France and then in honor of Charles I and Charles II of England. The Carolinas were divided into north and south in 1729.[91]

South Carolina's rice production lends it the nicknames the Rice State and the Swamp State. Its shape, that of a wedge, gives it the nickname of the Keystone of the South Atlantic Seaboard. The Iodine State is a nickname that refers to the iodine content of South Carolina plants, and the Palmetto State refers to South Carolina's state tree, the palmetto.[92]

South Dakota

The Dakota Territory was named for the Dakota tribe that inhabited the region. The territory was divided into north and south in 1889. Dakota is a Sioux word meaning "friends" or "allies."[93]

South Dakota recognizes two nicknames: the Sunshine State and the Coyote State.[94] The former nickname is frequently used in state publications promoting tourism, and the latter nickname refers to South Dakota's large population of coyotes.[95] South Dakota has also been called the Blizzard State for its severe winter weather and the Artesian State for its artesian wells.[96]

Tennessee

The original form of the name Tennessee was the Cherokee name "Tanasi." The Cherokee called two villages on the Little Tennessee River "Tanasi." The river was named after the villages and the region after the river. The meaning of the Cherokee name is unknown.[97]

Tennessee is widely known as the Volunteer State, a nickname resulting from the valor displayed by Tennessee volunteer soldiers fighting under Andrew Jackson in the Battle of New Orleans. Tennessee is also called the Big Bend State in reference to the Tennessee River and the Mother of Southwestern Statesmen for the three United States presidents it has spawned. At one time, Tennessee was called the Hog and the Hominy State for its pork and corn product production, but this nickname is no longer used.[98]

Texas

Texas, or "teysha" in the language of the Caddo, means "hello friend." The Spanish used this term to refer to friendly tribes throughout Louisiana, Oklahoma, and Texas. The tribes of the Caddo confederacy, who lived in Louisiana and eastern Texas, came to be called "the kingdom of the Texas." The name of Texas was firmly established in 1690 when the Spanish named their first mission St. Francis of the Texas.[99]

Texas is popularly called the Lone Star State. The lone star on the state flag connotes the history of Texas as an independent republic fighting alone against great odds for its freedom. Texas is also called the Beef State for its cattle production and the Banner State for its leading position in many pursuits.[100]

Utah

The White Mountain Apache referred to the Navajo as "Yuttahih" or "one that is higher up." European settlers and explorers understood the Apache term to refer to the Utes, who dwelled farther up the mountains than the Navajo. The land of the Utes came to be called Utah.[101]

Utah's state emblem, the beehive, gives it the nickname of the Beehive State. The beehive is a symbol of industry. Utah's Mormon heritage provides Utah with two nicknames: the Mormon State and the Land of the Saints (the Mormon church is officially called The Church of Jesus Christ of the Latter-Day Saints). Finally, Utah's Great Salt Lake gives it the additional nickname of the Salt Lake State.[102]

Vermont

The French explorer Champlain, who saw Vermont's Green Mountains only from a distance, designated them as "Verd Mont" or "green mountain" in a 1647 map. The English name Vermont is therefore directly derived from Champlain's naming of the Green Mountains.[103] Vermont's mountains lend it the nickname of the Green Mountain State.[104]

Virginia

Virginia was named in 1584 in honor of Queen Elizabeth of England, who was popularly called the "Virgin Queen." The name Virginia is the feminine form of the Latin word *virginius*.[105]

Virginia has long been nicknamed the Old Dominion or the Ancient Dominion. Charles II of England quartered the arms of Virginia on his shield in 1663 thus adding Virginia to his dominions of France, Ireland, and Scotland. Virginia is often called the Cavalier State for its early settlers who were loyal to England and the Mother of States because it was the first to be colonized. The predominance of the Virginia aristocracy in early United States politics and diplomacy lends Virginia the additional nicknames of the Mother of Presidents and the Mother of Statesmen.[106]

Washington

Washington Territory was carved out of Oregon Territory in 1853. It was named in honor of George Washington.[107]

The state of Washington is best known as the Evergreen State for its many large fir and pine trees. The Chinook State, a nickname referring to Washington's salmon industry and the Chinook Indians, is no longer in common use.[108]

West Virginia

West Virginia was not separated from Virginia until 1861. West Virginia, as part of Virginia, was named after Queen Elizabeth of England, who was called the "Virgin Queen."[109]

West Virginia's scenic Allegheny Mountains lend it the nicknames the Switzerland of America and the Mountain State. Its shape gives it the additional name of the Panhandle State.[110]

Wisconsin

The state of Wisconsin is named after the Wisconsin River. In Chippewa, Wisconsin means "grassy place." When Hennepin first recorded the name in 1695, it referred either to the river itself or to a place on the river.[111]

Wisconsin is popularly, but unofficially, called the Badger State after the early lead miners who lived underground and were called badgers. The badger is also the state animal of Wisconsin. Wisconsin is also known as the Copper State for its copper mines in the north.[112]

Wyoming

The name Wyoming comes from two Delaware words "mecheweami-ing" meaning "at the big flats." A popular interpretation translates the Delaware words as "large plains." Legh Richmond Freeman, publisher of *The Frontier Index* in Kearney, Nebraska, claimed to have been the first to suggest the name Wyoming for the southwest half of the Dakota Territory.[113]

Wyoming has three nicknames currently in use. The Equality State recognizes Wyoming as the first state to extend women the right to vote; "Equality" is also the state motto. Wyoming is also called Big Wyoming and the Cowboy State.[114]

Notes

1. *Alabama State Emblems* (Montgomery: Alabama State Department of Archives and History, n.d.), p. 2; "The Name Alabama," *Arrow Points* 10 (January 1925): 19–20.

2. *Alabama State Emblems*, pp. 3–4.

3. J. Ellis Ransom, "Derivation of the Word 'Alaska,'" *American Anthropologist* 42 (July–September 1940): 551.

4. John P. Harrington, "Our State Names," *Smithsonian Institution Annual Report* (1954): 376.

5. *Welcome to Arizona* (Phoenix: Arizona Office of Tourism, n.d.); Harrington, "Our State Names," p. 376; Adlai Feather, "Origin of the Name Arizona," *New Mexico Historical Review* 39 (April 1964): 90–100.

6. Ark. Stat. Ann. § 5–102.

7. Harrington, "Our State Names," p. 376.
8. *A Brief History of Arkansas* (n.p., n.d.).
9. Ark. Stat. Ann. § 5–110.
10. *A Brief History of Arkansas.*
11. *California's Legislature, 1984*, pp. 212–13.
12. Cal. Gov't. Code § 420.75 (West).
13. *California's Legislature, 1984*, p. 203.
14. *Colorado State Capitol* (Denver: Colorado Department of Education, n.d.); Harrington, "Our State Names," p. 377.
15. Harrington, "Our State Names," p. 377.
16. *State of Connecticut Register and Manual, 1983*, p. 909.
17. Conn. Gen. Stat. Ann. § 3–110a (West).
18. George Shankle, *State Names, Flags, Seals, Songs, Birds, and Flowers, and Other Symbols*, rev. ed. (Westport: Greenwood Press, 1970, c 1938), pp. 105–6.
19. Harrington, "Our State Names," pp. 377–78.
20. *Delaware; Small Wonder* (Dover: Delaware State Travel Service, n.d.).
21. Harrington, "Our State Names," p. 378; *A Short History of Florida* (Tallahassee: Florida Department of State, n.d.), p. 1.
22. *Georgia's Capitol* (Atlanta: Max Cleland, n.d.).
23. Ibid.; Shankle, *State Names*, pp. 109–10.
24. *Hawaii, The Aloha State* (Honolulu: State of Hawaii, Hawaii Visitors Bureau, Chamber of Commerce of Hawaii, n.d.).
25. Haw. Rev. Stat. § 5–7.
26. *Idaho Blue Book, 1981–1982*, pp. 14–15.
27. Harrington, "Our State Names," p. 379.
28. Ill. Ann. Stat. ch. 1, § 3007 (Smith-Hurd).
29. Ibid., ch. 1, § 3131.
30. *Here Is Your Indiana Government*, 18th ed. (Indianapolis: Indiana State Chamber of Commerce, 1977), p. 135.
31. 1937 Indiana Acts, 1389.
32. *Here Is Your Indiana Government*, p. 135.
33. Benjamin F. Shambaugh, "The Naming of Iowa," *The Palimpsest* 38 (March 1957): 97–98; Harrington, "Our State Names," p. 379.
34. Shambaugh, "The Naming of Iowa," p. 98.
35. Harrington, "Our State Names," pp. 379–80.
36. Shankle, *State Names*, pp. 115–16; *Kansas Directory 1982*, pp. 134–35.
37. Harrington, "Our State Names," p. 380.
38. *Oh! Kentucky* (Frankfort: Department of Travel Development, n.d.).
39. Frederick W. Lawrence, "The Origin of American State Names," *National Geographic* 38 (July 1920): 129.
40. *Louisiana Facts* (Baton Rouge: Louisiana Department of State, n.d.); Harrington, "Our State Names," p. 380.
41. Shankle, *State Names*, p. 119.
42. *Quick Facts About Maine* (Augusta: John L. Martin, n.d.).
43. Ibid.
44. Shankle, *State Names*, pp. 119–20.
45. Harrington, "Our State Names," p. 380.
46. Gregory A. Stiverson and Edward C. Papenfuse, *Maryland and Its Govern-

ment in Brief (Annapolis: Archives Division, Hall of Records Commission, Department of General Services, n.d.), p. 14.

47. Harrington, "Our State Names," p. 381.
48. Shankle, *State Names*, p. 123; information provided by the Citizen Information Service, State of Massachusetts.
49. Harrington, "Our State Names," p. 381.
50. Shankle, *State Names*, p. 124.
51. *Minnesota Facts* (St. Paul: Minnesota Historical Society, Education Division, December 1983); Harrington, "Our State Names," p. 381.
52. Shankle, *State Names*, pp. 125–26.
53. *Souvenir of Mississippi* (Jackson: Dick Molpus, n.d.), p. 19; Harrington, "Our State Names," p. 382.
54. Shankle, *State Names*, p. 127.
55. Harrington, "Our State Names," p. 382.
56. Shankle, *State Names*, pp. 128–29.
57. *Montana Highway Map, 1985–86* (Helena: Montana Promotion Division, 1985).
58. Ibid.; Shankle, *State Names*, p. 130.
59. Harrington, "Our State Names," p. 383.
60. 1895 Neb. Laws, 441.
61. *Nebraska Blue Book, 1982–1983*, p. 12.
62. Shankle, *State Names*, p. 130.
63. Harrington, "Our State Names," p. 383.
64. Shankle, *State Names*, pp. 131–32.
65. Harrington, "Our State Names," p. 383.
66. Shankle, *State Names*, pp. 132–33.
67. Harrington, "Our State Names," p. 383.
68. Shankle, *State Names*, pp. 133–34.
69. *Your Miniguide to New Jersey* (Trenton: New Jersey Department of Commerce and Economic Development, Division of Travel and Tourism, 1985).
70. Harrington, "Our State Names," pp. 383–84.
71. Shankle, *State Names*, p. 135.
72. *New Mexico USA: Where to Go, What to Do* (Santa Fe: Marketing Services Division, New Mexico Economic Development and Tourism Department, 1986); N. M. Stat. Ann. §12–3–9.
73. Harrington, "Our State Names," p. 384.
74. Shankle, *State Names*, p. 136.
75. Harrington, "Our State Names," p. 384.
76. Shankle, *State Names*, pp. 137–38.
77. *Facts About North Dakota* (Bismark: North Dakota Economic Development Commission, 1983), p. 32.
78. Harrington, "Our State Names," p. 384.
79. *Emblems of North Dakota* (Bismark: Ben Meier, n.d.), n.p.; Shankle, *State Names*, pp. 138–39.
80. Harrington, "Our State Names," pp. 384–85.
81. Shankle, *State Names*, pp. 139–40.
82. Harrington, "Our State Names," p. 385.
83. Shankle, *State Names*, pp. 140–41.

84. Harrington, "Our State Names," p. 385.
85. Shankle, *State Names*, pp. 141–42.
86. Harrington, "Our State Names," p. 385.
87. Shankle, *State Names*, p. 143.
88. *1976–77 Pennsylvania Manual*, p. 846.
89. Harrington, "Our State Names," pp. 385–86.
90. *State of Rhode Island Official Emblems* (Providence: Office of the Secretary of State, n.d.); Shankle, *State Names*, p. 144.
91. Harrington, "Our State Names," p. 384.
92. Shankle, *State Names*, pp. 144–45.
93. Harrington, "Our State Names," p. 384.
94. *Great Seal of South Dakota* (Pierre: Alice Kundert, n.d.).
95. *South Dakota Signs & Symbols*, n.p., n.d.
96. Shankle, *State Names*, pp. 146–47.
97. Harrington, "Our State Names," p. 386.
98. *Tennessee Blue Book, 1985–1986*, p. 341.
99. Harrington, "Our State Names," p. 386.
100. Shankle, *State Names*, pp. 148–49.
101. Harrington, "Our State Names," p. 386.
102. Shankle, *State Names*, p. 150.
103. Harrington, "Our State Names," pp. 386–87.
104. Shankle, *State Names*, pp. 150–51.
105. Harrington, "Our State Names," p. 387.
106. Shankle, *State Names*, pp. 151–52.
107. Harrington, "Our State Names," p. 387.
108. *Our State Seal, Flag, Flower, etc.* (Olympia: Washington State Superintendent of Public Instruction, n.d.).
109. Harrington, "Our State Names," p. 387.
110. Shankle, *State Names*, p. 154.
111. Harrington, "Our State Names," p. 387.
112. Shankle, *State Names*, pp. 154–55.
113. *Wyoming; Some Historical Facts* (Cheyenne: Wyoming State Archives, Museums and Historical Department, n.d.), p. 2.
114. Ibid., p. 1.

2 | State Mottoes

The use of mottoes accompanied the development of heraldry, which began to take hold in the twelfth century. A motto might be considered a terse statement, sometimes humorous, sometimes serious, that describes a certain spirit of the bearer. State mottoes, whether in English, Latin, French, or Spanish, or a native American language, express simply the character and beliefs of the citizenry.

Many state mottoes express a fundamental belief in God. Arizona's motto, *Ditat Deus*, means "God enriches." Florida's motto, taken from United States coinage, states simply "In God We Trust." Colorado's motto states that there is "Nothing without Providence" and Ohio's, that "With God, All Things Are Possible." South Dakota combines two common themes: "Under God the People Rule." Arkansas' motto boldly states that "The People Rule." Some statements of democratic belief are more pugnacious than religious: Alabama, "We Dare Maintain Our Rights," Massachusetts, "By the Sword We Seek Peace, but Peace Only Under Liberty," and New Hampshire, more direct, "Live Free or Die." Still other mottoes are designed as slogans rather than philosophical statements. Alaska promotes itself with the motto "North to the Future." Indiana calls itself "The Crossroads of America." Tennessee touts "Agriculture and Commerce," and Utah's motto is one word—"Industry."

Alabama

Motto: *Audemus Jura Nostra Defendere*[1]

Translation: "We Dare Maintain Our Rights"

Origin: This motto was selected by Marie Bankhead Owen, director of the State Department of Archives and History, when she requested B. J.

Tieman to design a coat of arms in 1923. The motto was translated into Latin by University of Alabama Professor W. B. Saffold. The positive statement made by this motto replaced what was considered a negative statement imposed by outsiders during Reconstruction through the motto "Here We Rest."[2]

Alaska

Motto: "North to the Future"[3]

Origin: In 1963, the Alaska Centennial Commission announced a competition to determine a distinctive centennial motto and emblem for Alaska.[4] During the competition, which carried a $300 prize, 761 entries were received. In December 1963, the commission announced that "North to the Future," the entry submitted by Juneau newsman Richard Peter, had won.[5] The legislature adopted this motto officially in 1967.

Arizona

Motto: *Ditat Deus*[6]

Translation: "God Enriches"

Origin: The motto remains unchanged since its introduction by Richard Cunningham McCormick in 1864. It is an expression, probably biblical in origin, of deep religious sentiment.

Arkansas

Motto: *Regnat Populus*[7]

Translation: "The People Rule"

Origin: A 1907 act changed the motto to its current language from "Regnant Populi," the motto selected in 1864. While the direct origin of this motto is somewhat obscure, it clearly voices the democratic tradition of the state and the nation.

California

Motto: *Eureka*[8]

Translation: "I Have Found It"

Origin: The great seal of California, first designed in 1849, included this Greek motto to signify either the admission of the state into the Union or a miner's success.[9] Clearly, this ancient expression refers to the discovery of gold in California.

Colorado

Motto: *Nil Sine Numine*[10]

Translation: "Nothing without Providence"

Origin: This motto is credited to William Gilpin, first territorial governor of Colorado. It may actually be an adaptation of a line from Virgil's *Aeneid*.[11]

Connecticut

Motto: *Qui Transtulit Sustinet*[12]

Translation: "He Who Transplanted Still Sustains"

Origin: This motto, dating back to the early colonial history of Connecticut, was part of the colonial seal that depicted a vineyard. The words are adapted from the Book of Psalms 79:3.

Delaware

Motto: "Liberty and Independence"[13]

Origin: This motto was added to the state's great seal in 1847 as an expression of the ideals of American government.[14]

Florida

Motto: "In God We Trust"[15]

Origin: The state seal, adopted in 1868, is declared to be the size of a silver dollar. This motto is evidently taken from the motto used on the silver dollar.

Georgia

Mottoes: "Agriculture and Commerce, 1776"
        "Wisdom, Justice, Moderation"[16]

Origins: These mottoes appear on the great seal of the state—one on the obverse, the other on the reverse. Agriculture and commerce, of course, describe the mainstay of Georgia's economic well-being. In 1914, the date of 1799 was changed to 1776, the date of national independence rather than the date of Georgia's admission to the Union. Wisdom, justice, and moderation refer to the virtues that should guide legislative, judicial, and executive branches of government.

Hawaii

Motto: *Ua Mau ke Ea o ka Aina i ka Pono*[17]

Translation: "The Life of the Land Is Perpetuated in Righteousness"

Origin: Before becoming the state of Hawaii's official motto, these words were part of the coat of arms of the Kingdom of Hawaii and the seals of the Republic of Hawaii and the Territory. King Kamehameha III issued this motto upon the restoration of the Hawaiian flag to the kingdom by the British in 1843.[18]

Idaho

Motto: *Esto Perpetua*[19]

Translation: "It Is Forever"

Origin: This motto is attributed to Venetian theologian and mathematician Pietro Sarpi (1552–1623) who, in 1623, applied it to the Republic of Venice.[20] This motto was chosen by the Grange in 1867 and by the state of Idaho in 1891.

Illinois

Motto: "State Sovereignty, National Union"

Origin: These words were inscribed on the original state seal adopted in 1818. The seal that came into use in 1868, contrary to an amendment disallowing it, reversed the motto and placed "National Union" above "State Sovereignty." Nevertheless, the official motto places "State Sovereignty" first.[21]

Indiana

Motto: "The Crossroads of America"[22]

Origin: The 1937 law designates "The Crossroads of America" as Indiana's official state motto or slogan. When this motto was chosen, the theoretical center of the United States was in Indiana; furthermore, a number of north-south and east-west routes intersect in Indiana.

Iowa

Motto: "Our Liberties We Prize, and Our Rights We will Maintain"[23]

Origin: This motto, expressing the sentiment of Iowans as they entered the Union in 1846, was placed on the state seal by the first General Assembly in 1847.

Kansas

Motto: *Ad Astra per Aspera*[24]

Translation: "To the Stars Through Difficulties"

Origin: John J. Ingalls was responsible for including this motto in the design of the great seal in 1861. He was at the time secretary of the Senate. Ingalls claimed the phrase was "as old as Josephus," quite common in heraldry, and the most melodious of various phrases that express similar sentiments. He had first noticed it in the office of the gentleman under whom he had read law.[25]

Kentucky

Motto: "United We Stand, Divided We Fall"[26]

Origin: This familiar motto paraphrases a line from John Dickinson's "Liberty Song of 1768," which says "By uniting we stand; by dividing we fall." George Pope Morris, who wrote the poem "The Flag of Our Union," probably got the phrase from the original song.[27]

Louisiana

Motto: "Union, Justice and Confidence"

Origin: An exact explanation for the choice of this motto has been lost in time. Clearly, however, it represents the sentiments present at Louisiana's joining the Union. Until 1864, the motto had been "Justice, Union, and Confidence."[28]

Maine

Motto: *Dirigo*[29]

Translation: "I Direct" or "I Guide"

Origin: In the design of the seal, the star above the motto is intended to symbolize the state. The motto continues a navigational metaphor to the effect that the state should be a guiding light to its citizens just as the citizens should direct their efforts to the well-being of the state.[30]

Maryland

Mottoes: *Fatti Maschii Parole Femine*

Scuto Bonae Voluntatis Tuae Coronasti Nos[31]

Translation: "Manly Deeds, Womanly Words"

"With Favor Wilt Thou Compass Us As with a Shield"

Origins: The first motto is the motto of the Calvert family, whose history is closely tied to the state. The second motto is derived directly from the twelfth verse of the Fifth Psalm.[32]

Massachusetts

Motto: *Ense Petit Placidam Sub Libertate Quietem*[33]

Translation: "By the Sword We Seek Peace, but Peace Only under Liberty"

Origin: This motto was first used on the seal commissioned in 1775, after which time royal authority, and therefore royal seals, lost legitimacy. The motto is attributed to Algernon Sydney, who penned it in 1659.[34]

Michigan

Motto: *Si Quaeris Peninsulam Amoenam Circumspice*[35]

Translation: "If You Seek a Pleasant Peninsula, Look About You"

Origin: This motto was placed on the 1835 great seal, which was designed by Lewis Cass. Cass, by one story, paraphrased the inscription on the north door of St. Paul's Cathedral in London, so that the lower peninsula took the place of the monument by which Christopher Wren wished to be remembered.[36]

Minnesota

Motto: *L'Etoile du Nord*[37]

Translation: "Star of the North"

Origin: This motto was substituted for the Latin motto on the territorial seal when Governor Sibley designed a new state seal. The seal was approved in 1861. This motto lies behind Minnesota's having become known as the North Star State.[38]

Mississippi

Motto: *Virtute et Armis*[39]

Translation: "By Valor and Arms"

Origin: James Rhea Preston, the superintendent of education, suggested this motto when the coat of arms was under consideration in 1894.[40]

Missouri

Motto: *Salus Populi Suprema Lex Esto*[41]

Translation: "The Welfare of the People Shall Be the Supreme Law"

Origin: This motto has always been found on the state seal, which was adopted in 1822. Its source is Cicero's *De Legibus*.[42]

Montana

Motto: *Oro y Plata*[43]

Translation: "Gold and Silver"

Origin: This motto first appeared on the territorial seal adopted in 1865. It had been suggested by a special committee charged with designing the seal. Curiously, it was decided that the motto should be Spanish, but no one knew enough Spanish to formulate the motto correctly in the committee report. The error was corrected before the seal was struck.[44]

Nebraska

Motto: "Equality Before the Law"[45]

Origin: This motto was adopted in 1867 along with the state seal. It speaks to the cornerstone of the American system of justice. In 1963, the legislature also adopted a state symbol, a sooner, and a slogan: "Welcome to Nebraskaland, where the West begins."[46]

Nevada

Motto: "All for Our Country"[47]

Origin: This motto was adopted in 1866 along with the state seal. It is clearly an expression of patriotism.

New Hampshire

Motto: "Live Free or Die"[48]

Origin: These words were written as a toast for a veterans' reunion on July 31, 1809, by General John Stark. The motto was adopted by the legislature in 1945.[49]

New Jersey

Motto: "Liberty and Prosperity"[50]

Origin: The state had used this patriotic, hopeful motto informally for at least a century before it was officially adopted in 1928 along with a new design of the state seal.[51]

New Mexico

Motto: *Crescit Eundo*[52]

Translation: "It Grows As It Goes"

Origin: This motto, which has its origins in classical Latin literature, has been in use since 1851, when the territorial seal was first designed. It is a statement of belief in growth and progress. True to New Mexico's belief in growth and progress, the legislature adopted a slogan in 1975; the official state slogan for business, commerce, and industry in New Mexico is "Everybody Is Somebody in New Mexico."[53]

New York

Motto: *Exselsior*[54]

Translation: "Higher"

Origin: This ancient motto signifying progress has been New York's motto since 1778, when its original coat of arms was adopted.

North Carolina

Motto: *Esse Quam Videri*[55]

Translation: "To Be Rather than to Seem"

Origin: This motto, adopted with the great seal in 1893, can be found in Cicero. It is an expression of the character of the citizens of North Carolina.

North Dakota

Motto: "Liberty and Union Now and Forever, One and Inseparable"[56]

Origin: This motto is a quotation from Daniel Webster's *Reply to Hayne*. When the state seal was adopted in 1889, the law changed the wording of the motto used on the territorial seal to its present form.

Ohio

Motto: "With God, All Things Are Possible"[57]

Origin: Ohio's motto, adopted in 1959, is taken from the Bible, Matthew 19:26.

Oklahoma

Motto: *Labor Omnia Vincit*[58]

Translation: "Labor Conquers All Things"

Origin: The classical quotation from Virgil speaks to the virtue of hard work in the settlement and growth of Oklahoma. It was adopted in 1906 as part of the state's seal.

Oregon

Motto: "The Union"[59]

Origin: Although this motto had been recommended for Oregon by a legislative committee in 1857 and adopted in 1859, an 1849 seal included the motto *Alis Volat Propriis* ("She Flies with Her Own Wings"). Confusion reigned until 1957, when "The Union" was adopted officially as the state motto.[60]

Pennsylvania

Motto: "Virtue, Liberty, and Independence"[61]

Origin: This motto was included in the state coat of arms designed in 1778 by Caleb Lownes of Philadelphia. In 1875, it was approved.

Rhode Island

Motto: "Hope"[62]

Origin: The simple motto was added to the seal after the colony received a more liberal charter in 1644. The anchor, the symbol of hope, had been the colonial seal since the beginning.

South Carolina

Mottoes: *Animis Opibusque Parati*
         Dum Spiro Spero

Translations: "Prepared in Mind and Resources"
             "While I Breathe I Hope"

Origins: These mottoes and the state seal on which they appear symbolize the June 28, 1776, battle between what is now Fort Moultrie and the British fleet. These mottoes declaring South Carolina's determination, strength, and hope were chosen in 1776 after the colony had declared itself independent.[63]

South Dakota

Motto: "Under God the People Rule"[64]

Origin: This motto was adopted in the 1885 and 1889 South Dakota constitutions at the suggestion of Dr. Joseph Ward, the founder of Yankton College.[65]

Tennessee

Motto: "Agriculture and Commerce"

Origin: Tennessee actually has no official motto. The motto noted above, found on the state seal, has been used in the place of an official motto.[66] In 1965, however, the legislature adopted a state slogan: "Tennessee—America at Its Best."[67]

Texas

Motto: "Friendship"[68]

Origin: This motto was adopted in 1930 in recognition that the name of the state is derived from the Indian word *tejas*, which means friendship.

Utah

Motto: "Industry"[69]

Origin: This motto, adopted in 1896, is an appropriate motto for a state which uses the beehive as a symbol.

Vermont

Motto: "Freedom and Unity"[70]

Origin: This motto, on the seal designed by Ira Allen in 1778 and adopted in 1779, expresses the desire that states remain free, but united.

Virginia

Motto: *Sic Semper Tyrannis*[71]

Translation: "Thus Ever to Tyrants"

Origin: This motto, dating back to the revolutionary times of 1776, evokes the sentiment for independence among the colonists.

Washington

Motto: *Alki*

Translation: "Bye and Bye"

Origin: This Indian word appeared on the territorial seal designed by Lt. J. K. Duncan. When settlers landed at Alki Point in Seattle, they named their settlement New York-Alki. They had hoped Seattle would become the New York of the West Coast.[72]

West Virginia

Motto: *Montani Semper Liberi*[73]

Translation: "Mountaineers Are Always Free"

Origin: This motto was adopted with the state seal in 1863. The seal was based on suggestions and designs by Joseph H. Diss Debar.

Wisconsin

Motto: "Forward"[74]

Origin: This motto, part of the coat of arms, became Wisconsin's motto when the seal and coat of arms were revised in 1851. The seal was designed by Edward Ryan and John H. Lathrop. The motto "Forward" was a compromise between the two men when Ryan objected to Lathrop's Latin motto.[75]

Wyoming

Motto: "Equal Rights"[76]

Origin: This motto, which had been used on the seal, was officially adopted in 1955. It was chosen in recognition of the fact that Wyoming women had attained political rights in 1869, long before they could vote in national elections.

Notes

1. Ala. Code § 1–2–1.
2. *Alabama State Emblems* (Montgomery: Alabama State Department of Archives and History, n.d.), pp. 9–11.
3. Alaska Stat. § 44.09.045.
4. *Centennial Press* 1 (September 1963): 1.
5. *Centennial Press* 1 (December 1963): 1.
6. Ariz. Rev. Stat. Ann. art. 22, § 20.

7. Ark. Stat. Ann. § 5–103.

8. Cal. Gov't. Code § 420.5 (West).

9. *California's Legislature, 1984*, p. 207.

10. Colo. Rev. Stat. § 24–80–901.

11. George E. Shankle, *State Names, Flags, Seals, Birds, Flowers, and Other Symbols*, rev. ed. (Westport: Greenwood Press, 1970, c 1938), pp. 158–59.

12. Conn. Gen. Stat. Ann. § 3–105.

13. Del. Code Ann. tit. 29, § 301.

14. *Official Insignia of Delaware* (Dover: Delaware State Development Department, n.d.).

15. Fla. Stat. Ann. § 15.03 (West).

16. Ga. Code Ann. § 50–3–30.

17. Haw. Rev. Stat. § 5–9.

18. 1959 Haw. Sess. Laws 365.

19. Idaho Code § 59–1005.

20. Shankle, *State Names*, p. 160.

21. *Illinois Blue Book, 1983–1984*, pp. 439–40.

22. 1937 Indiana Acts, 1389.

23. Iowa Code Ann. § 1A.1 (West).

24. Kan. Stat. Ann. § 75–201.

25. *Kansas Historical Collections* 8 (1903–04): 299.

26. Ky. Rev. Stat. Ann. § 2.020 (Baldwin).

27. *Louisville Times*, 19 November 1940 (copy supplied by Kentucky Department for Libraries and Archives).

28. La. Rev. Stat. Ann. § 49–153 (West); information provided by Richard H. Holloway, Archives, State of Louisiana, Division of Archivist, Records Management, and History.

29. Me. Rev. Stat. tit. 1, § 205.

30. *Resolves of the Legislature of the State of Maine . . .* (Portland: Francis Douglas, State Printer, 1820), p. 22.

31. Md. Ann. Code § 13–102.

32. Shankle, *State Names*, p. 162.

33. Mass. Gen. Laws Ann. ch. 2, § 1 (West).

34. "The History of the Seal of the Commonwealth" (copied material supplied by the Massachusetts Secretary of State, Citizen Information Service).

35. Mich. Comp. Laws Ann. § 2.21; § 2.22.

36. *Michigan History Magazine* 13 (1929): 663–64; *The Great Seal of Michigan* (Lansing: Richard H. Austin, n.d.).

37. Minn. Stat. Ann. § 1.135 (West).

38. *Minnesota Legislative Manual, 1985*, p. 11.

39. *Souvenir of Mississippi* (Jackson: Dick Molpus, n.d.), p. 19.

40. *Mississippi Official and Statistical Register, 1980–1984*, p. 27.

41. Mo. Ann. Stat. § 10.060 (Vernon).

42. Shankle, *State Names*, p. 163.

43. Mont. Rev. Codes Ann. § 1–1–501.

44. Rex C. Myers, *Symbols of Montana* (Helena: Montana Historical Society, 1976), p. 4.

45. Neb. Rev. Stat. § 84–501.

46. Ibid., § 90–105.

47. Nev. Rev. Stat. § 235.010.

48. N.H. Rev. Stat. Ann. § 3:8.

49. *Manual for the General Court, 1981.*

50. N.J. Stat. Ann. § 52:2–1 (West).

51. 1928 N.J. Laws 801.

52. N.M. Stat. Ann. § 12–3–1.

53. Ibid., § 12–3–9.

54. N.Y. State Law § 70 (McKinney).

55. N.C. Gen. Stat. § 144–2.

56. N.D. Cent. Code art. XI, § 2.

57. Ohio Rev. Code Ann. § 5.06 (Baldwin).

58. Okla. Stat. Ann. art. 6, § 35 (West).

59. Or. Rev. Stat. § 186.040.

60. "Motto (Oregon's)" (information supplied by the Office of the Secretary of State of Oregon).

61. *Pennsylvania Symbols* (Harrisburg: House of Representatives, n.d.).

62. R.I. Gen. Laws § 42–4–2.

63. *South Carolina State Symbols and Emblems* (Columbia: House of Representatives, n.d.)

64. S.D. Codified Laws Ann. § 1–6–2.

65. *History of the South Dakota State Flag* (Pierre: Bureau of Administration, Division of Central Services, The State Flag Account, n.d.).

66. *Tennessee Blue Book, 1985–1986*, p. 341.

67. Tenn. Code Ann. § 4–1–304.

68. Texas Rev. Civ. Stat. Ann. art. 6143a (Vernon).

69. Utah Code Ann. § 63–13–11.

70. Vt. Stat. Ann. tit. 1, § 491.

71. Va. Code § 7.1–26.

72. *Our State Seal, Flag, Flower, etc.* (Olympia: Washington State Superintendent of Public Instruction, n.d.).

73. W. Va. Code art. 2, § 7.

74. Wis. Stat. Ann. § 1.07 (West).

75. *State of Wisconsin, 1983–1984 Blue Book*, p. 947.

76. Wyo. Stat. Ann. § 8–3–107.

3 | State Seals

Not merely decorative symbols of statehood, the seals of state have been used to designate official acts of state through the ages, and their use is strictly prescribed by law.

State seals are like snapshots of each state's history. Oklahoma's seal, for example, contains the symbols of the Cherokee, Chickasaw, Creek, Choctaw, and Seminole nations and forty-five small stars around a central star, representing the forty-five existing states before Oklahoma became the forty-sixth in 1907. The seal of Kansas, on which appear thirty-four stars for the thirty-fourth state, depicts a steamboat and a river to symbolize commerce, a settler's cabin and a mare plowing to represent agriculture and prosperity, a train of wagons heading west and a herd of buffalo retreating being chased by two Indians on horseback.

The symbols employed in the seals represent recurring themes—agriculture, commerce, mining, shipping, liberty, and union. These symbols celebrate the economic development of the state, the natural resources on which the state was built, and the freedom of a united people to pursue their lives in peace and harmony.

Alabama

In 1939, the Alabama legislature returned to the design of the great seal that had been used before 1868. At the same time, the legislature provided for an official coat of arms. The seal, which celebrates the historical importance of Alabama's river systems, is set out by law to be

> circular, and the diameter thereof two and a quarter inches; near the edge of the circle shall be the word 'Alabama,' and opposite this word, at the same distance from the edge, shall be the words, 'great seal.'

In the center of the seal there shall be a representation of a map of the state with its principal rivers.[1]

The coat of arms signifies the history of Alabama under five flags, its status as a maritime state, and the courage of its citizens. The law describes the coat of arms as

a shield upon which is carried the flags of four of the five nations which have at various times held sovereignty over a part or the whole of what is now the state of Alabama: Spain, France, Great Britain and the Confederacy. The union binding these flags shall be the shield of the United States. The shield upon which the flags and shield of the United States are placed shall be supported on either side by an eagle. The crest of the coat of arms shall be a ship representing the 'Badine' which brought the French colonists who established the first permanent white settlements in the state. Beneath the shield there shall be a scroll containing the sentence in Latin: 'Audemus jura nostra defendere,' the English interpretation of which is 'We Dare Maintain Our Rights.' The word 'Alabama' shall appear beneath the state motto.[2]

Alaska

Alaska's state seal is 2 1/8 inches in diameter and consists of "two concentric circles between which appear the words 'The Seal of the State of Alaska.' "[3] The design inside the inner circle represents northern lights, icebergs, railroads, and people native to the state as well as symbols for mining, agriculture, fisheries, and fur seal rookeries. This seal, with the substitution of the word "Territory" for "State," had been used as the territorial seal since 1913.[4] It officially became the state seal in 1960.

Arizona

The great seal of Arizona is set in the state's constitution, which was adopted in 1911.

The seal of the State shall be of the following design: In the background shall be a range of mountains, with the sun rising behind the peaks thereof, and at the right side of the range of mountains there shall be a storage reservoir and a dam, below which in the middle distance are irrigated fields and orchards reaching into the foreground, at the right of which are cattle grazing. To the left in the middle distance on a mountain side is a quartz mill in front of which and in the foreground is a miner standing with pick and shovel. Above this device shall be the motto: 'Ditat Deus.' In a circular band surrounding the whole device shall be inscribed: 'Great Seal of the State of Arizona,' with the year of admission of the State into the Union.[5]

The seal uses the symbols of Arizona's first primary enterprises: reclamation, farming, cattle raising, and mining.

Arkansas

The seal of Arkansas was adopted in 1864. Except for an editorial change affecting the motto made in 1907, the seal has remained the same.

An eagle at the bottom, holding a scroll in its beak, inscribed 'Regnat Populus,' a bundle of arrows in one claw and an olive branch in the other; a shield covering the breast of the eagle, engraved with a steamboat at top, a bee-hive and plow in the middle, and sheaf of wheat at the bottom; the Goddess of Liberty at the top, holding a wreath in her right hand, a pole in the left hand, surmounted by a liberty cap, and surrounded by a circle of stars, outside of which is a circle of rays; the figure of an angel on the left, inscribed 'Mercy,' and a sword on the right hand, inscribed 'Justice,' surrounded with the words 'Seal of the State of Arkansas.'[6]

The Arkansas seal celebrates the importance of the steamboat in its development and the industry of its citizens in a peaceful, bountiful land.

California

The great seal of California was adopted by the 1849 constitutional convention. The code provides a pictorial description.[7] The seal as it now appears is the fourth design, a standardized representation adopted in 1937.

In the circular design is a seated figure of the goddess Minerva, at her feet a grizzly bear, in the background ships upon a mountain-rimmed bay, in the mid-distance a gold miner at work and, near the top centre, the motto EUREKA (I have found it!) beneath a semi-circle of 31 stars, the number of States in the Union after the admission of California (September 9, 1850).[8]

Colorado

The Colorado legislature adopted the state seal in 1877. The seal recalls the beauty of the Rocky Mountains and the significance of mining in the state's development.

The seal of the state shall be two and one-half inches in diameter, with the following device inscribed thereon: An heraldic shield bearing in chief, or upon the upper portion of the same, upon a red ground three snow-capped mountains; above surrounding clouds; upon the lower part thereof upon a golden ground a miner's badge, as prescribed by the rules of heraldry; as a crest above the shield, the eye of God, being golden rays proceeding from the lines of a triangle; below the crest and above the shield, as a scroll, the Roman fasces bearing upon a band of red, white, and blue the words 'Union and Constitution'; below the whole the motto, 'Nil Sine Numine'; the whole to be surrounded by the words, 'State of Colorado,' and the figures '1876.'[9]

Connecticut

The seal of the state of Connecticut has a history that goes back to colonial times. The seal has undergone several modifications, but essential elements have remained as the 1931 description indicates.

The great seal of the state shall conform to the following description: It shall be a perfect ellipse with its major axis two and one-half inches in length and its minor axis two inches in length, the major axis being vertical. Within such ellipse shall appear another ellipse with its major axis one and fifteen-sixteenths inches in length and its minor axis one and one-half inches in length. The inner ellipse is separated from the outer ellipse only by a line two points one-thirty-sixth of an inch in width and with the space between the two ellipses, being seven-thirty-seconds of an inch, forming a border. In said space shall appear, letter spaced and in letters one-eighth of an inch in height and of twelve point century Roman, the words 'SIGILLUM REIPUBLICAE CONNECTICUTENSIS,' beginning and ending one and one-sixteenth inches apart in the lower space along such border. In the center of the inner ellipse shall be three grape vines, two above and one below, each with four leaves and three clusters of grapes intertwined around a support nine-sixteenths of an inch high, and the base of the supports of the two upper vines one inch from the base of the inner ellipse and eleven-sixteenths of an inch apart. The base of the lower support shall be nine-sixteenths of an inch from the base of the inner ellipse and halfway between said bases shall appear the motto 'QUI TRANSTULIT SUSTINET,' in number three, six point card Roman letters, or engraver's Roman letters, on a ribbon gracefully formed, with the ends of the ribbon turned upward and inward and cleft.[10]

The official arms, seen on the seal and the flag, is described separately in the 1931 law.

The following-described arms shall be the official arms of the state: A shield of rococo design of white field, having in the center three grape vines, supported and bearing fruit. Below the shield shall be a white streamer, cleft at each end, bordered with two fine lines, and upon the streamer shall be in solid letters of medium bold Gothic the motto 'QUI TRANSTULIT SUSTINET.'[11]

Delaware

The great seal of Delaware is essentially the same design as the seal of 1777.

It is emblazoned as follows: Party per fess, or and argent, the first charged with a garb (wheat sheaf) in bend dexter and an ear of maize (Indian Corn) in bend sinister, both proper; the second charged with an ox statant, ruminating, proper; fess, wavy azure, supporters on the dexter a husbandman with a hilling hoe, on the sinister a rifleman armed and accoutred at ease. Crest, on a wreath azure and argent, a ship under full sail, proper, with the words 'Great Seal of the State of Delaware' and the words 'Liberty and Independence' engraved thereon.[12]

The seal symbolizes the importance of shipping and farming in Delaware's history as well as Delaware's role in carving out American independence.

Florida

The state seal was first designed in 1868 and remains substantially the same except for the substitution of the sabal palmetto for the cocoa tree in 1970.

The great seal of the state shall be of the size of the American silver dollar, having in the center thereof a view of the sun's rays over a highland in the distance, a sabal palmetto palm tree, a steamboat on water, and an Indian female scattering flowers in the foreground, encircled by the words 'Great Seal of the State of Florida: In God We Trust.'[13]

The seal signifies Florida's tropical climate and the importance of native Americans in its history and the steamboat in its modern development. In 1985, the seal was officially revised to correct previous errors and to bring it into conformity with the change made in 1970.

Georgia

The great seal of Georgia was adopted by the state constitution of 1798. It remains the same today except for changing the date 1799 to 1776.

The device on one side is a view of the seashore, with a ship bearing the flag of the United States riding at anchor near a wharf, receiving on board hogsheads of tobacco and bales of cotton, emblematic of the exports of this state; at a small distance a boat, landing from the interior of the state, with hogsheads, etc., on board, representing the state's internal traffic; in the back part of the same side a man in the act of plowing; and at a small distance a flock of sheep in different postures, shaded by a flourishing tree. The motto inscribed thereon is 'Agriculture and Commerce, 1776.'

The device on the other side is three pillars supporting an arch, with the word 'Constitution' engraved within the same, emblematic of the Constitution, supported by the three departments of government, namely the legislative, judicial, and executive. The first pillar has engraved upon it 'Wisdom,' the second, 'Justice,' the third, 'Moderation'; on the right of the last pillar a man stands with a drawn sword, representing the aid of the military in the defense of the Constitution, and the motto is 'State of Georgia, 1776.'[14]

Hawaii

Except for the legend "Republic of Hawaii" and the size of the seal, Hawaii's state seal is the same as that of the Republic of Hawaii.

The great seal of the State shall be circular in shape, two and three-quarters inches in diameter, and of the design being described, with the tinctures added as a basis for the coat of arms as follows:

Arms. An heraldic shield which is quarterly; first and fourth, stripes of the Hawaiian flag; second and third, on a yellow field, a white ball pierced on a black staff; overall, a green escutcheon with a five-pointed yellow star in the center.

Supporters. On the right side, Kamehameha I, standing in the attitude as represented by the bronze statue in front of Aliiolani Hale, Honolulu; cloak and helmet yellow; figure in natural colors. To the left, goddess of liberty, wearing a Phrygian cap and laurel wreath, and holding in right hand the Hawaiian flag, partly unfurled.

Crest. A rising sun irradiated in gold, surrounded by a legend 'State of Hawaii, 1959,' on a scroll, black lettering.

Motto. 'Ua mau ke ea o ka aina i ka pono' on the scroll at bottom, gold lettering.

Further accessories. Below the shield, the bird phoenix wings outstretched; arising from flames, body black, wings half yellow, half dark red; also eight taro leaves, having on either side banana foliage and sprays of maidenhair fern, trailed upwards.[15]

Idaho

The Idaho state seal, designed by Emma Edwards Green, was adopted in 1891.[16] The designer described the seal in these words:

The question of Woman Suffrage was being agitated somewhat, and as leading men and politicians agreed that Idaho would eventually give women the right to vote, and as mining was the chief industry, and the mining man the largest financial factor of the state at that time, I made the figure of the man the most prominent in the design, while that of the woman, signifying justice, as noted by the scales, liberty, as denoted by the liberty cap on the end of the spear, and equality with man as denoted by her position at his side, also signifies freedom. The pick and shovel held by the miner, and the ledge of rock beside which he stands, as well as the pieces of ore scattered about his feet, all indicate the chief occupation of the State. The stamp mill in the distance, which you can see by using a magnifying glass, is also typical of the mining interest of Idaho. The shield between the man and the woman is emblematic of the protection they unite in giving the state. The large fir or pine tree in the foreground in the shield refers to Idaho's immense timber interests. The husbandman plowing on the left side of the shield, together with the sheaf of grain beneath the shield, are emblematic of Idaho's agricultural resources, while the cornucopias, or horns of plenty, refer to the horticultural. Idaho has a game law, which protects the elk and moose. The elk's head, therefore, rises above the shield. The state flower, the wild Syringa or Mock Orange, grows at the woman's feet, while the ripened wheat grows as high as her shoulder. The star signifies a new light in the galaxy of states. . . . The river depicted in the shield is our mighty Snake or Shoshone River, a stream of great majesty.[17]

Illinois

The Illinois state seal, designed by Secretary of State Sharon Tyndale, dates back to 1867 and was first used in 1868. This seal, actually the third since statehood, is considerably altered from the earlier seals.[18]

The secretary of state is hereby authorized and required to renew the great seal of state, and to procure it as nearly as practicable of the size, form and intent of the seal now in use, and conforming with the original design, as follows: 'American eagle on a boulder in prairie— the sun rising in distant horizon,' and scroll in eagle's beak, on which shall be inscribed the words: 'State Sovereignty,' 'National Union,' to correspond with the original seal of state, in every particular.[19]

Indiana

Until 1963, Indiana had no officially authorized state seal although pioneer scenes were used on territorial seals as early as 1801.[20] The 1963 law sets out this description:

The official seal for the state of Indiana shall be described as follows:

A perfect circle, two and five eighths (2 5/8) inches in diameter, inclosed by a plain line. Another circle within the first, two and three eighths (2 3/8) inches in diameter inclosed by a beaded line, leaving a margin of one quarter (1/4) of an inch. In the top half of this margin are the words 'Seal of the State of Indiana.'

At the bottom center, 1816, flanked on either side by a diamond, with two (2) dots and a leaf of the tulip tree (liriodendron tulupifera), at both ends of the diamond. The inner circle has two (2) trees in the left background, three (3) hills in the center background with nearly a full sun setting behind and between the first and second hill from the left.

There are fourteen (14) rays from the sun, starting with two (2) short ones on the left, the third being longer and then alternating, short and long. There are two (2) sycamore trees on the right, the larger one being nearer the center and having a notch cut nearly half way through, from the left side, a short distance above the ground. The woodsman is wearing a hat and holding his ax nearly perpendicular on his right. The ax blade is turned away from him and is even with his hat.

The buffalo is in the foreground, facing to the left of front. His tail is up, front feet on the ground with back feet in the air—as he jumps over a log.

The ground has shoots of blue grass, in the area of the buffalo and woodsman.[21]

Iowa

In 1847, the first General Assembly of Iowa adopted the following act designating a state seal:

The secretary of state be, and he is, hereby authorized to procure a seal which shall be the great seal of the state of Iowa, two inches in diameter, upon which shall be engraved the following device, surrounded by the words, 'The Great Seal of the State of Iowa'—a sheaf and field of standing wheat, with a sickle and other farming utensils, on the left side near the bottom; a lead furnace and pile of pig lead on the right side; the citizen soldier, with a plow in his rear, supporting the American flag and liberty cap with his right hand, and his gun with his left, in the center and near the bottom; the Mississippi river in the rear of the whole, with the steamer Iowa under way; an eagle near the upper edge, holding in his beak a scroll, with the following inscription upon it: Our liberties we prize, and our rights we will maintain.[22]

Kansas

The 1861 resolution creating the great seal of Kansas describes the seal as follows:

The east is represented by a rising sun, in the right-hand corner of the seal; to the left of it, commerce is represented by a river and a steamboat; in the foreground, agriculture is represented as the basis of the future prosperity of the state, by a settler's cabin and a man plowing with a pair of horses; beyond this is a train of ox-wagons, going west; in the background is seen a herd of buffalo, retreating, pursued by two Indians, on horseback; around the top is the motto, 'Ad astra per aspera,' and beneath a cluster of thirty-four stars. The circle is surrounded by the words, 'Great seal of the state of Kansas. January 29, 1861.'[23]

Kentucky

Kentucky's seal has remained essentially unchanged since 1792. It combines friendship with a slogan of revolutionary fervor.

The seal of the Commonwealth shall have upon it the device, two (2) friends embracing each other, with the words 'Commonwealth of Kentucky' over their heads and around them the words, 'United We Stand, Divided We Fall.'[24]

Louisiana

The code of Louisiana empowers the governor of the state to devise a public seal to authenticate official governmental acts.[25] In 1902, Governor William Wright Heard prescribed this description of the seal:

A Pelican, with its head turned to the left, in a nest with three young; the Pelican, following the tradition in act of tearing its breast to feed its young; around the edge of the seal to be inscribed 'State of Louisiana.' Over the head of the Pelican to be inscribed 'Union, Justice,' and under the Pelican to be inscribed 'Confidence.'[26]

The motto and the pelican have been employed in Louisiana seals since at least 1804.

Maine

In 1820, when Maine became a state, a law was passed describing the state seal. The current law provides a bit more detail and retains all the features of the original seal.

The seal of the State shall be a shield; argent, charged with a pine tree (Americana, quinis ex uno folliculo setis) with a moose deer (cervus alces), at the foot of it, recumbent; supporters: on dexter side, a husbandman, resting on a scythe; on sinister side, a seaman, resting on an anchor.

In the foreground, representing sea and land, and under the shield, shall be the name of the State in large Roman capitals, to wit: MAINE. The whole shall be surrounded by a crest, the North Star. The motto, in small Roman capitals, shall be in a label interposed between the shield and crest, viz.:—DIRIGO.[27]

Maryland

The Maryland seal, readopted in 1876, is the seal sent from England shortly after the colony was settled. The reverse of the seal is the official state seal. The obverse is used only for decorative purposes.[28]

Description of Great Seal.

(a) Obverse. On the obverse of the Great Seal of Maryland is an equestrian figure of the Lord Proprietary, arrayed in complete armour and bearing a drawn sword in his hand. The caparisons of the horse are adorned with the family coat of arms. On the ground below is represented a sparse growth of grass on sand soil, with a few small blue and yellow flowers. On the circle, surrounding the obverse of the seal, is the Latin inscription 'Caecilius Absolutus Dominus Terrae Mariae et Avaloniae Baro de Baltemore' meaning 'Cecil Absolute Lord of Maryland and Avalon Baron of Baltimore' (Avalon refers to Lord Baltimore's first settlement in the new world, in Newfoundland).

(b) Reverse. On the reverse of the Great Seal of Maryland is Lord Baltimore's hereditary coat of arms. The 1st and 4th quarters represent the arms of the Calvert family described in heraldic language as a paly of 6 pieces, or (gold) and sable (black) a bend counterchanged. The 1st and 4th quarters are the left-hand top quarter and the right-hand bottom quarter. The 2nd and 3rd quarters show the arms of the Crossland family, which Cecil inherited from his grandmother, Alicia, wife of Leonard Calvert, the father of George, 1st Lord Baltimore. This coat of arms is in quarters also, argent (silver) and gules (red) a cross bottony (boutonne, with a button or a three-leaf clover at the end of each radius of the cross) counterchanged. Above the shield is placed an Earl's coronet (indicating that though only a baron in England, Calvert was an earl or court palatine in Maryland). Above that, a helmet set full faced and over that the Calvert crest, (2 pennons, the dexter or the right one or (gold), the other sable (black) staffs gules (red) issuing from the ducal coronet). The supporters of the shield are a plowman and a fisherman with their hands on the shield, designated respectively by a spade held in the right hand of the plowman and a fish held in the left hand of the fisherman (the fish is heraldic and cannot, therefore, be identified as to any species). The plowman wears a high-crowned, broad-brimmed beaver hat; the fisherman wears a knitted cap (somewhat resembling a stocking cap). The motto in Italian on a ribbon at the feet of the plowman and fisherman is the motto of the Calvert family 'Fatti maschii parole femine' loosely translated as 'Manly deeds, womanly words.' Behind and surrounding both shield and supporters is an ermine-lined mantle and on the circle around this part of the seal are the words 'Scuto bonae voluntatis tuae coronasti nos' (5th Psalm, 12th verse: 'With favor wilt thou compass us as with a shield') and the date 1632. The date refers to the year the charter was granted.[29]

Massachusetts

The seal and coat of arms of Massachusetts were adopted in 1885; some revisions were made in 1898 and 1971. The current law holds that the seal

shall be circular in form, bearing upon its face a representation of the arms of the commonwealth encircled with the inscription within a beaded border, 'Sigillum Reipublicae Massachusettensis.' The colors of the arms shall not be an essential part of said seal, and an impression from a seal engraved according to said design, on any commission, paper, or document shall be valid without such colors or the representation thereof by heraldic lines or marks.[30]

The coat of arms is described as consisting of

a blue shield with an Indian thereon, dressed in a shirt, leggings, and moccasins, holding in his right hand a bow, and in his left hand an arrow, point downward, all of gold; and, in the upper right-hand corner of the field a silver star of five points. The crest shall be, on a wreath of gold and blue, a right arm, bent at the elbow, clothed and ruffled, and grasping a broad-sword, all of gold. The motto 'Ense petit placidam sub libertate quietem' shall appear in gold on a blue ribbon.[31]

Michigan

The great seal of Michigan, adopted in 1911, is the 1835 seal designed by Lewis Cass. The law now reads that

the great seal shall be comprised of the coat of arms of the state around which shall appear the words 'great seal of the state of Michigan, A.D. MDCCCXXXV.'[32]

The coat of arms, simply the seal without the legend, was also adopted in 1911. It is described as follows:

The coat-of-arms shall be blazoned as follows:

Chief, Azure, motto argent Tuebor;

Charge, Azure, sun-rayed rising sinister proper, lake wavey proper, peninsula dexter grassy proper, man dexter on peninsula, rustic, habited, dexter arm-raised, dexter turned, sinister arm with gun stock resting, all proper;

Crest, On a wreath azure and or, an American eagle rising to the dexter, tips of wings partly lowered to base, all proper, dexter talon holding an olive branch with 13 fruit, sinister talon holding a sheaf of 3 arrows, all proper. Over his head a sky azure environed with a scroll gules with the motto 'E Pluribus Unum' argent;

Supporters:

Dexter, An elk rampant, proper;

Sinister, A moose rampant, proper;

Mottoes, On the scroll unending superior narrow argent, in sable, the motto, 'Si quaeris peninsulam, amoenam.'

On the scroll unending inferior, broader argent in sable the motto 'circumspice.'

Observations:

Scroll support and conventional leaf design between shield and scroll superior or;

Escutcheon supporters rest on the scroll supports and leaf design.[33]

Minnesota

Even though Minnesota became a state in 1858, the territorial seal remained in use until 1861 when the Minnesota legislature approved Governor Sibley's design for a state seal.[34] The design was revised in 1983 to read as follows:

(a) The seal is composed of two concentric borders. The outside forms the border of the seal and the inside forms the border for the illustrations within the seal. The area between the two borders contains lettering.

(b) The seal is two inches in diameter. The outside border has a radius of one inch and resembles the serrated edge of a coin. The width of the border is 1/16 of an inch.

(c) The inside border has a radius of three-fourths of an inch and is composed of a series of closely spaced dots measuring 1/32 of an inch in diameter.

(d) Within the area between the borders 'The Great Seal of the State of Minnesota.' is printed in capital letters. Under that is the date '1858.' with two dagger symbols separating the date and the letters. The lettering is 14 point century bold.

(e) In the area within the inside border is the portrayal of an 1858 Minnesota scene made up of various illustrations that serve to depict a settler plowing the ground near the falls of St. Anthony while he watches an Indian on horseback riding in the distance.

(f) For the purposes of description, when the area within the inside border is divided into quadrants, the following illustrations should be clearly visible in the area described.

(1) In the upper parts of quadrants one and two, the inscription, 'L'Etoile du Nord' is found on the likeness of a scroll whose length is equal to twice the length of the inscription, but whose ends are twice folded underneath and serve to enhance the inscription. The lettering is seven point century bold.

(2) In quadrant two is found a likeness of a rising sun whose ambient rays form a background for a male Indian in loincloth and plume riding on horseback at a gallop. The Indian is sitting erect and is holding a spear in his left hand at an upward 60-degree angle to himself and is looking toward the settler in quadrant four.

(3) In quadrant one, three pine trees form a background for a picturesque resemblance of St. Anthony Falls in 1858.

(4) In quadrants three and four, cultivated ground is found across the lower half of the seal, which provides a background for the scenes in quadrants three and four.

(5) In quadrant three, a tree stump is found with an ax embedded in the stump and a period muzzle loader resting on it. A powder flask is hanging towards the end of the barrel.

(6) In quadrant four, a white barefoot male pioneer wearing clothing and a hat of that period is plowing the earth, using an animal-drawn implement from that period. The animal is not visible. The torso of the man continues into quadrant two, and he has his legs spread apart to simulate movement. He is looking at the Indian.

Additional effects; size. Every effort shall be made to reproduce the seal with justification to the 12 o'clock position and with attention to the authenticity of the illustrations used to create the scene within the seal. The description of the scene in this section does not preclude the graphic inclusion of the effects of movement, sunlight, or falling water when the seal is reproduced. Nor does this section prohibit the enlargement, proportioned reduction, or embossment of the seal for its use in unofficial acts.

Historical symbolism of seal. The sun, visible on the western horizon, signifies summer in the northern hemisphere. The horizon's visibility signifies the flat plains covering much of Minnesota. The Indian on horseback is riding due south and represents the great Indian heritage of Minnesota. The Indian's horse and spear and the Pioneer's ax, rifle, and plow represent tools that were used for hunting and labor. The stump symbolizes the importance of the lumber industry in Minnesota's history. The Mississippi River and St. Anthony Falls are depicted to note the importance of these resources in transportation and industry. The cultivated ground and the plow symbolize the importance of agriculture in Minnesota. Beyond the falls three pine trees represent the state tree and three great pine regions of Minnesota; the St. Croix, Mississippi, and Lake Superior.[35]

Mississippi

The great seal of the state of Mississippi adopted by the legislature is the same seal that has been in use since statehood was attained in 1817.[36] The 1817 law reads:

The seal of this state, the inscription of which shall be 'the great seal of the state of Mississippi' around the margin, and in the center an eagle, with the olive branch and quiver of arrows in his claws.[37]

Missouri

The Missouri state seal, designed by a select committee of legislators, was adopted by the legislature and signed into law in 1822.

The device for an armorial achievement for the state of Missouri is as follows: Arms, parted per pale, on the dexter side; gules, the white or grizzly bear of Missouri, passant guardant, proper on a chief engrailed; azure, a crescent argent; on the sinister side, argent, the arms of the United States, the whole within a band inscribed with the words 'UNITED WE STAND, DIVIDED WE FALL.' For the crest, over a helmet full-faced, grated with six bars; or a cloud proper, from which ascends a star argent, and above it a constellation of twenty-three smaller stars, argent, on an azure field, surrounded by a cloud proper. Supporters on each side, a white or grizzly bear of Missouri, rampant, guardant proper, standing on a scroll, inscribed with the motto, 'Salus populi suprema lex esto,' and under the scroll numerical letters

MDCCCXX. And the great seal of the state shall be so engraved as to present by its impression the device of the armorial achievement aforesaid, surrounded by a scroll inscribed with the words, 'THE GREAT SEAL OF THE STATE OF MISSOURI,' in Roman capitals, which seal shall be in a circular form and not more than two and a half inches in diameter.[38]

Montana

The Montana territorial seal, slightly altered since 1865, became the state seal by legislative act in 1893.[39]

The great seal of the state is as follows: a central group representing a plow and a miner's pick and shovel; upon the right, a representation of the Great Falls of the Missouri River; upon the left, mountain scenery; and underneath, the words 'Oro y Plata.' The seal must be 2 1/2 inches in diameter and surrounded by these words, 'The Great Seal of the State of Montana.'[40]

Nebraska

The great seal of the state of Nebraska was laid by an 1867 law, which reads in part:

The eastern part of the circle to be represented by a steamboat ascending the Missouri river; the mechanic arts to be represented by a smith with hammer and anvil; in the foreground, agriculture to be represented by a settler's cabin, sheaves of wheat and stalks of growing corn; in the background a train of cars heading towards the Rocky Mountains, and on the extreme west, the Rocky Mountains to be plainly in view; around the top of this circle to be in capital letters, the motto, 'EQUALITY BEFORE THE LAW,' and the circle to be surrounded with the words, 'Great Seal of the State of Nebraska, March 1st, 1867.'[41]

Nevada

The state seal was officially adopted in 1866. The current law states that

1. There shall be a seal of the State of Nevada called The Great Seal of the State of Nevada, the design of which shall be as follows: In the foreground, there shall be two large mountains, at the base of which, on the right, there shall be located a quartz mill, and on the left a tunnel, penetrating the silver leads of the mountain, with a miner running out a carload of ore, and a team loaded with ore for the mill.

Immediately in the foreground, there shall be emblems indicative of the agricultural resources of the state, as follows: A plow, a sheaf and sickle. In the middle ground, there shall be a railroad train passing a mountain gorge and a telegraph line extending along the line of the railroad. In the extreme background, there shall be a range of snow-clad mountains, with the rising sun in the east. Thirty-six stars and the motto of our state, 'All for Our Country,' shall encircle the whole group. In an outer circle, the words 'The Great Seal of the State of Nevada' shall be engraved with 'Nevada' at the base of the seal and separated from the other words by two groups of three stars each.

2. The size of the seal shall not be more than 2 3/4 inches in diameter.[42]

New Hampshire

The current seal was adopted in 1931, when a committee was formed to recommend improvements in the seal of 1784. The law states that

The seal of the state shall be two inches in diameter, circular, with the following detail and no other: A field crossed by a straight horizon line of the sea, above the center of the field; concentric with the field the rising sun, exposed above the horizon about one third of its diameter; the field encompassed with laurel; across the field for the full width within the laurel a broadside view of the frigate Raleigh, on the stocks; the ship's bow dexter and higher than the stern; the three lower masts shown in place, together with the fore, main and mizzen tops, shrouds and mainstays; an ensign staff at the stern flies the United States flag authorized by act of Congress June 14, 1777; a jury staff on the mainmast and another on the foremast each flies a pennant; flags and pennants are streaming to the dexter side; the hull is shown without a rudder; below the ship the field is divided into land and water by a double diagonal line whose highest point is sinister; no detail is shown anywhere on the water, nor any on the land between the water and the stocks except a granite boulder on the dexter side; encircling the field is the inscription, SEAL OF THE STATE OF NEW HAMPSHIRE, the words separated by round periods, except between the parts of New Hampshire; at the lowest point of the inscription is the date 1776, flanked on either side by a five-pointed star, which group separates the beginning and end of the inscription . . . [43]

In 1945, the legislature also adopted a state emblem. The law, slightly amended in 1957, reads as follows:

The state emblem shall be of the following design: With an elliptical panel, the longest dimension of which shall be vertical, there shall appear an appropriate replica of the Old Man of the Mountains;

surrounding the inner panel, and enclosed within another ellipse, there shall be at the bottom of the design the words of any state motto which may be adopted by the general court; and at the top of the design, between the inner and outer elliptical panels, the words, New Hampshire, appropriately separated from the motto, if adopted, by one star on each side. Said emblem may be placed on all printed or related material issued by the state and its subdivisions relative to the development of recreational, industrial, and agricultural resources of the state.[44]

New Jersey

The great seal was authorized in 1776 and its design amended in 1928. The law describes the seal accordingly:

The great seal of this state shall be engraved on silver, which shall be round, of two and a half inches in diameter and three-eighths of an inch thick; the arms shall be three ploughs in an escutcheon, azure; supporters, Liberty and Ceres. The Goddess Liberty to carry in her dexter hand a pole, proper, surmounted by a cap gules, with band azure at the bottom, displaying on the band six stars, argent; tresses falling on shoulders, proper; head bearing over all a chaplet of laurel leaves, vert; overdress, tenne; underskirt, argent; feet sandaled, standing on a scroll. Ceres: Same as Liberty, save overdress, gules; holding in left hand a cornucopia, or, bearing apples, plums and grapes surrounded by leaves, all proper; head bearing over all a chaplet of wheat spears, vert. Shield surmounted by sovereign's helmet, six bars, or; wreath and mantling, argent and azure. Crest: A horse's head, proper. Underneath the shield and supporting the goddesses, a scroll azure, bordered with tenne, in three waves or folds; on the upper folds the words 'Liberty and Prosperity'; on the under fold in Arabic numerals, the figures '1776.' These words to be engraved round the arms, viz., 'The Great Seal of the State of New Jersey.'[45]

New Mexico

The great seal of New Mexico is essentially the one that was designed for the Territory of New Mexico in 1851 and adopted in 1887. After becoming a state in 1912, the state legislature adopted the old territorial seal, appropriately changed for New Mexico's new status, as the state seal.[46]

The coat of arms of the state shall be the Mexican eagle grasping a serpent in its beak, the cactus in its talons, shielded by the American eagle with outspread wings, and grasping arrows in its talons; the date 1912 under the eagles and, on a scroll, the motto: 'Crescit Eundo.'

The great seal of the state shall be a disc bearing the coat of arms and having around the edge the words 'Great Seal of the State of New Mexico.'[47]

New York

The great seal of New York was officially designated in 1882. The 1882 law seeks to describe the seal first adopted in 1778.

The secretary of state shall cause to be engraved upon metal two and one-half inches in diameter the device of arms of this state, accurately conformed to the description thereof given in this article, surrounded with the legend, 'The great seal of the state of New York.'[48]

North Carolina

North Carolina's seal was adopted first in 1893 and has undergone some modifications since then. The current law is as follows:

The Governor shall procure for the State a seal, which shall be called the great seal of the State of North Carolina, and shall be two and one-quarter inches in diameter, and its design shall be a representation of the figures of Liberty and Plenty, looking toward each other, but not more than half-fronting each other and otherwise disposed as follows: Liberty, the first figure, standing her pole with cap on it in her left hand and a scroll with the word 'Constitution' inscribed thereon in her right hand. Plenty, the second figure, sitting down, her right arm half extended towards Liberty, three heads of grain in her right hand, and in her left, the small end of her horn, the mouth of which is resting at her feet, and the contents of the horn rolling out.

The background on the seal shall contain a depiction of mountains running from left to right to the middle of the seal and an ocean running from right to left to the middle of the seal. A side view of a three-masted ship shall be located on the ocean and to the right of Plenty. The date 'May 20, 1775' shall appear within the seal and across the top of the seal and the words 'esse quam videri' shall appear at the bottom around the perimeter. The words 'THE GREAT SEAL of the STATE of NORTH CAROLINA' shall appear around the perimeter. No other words, figures or other embellishments shall appear on the seal.[49]

North Dakota

This North Dakota seal is described in the 1889 state constitution. It is essentially the same as the territorial seal approved in 1863.

The following described seal is hereby declared to be and hereby constituted the great seal of the state of North Dakota, to wit: a tree in the open field, the trunk of which is surrounded by three bundles of wheat; on the right a plow, anvil and sledge; on the left, a bow crossed with three arrows, and an Indian on horseback pursuing a buffalo toward the setting sun; the foliage of the tree arched by a half circle of forty-two stars, surrounded by the motto 'Liberty and Union Now and Forever, One and Inseparable'; the words 'Great Seal' at the top; the words 'State of North Dakota' at the bottom; 'October 1st' on the left and '1889' on the right. The seal to be two and one-half inches in diameter.[50]

Ohio

The current seal of Ohio was revised in 1967, but the revision is based on the first seal, adopted in 1803.

The great seal of the state shall be two and one-half inches in diameter and shall consist of the coat of arms of the state within a circle having a diameter of one and three-fourths inches, surrounded by the words 'THE GREAT SEAL OF THE STATE OF OHIO' in news gothic capitals.[51]

The coat of arms used in the seal was also revised in 1967.

The coat of arms of the state shall consist of the following device: a circular shield; in the right foreground of the shield a full sheaf of wheat bound and standing erect; in the left foreground, a cluster of seventeen arrows bound in the center and resembling in form the sheaf of wheat; in the background, a representation of Mount Logan, Ross county, as viewed from Adena state memorial; over the mount, a rising sun three-quarters exposed and radiating seventeen rays, the exterior extremities of which form a semicircle; and uniting the background and foreground, a representation of the Scioto river and cultivated fields ...

When the coat of arms of the state is reproduced in color, the colors used shall be substantially the same as the natural color of the terrain and objects shown.[52]

Oklahoma

The design of Oklahoma's seal is laid out thusly in the 1906 state constitution:

In the center shall be a five pointed star, with one ray directed upward. The center of the star shall contain the central device of the seal of the Territory of Oklahoma, including the words, 'Labor Omnia Vincit.' The upper left hand ray shall contain the symbol of the ancient seal of the Cherokee Nation, namely: A seven pointed star partially surrounded by a wreath of oak leaves. The ray directed upward shall contain the symbol of the ancient seal of the Chickasaw Nation, namely: An Indian warrior standing upright with bow and shield. The lower left hand ray shall contain the symbol of the ancient seal of the Creek Nation, namely: A sheaf of wheat and a plow. The upper right hand ray shall contain the symbol of the ancient seal of the Choctaw Nation, namely: A tomahawk, bow, and three crossed arrows. The lower right hand ray shall contain the symbol of the ancient seal of the Seminole Nation, namely: A village with houses and a factory beside a lake upon which an Indian is paddling a canoe. Surrounding the central star and grouped between its rays shall be forty-five small stars, divided into five clusters of nine stars each, representing the forty-five states of the Union, to which the forty-sixth is now added. In a circular band surrounding the whole device shall be inscribed, 'GREAT SEAL OF THE STATE OF OKLAHOMA 1907.'[53]

Oregon

The seal of the state of Oregon was designed by a legislative committee in 1857 and officially adopted in 1903.

The description of the seal of the State of Oregon shall be an escutch-eon, supported by 33 stars, and divided by an ordinary, with the inscription, 'The Union.' In chief—mountains, an elk with branching antlers, a wagon, the Pacific Ocean, on which there are a British man-of-war departing and an American steamer arriving. The second—quartering with a sheaf, plow and a pickax. Crest—the American eagle. Legend—State of Oregon, 1859.[54]

Pennsylvania

A seal for the Commonwealth was designed in 1776 and approved in 1791. In 1809, a new die was cut. The seal currently in use was adopted in 1893.[55] The three symbols used in the seal were originally used in county seals. The ship was the crest of Philadelphia County; the plough, the crest of Chester County; and the sheaf of wheat, the crest of Sussex County, which is now in Delaware.[56]

The shield shall be parted PER FESS, or, charged with a plough, PROPER, in chief; on a sea WAVY; PROPER, a ship under full sail, surmounted with a sky, Azure; and in BASE, on a field VERT, three GARBS, OR. On the SINISTER a stock of maize, and DEXTER an olive branch. And on the wreath of its colours a bald eagle—PROPER, PERCHED, wings extended, for the CREST. MOTTO: VIRTUE, LIBERTY, and INDEPENDENCE. Round the margin of the seal, COMMONWEALTH OF PENNSYLVANIA. The reverse, Liberty, trampling on a Lyon, Gules, the emblem of Tyranny. MOTTO—'BOTH CAN'T SURVIVE.'[57]

Rhode Island

The state seal was adopted in 1875. The anchor was adopted in the 1647 seal by the assembly. The law states that

There shall continue to be one (1) seal for the public use of the state; the form of an anchor shall be engraven thereon; the motto thereof shall be the word Hope; and in a circle around the same shall be engraven the words, Seal of the State of Rhode Island and Providence Plantations, 1636.[58]

The arms, found on the flag, are officially described as follows:

The arms of the state are a golden anchor on a blue field, and the motto thereof is the word Hope.[59]

South Carolina

The seal of South Carolina was commissioned in 1776 and first used in 1777. The design for the arms was made by William Henry Drayton and that for the reverse, by Arthur Middleton. The seal is a circle four inches in diameter and is described as follows:

Arms: A Palmetto tree growing on the seashore erect (symbolical of the fort on Sullivan's Island, built on Palmetto logs); at its base, a torn up oak tree, its branches lopped off, prostrate, typifying the British Fleet, constructed of oak timbers and defeated by the fort; both proper. Just below the branches of the Palmetto, two shields, pendant; one of them on the dexter side is inscribed MARCH 26, (the date of ratification of the Constitution of S.C.)—the other on the sinister side JULY 4, (the date of Declaration of Independence): Twelve spears proper, are bound crosswise to the stem of the Palmetto, their points raised, (representing the 12 states first acceding to the Union); the band uniting them together bearing the inscription QUIS SEPARABIT (Who shall separate?) under the prostrate oak, is inscribed MELIOREM LAPSA LOCAVIT (having fallen it has set up a better); below which appears in large figures, 1776 (the year the Constitution of S.C. was passed, the year of the Battle at Sullivan's Island and of the Declaration of Independence, and the year in which the Seal was ordered made). At the summit of Exergue, are the words SOUTH CAROLINA; and at the bottom of the same ANIMIS OPIBUSQUE PARATI (prepared in mind and resources).

Reverse: A woman walking on the seashore, over swords and daggers (typifying Hope overcoming dangers, which the sun, just rising, was about to disclose); she holds in her dexter hand, a laurel branch, (symbolical of the honors gained at Sullivan's Island), and in her sinister hand, the folds of her robe; she looks toward the sun, just rising above the sea, (indicating that the battle was fought on a fine day, and also bespeaking good fortune); all proper. On the upper part is the sky azure. At the summit of Exergue, are the words DUM SPIRO SPERO (While I breathe I hope) and within the field below the figure, is inscribed the word SPES (Hope).[60]

South Dakota

The design of the state seal was set out in the constitutions of 1885 and 1889. In 1961, the legislature adopted the same design, but specified the colors to be used.

The design of the colored seal of the state of South Dakota shall be as follows: An inner circle, whose diameter shall be five-sevenths of the diameter of the outer circle of any seal produced in conformity herewith; within which inner circle shall appear; in the left foreground on the left bank of a river, a rust-colored smelting furnace from which grey smoke spirals upward and adjacent to which on the left are a rust-colored hoist house and mill, and to the left a grey dump; these three structures being set in a yellow field and above and back of a light green grove on the left bank of the river. In the left background is a series of three ranges of hills, the nearer range being a darker green than the said grove, the intermediate range of a blue-green and the higher range of blue-black coloration.

In the right foreground is a farmer with black hat, red shirt, navy-blue trousers and black boots, holding a black and silver breaking plow, drawn by a matched team of brown horses with a black harness. In the right background and above the horses in a pasture of grey-green, a herd of rust-colored cattle graze in front of a field of yellow-brown corn, part in shock and part in cut rows to the rear and above which are blue and purple hills forming a low background and receding into the distance. Between the right and left foregrounds and back-grounds is a light-blue river merging in the distance into a sky-blue and cloudless sky. Moving upstream on the river is a white steamboat with a single black funnel from which grey smoke spirals upward. Green shrubbery appears on the near bank of the river, in the left foreground and on the right bank of the river near the pasture is a yellow field. The farmer is turning black-brown furrows which reach across the circle and in his foreground is a field of brown-green-yellow. Near the upper edge of the inner circle at the top on a golden quarter circle which is one-fifth in width the distance between the innermost and the outermost circles that compose the seal, shall appear in black, the state motto: 'Under God the People Rule.' This innermost circle is circumscribed by a golden band one-fourth as wide as the above-described quarter circle, which inner border, shall be circumscribed by a deep blue circle four and one-half times as wide as the above quarter circle, on which in golden letters one-third its width, in height, shall appear at the top the words, 'State of South Dakota.' In the lower half of the deep blue circle shall appear in words of equal height 'Great' and 'Seal' between which shall be the numerals '1889.' Between the above-stated names and on either side shall appear a golden star one-half in size the width of the deep blue circle. Circumscribing this deep blue circle shall be a band of gold of the same width as of the inner golden band.

Outside of this outer golden band shall be a serrated or saw-toothed edge of small triangles whose base shall be of the same width as the above quarter circle.[61]

Tennessee

Tennessee has no officially designated seal. The seal in use now, however, is essentially the same as that recommended in 1801 by a special committee:

> ... the said seal shall be a circle, two inches and a quarter in diameter, that the circumference of the circle contain the words THE GREAT SEAL OF TENNESSEE, that in the lower part of said circumference be inserted Feb. 6th 1796, the date of the constitution of this State; that in the inside of the upper part of said circle, be set in numerical letters XVI, the number of the state in chronological order; that under the base of the upper semicircle, there be the word AGRICULTURE; that above said base, there be the figure of a plough, sheaf of wheat and cotton plant; that in the lower part of the lower semicircle, there be the word COMMERCE, and said lower semicircle shall also contain the figure of a boat and boatman.

This seal was used until 1829, when a second seal began to come into use. The new seal was used until 1865. The so-called Brownlow Seal was used in 1865, after which time, two new seals came into use. The seal now used is the larger of the two new seals. It differs from the 1801 seal in that the boat is of different design and is pointed in the opposite direction, and the month and day have been dropped from the date.[62]

Texas

The seal of Texas is that adopted by the Republic of Texas in 1839. When Texas became a state in 1845, the word "Republic" was changed to "State." The seal is described as follows:

There shall be a Seal of the State which shall be kept by the Secretary of State, and used by him officially under the direction of the Governor. The Seal of the State shall be a star of five points encircled by olive and live oak branches, and the words 'The State of Texas.'[63]

Utah

The state seal of Utah, designed by Harry Edwards, was adopted in 1896. The symbols of the seal include the American eagle (protection in peace and war), the beehive (industry), and sego lilies (peace). The date 1847 represents the year the Mormons came to the Salt Lake Valley, and 1896 is the year in which Utah was granted statehood.[64]

The Great Seal of the state of Utah shall be 2–1/2 inches in diameter, and of the following device: the center a shield and perched thereon an American eagle with outstretching wings; the top of the shield pierced by six arrows crosswise; under the arrows the motto 'Industry'; beneath the motto a beehive, on either side growing sego lilies; below the beehive the figures '1847'; and on each side of the shield an American flag; encircling all, near the outer edge of the seal, beginning at the lower left-hand portion, the words 'The Great Seal of the State of Utah,' with the figures '1896' at the base.[65]

Vermont

In 1821, the original 1779 seal went into disuse. Until 1937, when the design of the first seal was adopted again, Vermont used a number of different seals. The current law reads as follows:

The state seal shall be the great seal of the state, a faithful reproduction, cut larger and deeper, of the original seal, designed by Ira Allen, cut by Reuben Dean of Windsor and accepted by resolution of the general assembly, dated February 20, 1779. The seal shall be kept by the secretary of civil and military affairs.[66]

The description of the coat of arms was set out in law in 1862:

The coat of arms, crest, motto and badge of the state shall be and are described as follows:

(1) Coat of arms. Green, a landscape occupying half of the shield; on

the right and left, in the background, high mountains, blue; the sky, yellow. From near the base and reaching nearly to the top of the shield, arises a pine tree of natural color and between three erect sheaves, yellow, placed diagonally on the right side and a red cow standing on the left side of the field.

(2) Motto and badge. On a scroll beneath the shield, the motto: Vermont; Freedom and Unity. The Vermonter's badge: two pine branches of natural color, crossed between the shield and scroll.

(3) Crest. A buck's head, of natural color, placed on a scroll, blue and yellow.[67]

Virginia

The seal of Virginia is described in a 1930 law:

The great seal of the Commonwealth of Virginia shall consist of two metallic discs, 2 1/4 inches in diameter, with an ornamental border one fourth of an inch wide, with such words and figures engraved thereon as will, when used, produce impressions to be described as follows: On the obverse, Virtus, the genius of the Commonwealth, dressed as an Amazon, resting on a spear in her right hand, point downward, touching the earth; and holding in her left hand, a sheathed sword, or parazonium, pointing upward; her head erect and face upturned; her left foot on the form of Tyranny represented by the prostrate body of a man, with his head to her left, his fallen crown nearby, a broken chain in his left hand, and a scourge in his right. Above the group and within the border conforming therewith, shall be the word 'Virginia,' and, in the space below, on a curved line, shall be the motto, 'Sic Semper Tyrannis.' On the reverse, shall be placed a group consisting of Libertas, holding a wand and pileus in her right hand; on her right, Aeternitas, with a globe and phoenix in her right hand; on the left of Libertas, Ceres, with a cornucopia in her left hand, and an ear of wheat in her right; over this device, in a curved line, the word 'Perseverando.'[68]

The law also provides for a lesser seal:

The lesser seal. The lesser seal of the Commonwealth shall be 1 9/16 inches in diameter, and have engraved thereon the device and inscriptions contained in the obverse of the great seal.[69]

Washington

The seal of the state of Washington was prescribed in the 1889 state constitution and added to the body of law in 1967.

The seal of the state of Washington shall be, a seal encircled with the words: 'The Seal of the State of Washington,' with the vignette of General George Washington as the central figure, and beneath the vignette the figures '1889'...[70]

West Virginia

The state constitution of West Virginia designates the seal designed by Joseph H. Diss Debar and chosen by a legislative committee in 1863 as the official state seal.

The present seal of the State, with its motto, 'Montani Semper Liberi,' shall be the great seal of the State of West Virginia, and shall be kept by the secretary of state, to be used by him officially, as directed by law.[71]

The report of the committee, which was then adopted by a joint resolution in 1863, described the seal:

The disc of the Great Seal is to be two and one-half inches in diameter; the obverse to bear the legend 'The State of West Virginia,' the constitutional designation of our Republic, which with the motto, 'Montani Semper Liberi—Mountaineers always free'—is to be inserted in the circumference. In the center a rock with ivy, emblematic of stability and continuance, and on the face of the rock the inscription, 'June 20, 1863,' the date of our foundation, as if graven with a pen of iron in the rock forever. On the right of the rock a farmer clothed in the traditional hunting garb, peculiar to this region, his right arm resting on the plow handles, and his left supporting a woodman's axe, indicating that while our territory is partly cultivated, it is still in the process of being cleared of the original forest. At his right hand a sheaf of wheat and a cornstalk on the left hand of the rock, a miner, indicated by a pick-axe on his shoulder, with barrels and lumps of mineral at his feet. On his left anvil, partly seen, on which rests a sledge hammer, typical of the mechanic arts, the whole indicating the principal pursuits and resources of the state. In front of the rock and the hunter, as if just laid down by the latter and ready to be resumed at a moment's notice, two hunters' rifles, crossed and surmounted at the place of contact by the Phrygian cap, or cap of liberty, indicating that our freedom and liberty were won and will be maintained by the force of arms.

The reverse of the Great Seal is to be encircled by a wreath composed of laurel and oak leaves, emblematical of valor and strength, with fruits and cereals, productions of the State. For device, a landscape. In the distance, on the left of the disc, a wooded mountain, and on the right a cultivated slope with the log farmhouse peculiar to this region. On the side of the mountain, a representation of the viaduct on the line of the Baltimore & Ohio Railroad in Preston County, one of the great engineering triumphs of the age, with a train of cars about to pass over it. Near the center a factory, in front of which a river with boats, on the bank and to the right of it nearer the foreground, a derrick and a shed, appertaining to the production of salt and petroleum. In the foreground a meadow with cattle and sheep feeding and reposing, the whole indicating the leading characteristics, productions and pursuits of the State at this time. Above the mountain, etc., the sun merging from the clouds, indicating that former obstacles to our prosperity are now disappearing. In the rays of the sun the motto 'Libertas et Fidelitate' Freedom and Loyalty—indicating that our liberty and independence are the result of faithfullness to the Declaration and the National Constitution.

The committee further recommend that the above device and motto, for the obverse of the Great Seal be also adopted as the Coat-of-Arms of the State.[72]

Wisconsin

When Wisconsin became a state in 1848, a new seal was designed to replace the revised territorial seal of 1839. The state seal was itself revised in 1851 and finally prescribed by law in 1881.[73] The law sets out the following description:

The great seal of the state consists of a metallic disc, 2–3/8 inches in diameter, containing, within an ornamental border, the following devices and legend: The coat of arms of the state . . . above the arms, in a line parallel with the border, the words, 'Great Seal of the State of Wisconsin'; in the exergue, in a curved line, 13 stars.[74]

The coat of arms is prescribed as follows:

The coat of arms of the state of Wisconsin is declared to be as follows:

Arms. Or, quartered, the quarters bearing respectively a plow, a crossed shovel and pick, an arm and held hammer, and an anchor, all proper; the base of shield resting upon a horn of plenty and pyramid of pig lead, all proper; overall, on fesse point, the arms and motto of the United States, namely: Arms, palewise of 13 pieces argent and gules; a chief azure; motto (on garter surrounding inescutcheon), 'E pluribus unum.'

Crest. A badger, passant, proper.

Supporters. Dexter, a sailor holding a coil of rope, proper; sinister, a yeoman resting on a pick, proper.

Motto. Over crest, 'Forward.'[75]

Wyoming

Wyoming's seal was adopted in 1893 and revised in 1921. The current law is as follows:

There shall be a great seal of the state of Wyoming, which shall be of the following design, viz: A circle one and one-half (1–1/2) inches in diameter, on the outer edge or rim of which shall be engraved the words 'Great Seal of the State of Wyoming.' The design shall conform substantially to the following description: A pedestal, showing on the front thereof an eagle resting upon a shield, the shield to have engraved thereon a star and the figures, '44,' being the number of Wyoming in the order of admission to statehood. Standing upon the pedestal shall be a draped figure of a woman, modeled after the statute of the 'Victory of the Louvre,' from whose wrists shall hang links of a broken chain, and holding in her right hand a staff from the top of which shall float a banner with the words 'Equal Rights' thereon, all suggesting the political position of woman in this state. On either side of the pedestal and standing at the base thereof, shall be male figures typifying the livestock and mining industries of Wyoming. Behind the pedestal, and in the background, shall be two (2) pillars, each supporting a lighted lamp, signifying the light of knowledge. Around each pillar shall be a scroll with the following words thereon: On the right of the central figure the words 'Livestock' and 'Grain,' and on the left the words 'Mines' and 'Oil.' At the base of the pedestal, and in front, shall appear the figures '1869–1890,' the former date signifying the organization of the territory of Wyoming and the latter date of its admission to statehood.[76]

Notes

1. Ala. Code § 1–2–4.
2. Ibid., § 1–2–1.
3. Alaska Stat. § 44.09.010.
4. *Alaska Blue Book, 1977*, p. i.
5. Ariz. Rev. State. Ann. art. 22, § 20.
6. Ark. Stat. Ann. § 5–104.
7. Cal. Govt. Code tit. 1, § 400 (West).
8. *State Emblems* (Sacramento (?): n.d.).
9. Colo. Rev. Stat. § 24–80–901.
10. Conn. Gen. Stat. Ann. § 3–106 (West).

11. Ibid., § 3–105 (West).
12. Del. Code Ann. tit. 29, § 301.
13. Fla. Stat. Ann. § 15.03 (West).
14. Ga. Code Ann. § 50–3–30.
15. Haw. Rev. Stat. § 5–5.
16. Idaho Code § 59–1005.
17. "Description of the Idaho State Seal" (Idaho Historical Society Reference Series No. 61, reissued in 1970).
18. *Illinois Blue Book, 1983–1984*, pp. 439–40.
19. 1867 Ill. Laws 36.
20. *Indiana Emblems* (Indianapolis: Indiana Historical Bureau, 1982), p. 5.
21. Ind. Code Ann. § 1–2–4 (West).
22. Iowa Code Ann. § 1A.1 (West).
23. Kan. Stat. Ann. § 75–201.
24. Ky. Rev. Stat. § 2.020 (Baldwin).
25. La. Rev. Stat. Ann. § 49–151 (West).
26. *Louisiana Facts* (Baton Rouge: Department of State, n.d.).
27. Me. Rev. Stat. tit. 1, § 201.
28. *Maryland Manual, 1981–1982*, p. 9.
29. Md. Ann. Code § 13–302.
30. Mass. Gen. Laws Ann. ch. 2, § 2 (West).
31. Ibid., ch. 2, § 1 (West).
32. Mich. Comp. Laws Ann. § 2.41.
33. Ibid., § 2.22.
34. *Minnesota Legislative Manual, 1985*, p. 11.
35. Minn. Stat. Ann. § 1.135 (West).
36. Miss. Code Ann. § 7–1–9.
37. *Souvenir of Mississippi* (Jackson: Dick Molpus, n.d.), p. 16.
38. Mo. Stat. Ann. § 10.060 (Vernon).
39. Rex C. Myers, *Symbols of Montana* (Helena: Montana Historical Society, 1976), p. 10.
40. Mont. Rev. Codes Ann. § 1–1–501.
41. 1867 Neb. Stats. 863.
42. Nev. Rev. Stat. § 235.010.
43. N.H. Rev. Stat. Ann. § 3:9.
44. Ibid., § 3:1.
45. N.J. Stat. Ann. § 52:2–1 (West).
46. "The Great Seal of the State of New Mexico" (information provided by the New Mexico State Library).
47. N.M. Stat. Ann. § 12–3–1.
48. N.Y. Stat. Law § 73 (McKinney).
49. N.C. Gen. Stat. § 147–26.
50. N.D. Cent. Code art. XI, § 2.
51. Ohio Rev. Code Ann. § 5.10 (Baldwin).
52. Ibid., § 5.04 (Baldwin).
53. Okla. Stat. Ann. art. 6, § 35 (West).
54. Or. Rev. Stat. § 186.020.
55. *Pennsylvania Symbols* (Harrisburg: House of Representatives, n.d.).

56. *Pennsylvania Manual, 1976–1977*, pp. 846–47.
57. *Commonwealth of Pennsylvania Official Documents, 1893*, vol. 4, pp. 215–16.
58. R. I. Gen. Laws § 42–4–2.
59. Ibid., § 42–4–1.
60. *South Carolina State Symbols and Emblems* (Columbia: House of Representatives, n.d.).
61. S.D. Codified Laws Ann. § 1–6–2.
62. *Tennessee Blue Book, 1985–1986*, pp. 337–38.
63. Tex. Gov't. Code art. 4, § 19 (Vernon).
64. *Symbols of the Great State of Utah* (Salt Lake City (?): n.d.).
65. Utah Code Ann. § 67–1a–8.
66. Vt. Stat. Ann. tit. 1, § 493.
67. Ibid., tit. 1, § 491.
68. Va. Code § 7.1–26.
69. Ibid., § 7.1–27.
70. Wash. Rev. Code Ann. § 1.20.080.
71. W.Va. Code art 2, § 7.
72. *The Great Seal of West Virginia* (Charleston: A. James Manchin, n.d.).
73. *State of Wisconsin 1983–1984 Blue Book*, p. 947.
74. Wis. Stat. Ann. § 14.45 (West).
75. Ibid., § 1.07 (West).
76. Wyo. Stat. Ann. § 8–3–101.

4 | State Flags

Flags, like seals, are symbols that legitimize the sovereignty of each state, linked by vote of the people into the union of the United States.

The flags of the states, often displaying the coats of arms, are also tableaux of each state's history. Hawaii's flag proudly symbolizes its founding by displaying Great Britain's Union Jack. New Mexico retains the yellow and red colors of Spain in its flag together with the Zia symbol, an ancient Indian symbol of friendship. The crossed peace pipe and olive branch of Oklahoma's flag and the Indian figure and steamboat of Florida's flag vividly recall the history of these states.

Alabama

The state flag of Alabama was officially designated in 1895. The law declares that the flag, reminiscent of the Confederate battle flag, "shall be a crimson cross of St. Andrew on a field of white. The bars forming the cross shall be not less than six inches broad, and must extend diagonally across the flag from side to side."[1]

The governor's flag is the state flag with the addition of the coat of arms or great seal in the upper portion above the cross, and in the lower portion, the military crest of the state.[2]

Alaska

In 1927, a contest was held among Alaska's school children for the design of a territorial flag. Benny Benson, then thirteen years old, submitted the winning design. In 1959, the territorial flag was declared to be the state flag.[3]

The design of the official flag is eight gold stars in a field of blue, so selected for its simplicity, its originality and its symbolism. The blue, one of the national colors, typifies the evening sky, the blue of the sea and of mountain lakes, and of wild flowers that grow in Alaskan soil, the gold being significant of the wealth that lies hidden in Alaska's hills and streams.

The stars, seven of which form the constellation Ursa Major, the Great Bear, the most conspicuous constellation in the northern sky, contains the stars which form the "Dipper," including the "Pointers" which point toward the eighth star in the flag, Polaris, the North Star, the ever constant star for the mariner, the explorer, hunter, trapper, prospector, woodsman, and the surveyor. For Alaska the northernmost star in the galaxy of stars and which at some future time will take its place as the forty-ninth star in the national emblem.[4]

The code goes on to describe the color of the stars as that of natural yellow gold and the shade of blue as that used in the United States flag. Standard proportions and size are also delineated.

Arizona

Arizona's flag was adopted in 1917. It symbolizes the importance of the state's copper industry.

The lower half of the flag a blue field and the upper half divided into thirteen equal segments or rays which shall start at the center on the lower line and continue to the edges of the flag, colored alternately light yellow and red, consisting of six yellow and seven red rays. In the center of the flag, superimposed, there shall be a copper-colored five pointed star, so placed that the upper points shall be one foot from the top of the flag and the lower points one foot from the bottom of the flag. The red and blue shall be the same shade as the colors in the flag of the United States. The flag shall have a four-foot hoist and a six-foot fly, with a two-foot fly, with a two-foot star and the same proportions shall be observed for flags of other sizes.[5]

Arkansas

In 1913, at the urging of the Pine Bluff Chapter of the Daughters of the American Revolution, the Arkansas legislature adopted a state flag designed by Willie K. Hocker, a member of that chapter. In 1923, an additional star was added to the flag.[6] The amended 1913 act holds that

Whereas, the present State Flag is a rectangular of red on which is placed a large white diamond bordered by a wide band of blue, across the diamond being the word "Arkansas" and three stars, one above and two below the word "Arkansas"; and

Whereas, the said three stars so placed are designed to represent the three nations, France, Spain, and the United States which have successively exercised dominion over Arkansas; and

Whereas, from the 1st day of May, 1861, to the 23rd day of May, 1865, the State of Arkansas was a part of and under dominion of the Confederate States of America...

Be it resolved by the House, the Senate concurring therein, that an additional star be added to the State flag, which star is designed to represent the Confederate States of America, said star to be placed above the letter "R" in the word "Arkansas," and the present star appearing above the word "Arkansas" be placed above the last letter "A" in the said word "Arkansas" and upon the adoption of this resolution such flag of the State of Arkansas be and the same shall be official Flag of our State.[7]

The diamond signifies the fact that Arkansas is the only state in which diamonds are found. The twenty-five stars in the border signify that Arkansas was the twenty-fifth state to enter the Union.

The code also sets out a salute to the flag: "I salute the Arkansas Flag with its diamond and stars. We pledge our loyalty to thee."[8]

California

The California Bear Flag was designed by an unknown person sometime between 1875 and 1899. In 1846, however, a bear flag had been chosen as the emblem of the republic. It was adopted by legislative action in 1911. A new color rendering was approved in 1953.

The Bear Flag is the State Flag of California. As viewed with the hoist end of the flag to the left of the observer there appears in the upper left-hand corner of a white field a five-pointed red star with one point vertically upward and in the middle of the white field a brown grizzly bear walking toward the left with all four paws on a green grass plot, with head and eye turned slightly toward the observer; a red stripe forms the length of the flag at the bottom, and between the grass plot and the red stripe appear the words CALIFORNIA REPUBLIC.[9]

The code goes on to specify exact colors and dimensions. The white background symbolizes purity, the red star and bar, courage. The star itself represents sovereignty and the grizzly bear, strength.

Colorado

The 1911 law, amended slightly in 1929 and 1964, adopting the state flag, describes it as follows:

The flag shall consist of three alternate stripes to be of equal width and at right angles to the staff, the two outer stripes to be blue of the same color as in the blue field of the national flag and the middle stripe to be white, the proportion of the flag being a width of two-thirds of its length. At a distance from the staff end of the flag of one-fifth of the total length of the flag there shall be a circular red C, of the same color as the red in the national flag of the United States. The diameter of the letter shall be two-thirds of the width of the flag. The inner line of the opening of the letter C shall be three-fourths of the width of its body or bar and the outer line of the opening shall be double the length of the inner line thereof. Completely filling the open space inside the letter C shall be a golden disk; attached to the flag shall be a cord of gold and silver intertwined, with tassels one of gold and one of silver.[10]

Connecticut

The General Assembly adopted the design of the state flag in 1897.

The dimensions of the flag shall be five feet and six inches in length, four feet and four inches in width. The flag shall be of azure blue silk, charged with a shield of rococo design of argent white silk, having embroidered in the center three grape vines, supported and bearing fruit in natural colors. The bordure to the shield shall be embroidered in two colors, gold and silver. Below the shield shall be a white streamer, cleft at each end, bordered by gold and browns in fine lines, and upon the streamer shall be embroidered in dark blue letters the motto "Qui Transtulit Sustinet"; the whole design being the arms of the state.[11]

Delaware

The state flag of Delaware was adopted in 1913.

The design of the official state flag shall be as follows: A background of colonial blue surrounding a diamond of buff in which diamond is placed the correct coat of arms of the State in the colors prescribed by law and in accordance with § 301 of this title, with the words, "December 7, 1787," to be inscribed underneath the diamond.[12]

The code goes on to describe the exact colors of each element of the flag. A governor's flag is also provided by law.[13]

Florida

The Florida state flag makes prominent use of the 1868 seal, which was changed in 1970, when the sabal palmetto replaced the cocoa tree as the state tree.

The state flag shall conform with standard commercial sizes, and be of the following proportions and description: The seal of the state, in diameter one-half the hoist, shall occupy the center of a white ground. Red bars, in width one-fifth the hoist, shall extend from each corner toward the center, to the outer rim of the seal.[14]

Georgia

The Georgia state flag, designed by John Sammons Bell, was adopted in 1956. It replaced the flags adopted in 1799, 1861, 1879, and 1905. The current flag maintains many of the characteristics of the older flags.

The flag of the State of Georgia shall be a vertical band of blue occupying one-third of the entire flag nearest to the flagstaff. The remainder of the space shall be a square, two-thirds the length of the flag, having a red background with a broad saltire of blue bordered with white on which 13 white mullets or five-pointed stars, corresponding in number to that of the Confederate States of America as recognized by the Confederate States Congress, are emblazoned; so that such remainder shall be the same as the union of the flag of the Confederate States as approved and cited in Statutes at Large of the Confederate States Congress, 1st and 2nd Sessions, 1862–63, 1863–64, and approved May 1, 1863, such remainder being popularly known as the Battle Flag of the Confederacy. On the blue field shall be stamped, painted, or embroidered the coat of arms of the state. Every force of the organized militia shall carry this flag when on parade or review.[15]

The pledge of allegiance to the Georgia flag is set in the state code: "I pledge allegiance to the Georgia flag and to the principles for which it stands: Wisdom, Justice, and Moderation."[16]

Hawaii

The Hawaiian state flag is the same flag that was used for the Kingdom of Hawaii, the Republic of Hawaii, and the Territory of Hawaii. Its alternating white, red, and blue stripes represent the eight islands. The field resembles the Union Jack of Great Britain, from which the flag was originally designed.[17]

Idaho

The state flag was adopted in 1907. For twenty years, the state flag in actual use did not meet the specifications of the 1907 law. In 1927, this situation was corrected.

A state flag for the state of Idaho is hereby adopted, the same to be as follows:

A silk flag, blue field, five (5) feet six (6) inches fly, and four (4) feet four (4) inches on pike, bordered with gilt fringe two and one half (2 1/2) inches in width, with state seal of Idaho twenty-one (21) inches in diameter, in colors, in the center of a blue field. The words "State of Idaho" are embroidered in with block letters, two (2) inches in height on a red band three (3) inches in width by twenty-nine (29) inches in length, the band being in gold and placed about eight and one half (8 1/2) inches from the lower border of fringe and parallel with the same.[18]

Illinois

The first Illinois state flag, which incorporated the great seal on the banner, was adopted in 1915. In 1969, the legislature amended the 1915 act to include the name of the state on the flag and to standardize production of the flag. The amended act reads as follows:

The reproduction of the emblem only on the "great seal of the State of Illinois" is authorized and permitted when reproduced in black or in the national colors upon a white sheet or background and bearing underneath the emblem in blue letters the word "Illinois" and being an actual reproduction of the great seal except for the outer ring thereof for use as a State banner or insignia under the conditions and subject to the restrictions provided by the laws of the United States and the State of Illinois as to the United States or State flag or ensign.[19]

Indiana

The Indiana state flag, designed by Paul Hadley of Mooresville, Indiana, was adopted in 1917. In 1979, an amendment standardized the size of the flag, but the 1917 law otherwise remains in force.

A state flag is hereby adopted, and the same shall be of the following design and dimensions, to-wit: Its dimensions shall be three (3) feet fly by two (2) feet hoist; or five (5) feet fly by three (3) feet hoist; or any size proportionate to either of those dimensions. The field of the flag shall be blue with nineteen (19) stars and a flaming torch in gold or buff. Thirteen (13) stars shall be arranged in an outer circle, representing the original thirteen (13) states; five (5) stars shall be arranged in a half circle below the torch and inside the outer circle of stars, representing the states admitted prior to Indiana; and the nineteenth star, appreciably larger than the others and representing Indiana shall be placed above the flame of the torch. The outer circle of stars shall be so arranged that one (1) star shall appear directly in the middle at the top of the circle, and the word "Indiana" shall be placed in a half circle over and above the star representing Indiana and midway between it and the star in the center above it. Rays shall be shown radiating from the torch to the three (3) stars on each side of the star in the upper center of the circle.[20]

Iowa

The Iowa state banner was designed by Mrs. Dixie Cornell Gebhardt and sponsored by the Iowa Society of the Daughters of the American Revolution. It was approved in 1921.[21]

The banner designed by the Iowa society of the Daughters of the American Revolution and presented to the state, which banner consists of three vertical stripes of blue, white, and red, the blue stripe being nearest the staff and the white stripe being in the center, and upon the central white stripe being depicted a spreading eagle bearing in its beak blue streamers on which is inscribed, in white letters, the state motto, "Our liberties we prize and our rights we will maintain" and with the word "Iowa" in red letters below such streamers, as such design now appears on the banner in the office of the governor of the state of Iowa, is hereby adopted as a distinctive state banner, for use on all occasions where a distinctive state symbol in the way of a banner may be fittingly displayed.[22]

Kansas

The Kansas state flag was approved in 1927. In 1961, the name of the state was added to it. The laws describe the flag in this manner:

The official state flag of the state of Kansas shall be a rectangle of dark-blue silk or bunting, three (3) feet on the staff by five (5) feet fly.

The great seal of the state of Kansas, without its surrounding band of lettering, shall be located equidistant from the staff and the fly side of the flag, with the lower edge of the seal located eleven (11) inches above the base side of the flag. The great seal shall be surmounted by a crest and the word KANSAS shall be located underneath the seal.

The seal shall be seventeen (17) inches in diameter. The crest shall be on a wreath or an azure, a sunflower slipped proper, which divested of its heraldic language is a sunflower as torn from its stalk in its natural colors on a bar of twisted gold and blue. The crest shall be six (6) inches in diameter; the wreath shall be nine (9) inches in length. The top of the crest shall be located two (2) inches beneath the top side of the flag. The letters KANSAS shall be imprinted in gold block letters below the seal, the said letters to be properly proportioned, and five (5) inches in height, imprinted with a stroke one (1) inch wide; and the first letter K shall commence with the same distance from the staff side of the flag as the end of the last letter S is from the fly side of the flag. The bottom edge of the letters shall be two (2) inches above the base side of the flag. Larger or smaller flags will be of the same proportional dimensions.

The colors in the seal shall be as follows: Stars, silver; hills, purple; sun, deep yellow; glory, light yellow; sky, yellow and orange from hills half way to motto, upper half azure; grass, green; river, light blue; boat, white; house, dark brown; ground, brown; wagons, white; near horse, white; off horse, bay; buffalo, dark, almost black; motto, white; scroll, light brown.[23]

Kansas also has a state banner, which was approved in 1925. The law holds that the official state banner

shall be of solid blue and shall be of the same tint as the color of the field of the United States flag, whose width shall be three-fourths of its length, with a sunflower in the center having a diameter of two-thirds of the space.[24]

Kentucky

The 1918 act creating Kentucky's state flag was amended in 1962 to read as follows:

The official state flag of the Commonwealth of Kentucky shall be of navy blue silk, nylon, wool or cotton bunting, or some other suitable material, with the seal of the Commonwealth encircled by a wreath, the lower half of which shall be goldenrod in bloom and the upper half the words "Commonwealth of Kentucky," embroidered, printed, painted or stamped on the center thereof. The dimensions of the flag may vary, but the length shall be one and nine-tenths (1 9/10) times the width and the diameter of the seal and encirclement shall be approximately two-thirds (2/3) the width of the flag.[25]

Louisiana

Louisiana's flag was adopted officially in 1912 by the legislature.

The official flag of Louisiana shall be that flag now in general use, consisting of a solid blue field with the coat-of-arms of the state, the pelican feeding its young, in white in the center, with a ribbon beneath, also in white, containing in blue the motto of the state, "Union, Justice and Confidence."[26]

In 1981, the legislature adopted a state pledge of allegiance.

I pledge allegiance to the flag of the state of Louisiana and to the motto for which it stands: A state, under God, united in purpose and ideals, confident that justice shall prevail for all of those abiding here.[27]

Maine

The Maine legislature adopted the state flag in 1909. This flag uses the coat of arms in a field of blue.

The flag to be known as the official flag of the State shall be of blue, of the same color as the blue field in the flag of the United States, and of the following dimensions and designs; to wit, the length or height of the staff to be 9 feet, including brass spearhead and ferrule; the fly of said flag to be 5 feet 6 inches, and to be 4 feet 4 inches on the staff; in the center of the flag there shall be embroidered in silk on both sides of the flag the coat of arms of the State, in proportionate size; the edges to be trimmed with knotted fringe of yellow silk, 2 1/2 inches wide; a cord, with tassels, to be attached to the staff at the spearhead, to be 8 feet 6 inches long and composed of white and blue silk strands.[28]

Maine law also prescribes a merchant and marine flag.

The flag to be known as the merchant and marine flag of the State shall be of white, at the top of which in blue letters shall be the motto "Dirigo"; beneath the motto shall be the representation of a pine tree in green color, the trunk of which shall be entwined with the representation of an anchor in blue color; beneath the tree and anchor shall be the name "Maine" in blue color.[29]

Maryland

Maryland's flag was officially adopted in 1904, although the flag was first flown in 1888 at Gettysburg Battlefield. The flag described below employs the arms of the Calvert and Crossland families.[30]

(a) *In general.* The State flag is quartered.

(b) *First and fourth quarters.* The 1st and 4th quarters are paly of 6 pieces, or sable, a bend dexter counterchanged and the 2nd and 3rd, quarterly, are argent and gules, a cross bottony countersigned. Thus, the 1st and 4th quarters consist of 6 vertical bars alternately gold and black with a diagonal band on which the colors are reversed.

(c) *Second and third quarters.* The 2nd and 3rd quarters are a quartered field of red and white, charged with a Greek cross, its arms terminating in trefoils, with the coloring transported, red being on the white ground and white on the red, and all being as represented upon the escutcheon of the State seal.[31]

Massachusetts

The Massachusetts flag, like many other state flags, includes a representation of the coat of arms. Unlike most other states, the law also prescribes a naval and maritime flag.

The flag of the commonwealth shall consist of a white rectangular field, bearing on either side a representation of the arms of the commonwealth, except that the star shall be white. The naval and maritime flag of the commonwealth shall consist of a white rectangular field bearing on either side a representation of a green pine tree.[32]

In 1971, the governor's flag was prescribed by law.

The flag of the governor shall conform to the design of the flag of the commonwealth, except that the field of the flag of the governor shall be triangular in shape.[33]

Michigan

The 1911 law adopting the state flag states simply that "the state flag shall be blue charged with the arms of the state."[34] A pledge of allegiance, written by Harold G. Coburn, was adopted in 1972.

I pledge allegiance to the flag of Michigan, and to the state for which it stands, 2 beautiful peninsulas united by a bridge of steel, where equal opportunity and justice to all is our ideal.[35]

A governor's flag is also provided in the 1911 law: "The governor's flag shall be white charged with the arms of the state."[36]

Minnesota

In 1957, the legislature approved the design for a new flag. The 1893 flag had been a double flag. The new law, revised only for editorial purposes in 1984, simplifies the design of the first flag.[37]

The design of the flag shall conform substantially to the following description: The staff is surmounted by a bronze eagle with outspread wings; the flag is rectangular in shape and is on a medium blue background with a narrow gold border and a golden fringe. A circular emblem is contained in the center of the blue field. The circular emblem is on a general white background with a yellow border. The word MINNESOTA is inscribed in red lettering on the lower part of the white field. The white emblem background surrounding a center design contains 19 five pointed stars arranged symmetrically in four groups of four stars each and one group of three stars. The latter group is in the upper part of the center circular white emblem. The group of stars at the top in the white emblem consists of three stars of which the uppermost star is the largest and represents the north star. A center design is contained on the white emblem and is made up of the scenes from the great seal of the state of Minnesota, surrounded by a border of intertwining Cypripedium reginae, the state flower, on a blue field of the same color as the general flag background. The flower border design contains the figures 1819, 1858, 1893.

The coloring is the same on both sides of the flag, but the lettering and the figures appear reversed on one side.[38]

Mississippi

The Mississippi flag was created by a special committee appointed by the legislature in 1894. The original law described a flag

with width two-thirds length; with a union square, in width two-thirds of the width of the flag; the ground of the union to be red and a broak blue saltier thereon, bordered with white and emblazoned with thirteen (13) mullets or five-pointed stars, corresponding with the number of original states of the Union; the field to be divided into three bars of equal width, the upper one blue, the center one white, and the lower one, extending the whole length of the flag, red—the national colors ...[39]

The official pledge of the State of Mississippi reads as follows:

I salute the flag of Mississippi and the sovereign state for which it stands with pride in her history and achievements and with confidence in her future under the guidance of Almighty God.[40]

Missouri

The Missouri flag, designed by Marie Elizabeth Watkins Oliver and Mary Kochtitzky, was approved by the legislature in 1913.[41]

The official flag of the state of Missouri is rectangular in shape and its vertical width is to the horizontal length as seven is to twelve. It has one red, one white and one blue horizontal stripe of equal width; the red is at the top and the blue at the bottom. In the center of the flag there is a band of blue in the form of a circle enclosing the coat of arms in the colors as established by law on a white ground. The width of the blue band is one-fourteenth of the vertical width of the flag and the diameter of the circle is one-third of the horizontal length of the flag. In the blue band there are set at equal distances from each other twenty-four five pointed stars.[42]

Montana

The Montana flag had been the banner of the First Montana Infantry before it was adopted as the state flag in 1905. In 1981, the name of the state was added to the flag.

The state flag of Montana shall be a flag having a blue field with a representation of the great seal of the state in the center and with golden fringe along the upper and lower borders of the flag; the same being the flag borne by the 1st Montana Infantry, U.S.V., in the Spanish-American War, with the exception of the device, "1st Montana Infantry, U.S.V."; and above the great seal of the state shall be the word "MONTANA" in Roman letters of gold color equal in height to one-tenth of the total vertical measurement of the blue field.[43]

Nebraska

A state banner was adopted in 1925 according to a bill introduced by J. Lloyd McMaster. In 1963, the banner was designated the official state flag.[44]

The banner of the State of Nebraska shall consist of a reproduction of the Great Seal of the State, charged on the center in gold and silver on a field of national blue. The banner shall be the official state flag of the State of Nebraska and may be displayed on such occasions, at such times, and under such conditions as the flag of the United States of America.[45]

Nevada

The Nevada state flag has been modified several times since 1866, when a flag was first adopted. The current law prescribes the following:

The official flag of the State of Nevada is hereby created, to be designed of the following colors, with the following lettering and devices thereon: The body of the flag shall be of solid cobalt blue. On the field in the upper left quarter thereof shall be two sprays of sagebrush with the stems crossed at the bottom to form a half wreath. Within the sprays shall be a five-pointed silver star with one point up. The word "Nevada" shall also be inscribed within the sprays, and shall be inscribed in the same style of letters as the words, "Battle Born" and shall be inscribed in the following manner: Beginning at the upper point shall appear the letter "N," the other letters shall appear equally spaced between the points of the star. Above the wreath, and touching the tips thereof, shall be a scroll bearing the words "Battle Born"; the scroll shall be golden-yellow, and the lettering thereon black-colored roman capital letters.[46]

New Hampshire

New Hampshire's state flag was not adopted until 1909. The original flag was modified in 1931, when changes were made in the state seal. The law declares that

The state flag shall be of the following color and design: The body or field shall be blue and shall bear upon its center in suitable proportion and colors a representation of the state seal. The seal shall be surrounded by a wreath of laurel leaves with nine stars interspersed. When used for military purposes the flag shall conform to the regulations of the United States.[47]

New Jersey

The design of the state flag was adopted in 1896. The law states simply that

The state flag shall be of buff color, having in the center thereof the arms of the state emblazoned thereon.[48]

In 1965, the official state colors for use in the flag were designated:

The official colors of the State of New Jersey for use on the State Flag and for other purposes shall be buff and Jersey blue.

For the purposes of this act the specifications, references and designations for the official colors of the state are as follows:

Jersey Blue (Cable No. 70087, Royal Blue. The Color Association of the United States, Inc.)

Buff (Cable No. 65015, U.S. Army Buff. The Color Association of the United States, Inc.)[49]

New Mexico

The current New Mexico state flag, adopted in 1925, replaced a flag adopted in 1915. The Daughters of the American Revolution had supported the movement for a distinctive new flag, and the design of Dr. Harry Mera was finally chosen.[50] The law reads as follows:

That a flag be and the same is hereby adopted to be used on all occasions when the state is officially and publicly represented, with the privilege of use by all citizens upon such occasions as they may deem fitting and appropriate. Said flag shall be the ancient Zia sun symbol of red in the center of a field of yellow. The colors shall be the red and yellow of old Spain. The proportion of the flag shall be a width of two-thirds its length. The sun symbol shall be one-third of the length of the flag. Said symbol shall have four groups of rays set at right angles; each group shall consist of four rays, the two inner rays of the group shall be one-fifth longer than the outer rays of the group. The diameter of the circle in the center of the symbol shall be one-third of the width of the symbol. Said flag shall conform in color and design described herein.[51]

In 1953, the legislature adopted both an English and a Spanish salute to the state flag. The official salute to the state flag is:

I salute the flag of the state of New Mexico, the Zia symbol of perfect friendship among united cultures.[52]

The official Spanish language salute to the state flag is:

Saludo la bandera del estado de Nuevo Méjico, el símbolo zía de amistad perfecta, entre culturas unidas.[53]

New York

In 1882, the legislature adopted the arms of the state that had first been designated in 1778. The flag was adopted in 1901 and modified in 1909. The current law reads as follows:

The device of arms of this state, as adopted March sixteenth, seventeen hundred and seventy-eight, is hereby declared to be correctly described as follows:

Charge. Azure, in a landscape, the sun in fess, rising in splendor or, behind a range of three mountains, the middle one the highest; in base a ship and sloop under sail, passing and about to meet on a river, bordered below by a grassy shore fringed with shrubs, all proper.

Crest. On a wreath azure and or, an American eagle proper, rising to the dexter from a two-thirds of a globe terrestrial, showing the north Atlantic ocean with outlines of its shores.

Supporters. On a quasi compartment formed by the extension of the scroll.

Dexter. The figure of Liberty proper, her hair disheveled and decorated with pearls, vested azure, sandaled gules, about the waist a cincture or, fringed gules, a mantle of the last depending from the shoulders behind to the feet, in the dexter hand a staff ensigned with a Phrygian cap or, the sinister arm embowed, the hand supporting the shield at the dexter chief point, a royal crown by her sinister foot dejected.

Sinister. The figure of Justice proper, her hair disheveled and decorated with pearls, vested or, about the waist a cincture azure, fringed gules, sandaled and manteled as Liberty, bound about the eyes with a fillet proper, in the dexter hand a straight sword hilted or, erect, resting on the sinister chief point of the shield, the sinister arm embowed, holding before her scales proper.

Motto. On a scroll below the shield argent, in sable, Excelsior.

State Flag. The state flag is hereby declared to be blue, charged with the arms of the state in the colors as described in the blazon of this section.[54]

North Carolina

The flag of North Carolina was adopted in 1885.

The flag of North Carolina shall consist of a blue union, containing in the center thereof a white star with the letter "N" in gilt on the left and the letter "C" in gilt on the right of said star, the circle containing the same to be one third the width of said union. The fly of the flag shall consist of two equally proportioned bars, the upper bar to be red, the lower bar to be white; the length of the bars horizontally shall be equal to the perpendicular length of the union, and the total length of the flag shall be one third more than its width. Above the star in the center of the union there shall be a gilt scroll in semicircular form, containing in black letters this inscription: "May 20th, 1775," and below the star there shall be a similar scroll containing in black letters the inscription: "April 12th, 1776."[55]

North Dakota

The North Dakota state flag was first adopted in 1911. An amendment was made to the original act in 1959. The current law reads as follows:

The flag of North Dakota shall consist of a field of blue silk or material which will withstand the elements four feet four inches [132.08 centimeters] on the pike and five feet six inches [167.64 centimeters] on the fly, with a border of knotted yellow fringe two and one-half inches [6.35 centimeters] wide. On each side of said flag in the center thereof, shall be embroidered or stamped an eagle with outspread wings and with opened beak. The eagle shall be three feet four inches [101.6 centimeters] from tip to tip of wing, and one foot ten inches [55.88 centimeters] from top of head to bottom of olive branch hereinafter described. The left foot of the eagle shall grasp a sheaf of arrows, the right foot shall grasp an olive branch showing three red berries. On the breast of the eagle shall be displayed a shield, the lower part showing seven red and six white stripes placed alternately. Through the open beak of the eagle shall pass a scroll bearing the words "E Pluribus Unum." Beneath the eagle there shall be a scroll on which shall be borne the words "North Dakota." Over the scroll carried through the eagle's beak shall be shown thirteen five-pointed stars, the whole device being surmounted by a sunburst. The flag shall conform in all respects as to color, form, size, and device with the regimental flag carried by the First North Dakota Infantry in the Spanish American War and Philippine Insurrection, except in the words shown on the scroll below the eagle.[56]

Ohio

The flag of Ohio was first adopted in 1902. An amendment in 1953 was made so that the current law reads as follows:

The flag of the state shall be pennant shaped. It shall have three red and two white horizontal stripes. The union of the flag shall be seventeen five-pointed stars, white in a blue triangular field, the base of which shall be the staff end or vertical edge of the flag, and the apex of which shall be the center of the middle red stripe. The stars shall be grouped around a red disc superimposed upon a white circular "O." The proportional dimensions of the flag and of its various parts shall be according to the official design on file in the office of the secretary of state. One state flag of uniform dimensions shall be furnished to each company of the organized militia.[57]

In 1963, descriptions of other official flags were passed by the legislature.

The flag of the governor of this state will be of scarlet wool bunting, six feet eight inches hoist by ten feet six inches fly. In each of the four corners will be a white five-pointed star with one point upward. The centers of these stars will be twelve inches from the long edges and seventeen inches from the short edges of the flag. In the center of the flag will be a reproduction of the great seal of Ohio in proper colors, three feet in diameter, surrounded by thirteen white stars equally spaced with their centers on an imaginary circle four feet three inches in diameter. All stars shall be of such size that their points would lie on the circumference of an imaginary circle ten inches in diameter.

The official colors of the governor of Ohio will be of scarlet silk, four feet four inches on the pike by five feet six inches fly, of the same design as the flag of the governor of Ohio, with the seal and stars proportionately reduced in size and embroidered. The colors will be trimmed on three edges with a knotted fringe of yellow silk two and one half inches wide. Attached below the head of the pike will be a silk cord of scarlet and white eight feet six inches in length with a tassel at each end.

The naval flag of the governor of Ohio will be of scarlet wool bunting, three feet hoist by four feet fly. The design will be the same as the flag of the governor of Ohio with the seal and the stars proportionately reduced in size.

The automobile flag of the governor of Ohio will be of scarlet silk, or wool bunting, one foot six inches on the staff by two feet six inches on the fly. The design will be the same as the flag of the governor of Ohio with the seal and stars proportionately reduced in size. The flag will be trimmed on three edges with a knotted fringe of silk or wool one and one half inches wide.[58]

Oklahoma

The Oklahoma flag was adopted in 1925 and amended in 1941 to add the name of the state to the flag. The law reads as follows:

The banner, or flag, of the design prescribed by Senate Concurrent Resolution No. 25, Third Legislature of the State of Oklahoma shall be, and it hereby is superseded and replaced by one of the following design, to-wit:

A sky blue field with a circular rawhide shield of an American Indian

Warrior, decorated with six (6) painted crosses on the face thereof, the lower half of the shield to be fringed with seven (7) pendant eagle feathers and superimposed upon the face of the shield a calumet or peace pipe, crossed at right angles by an olive branch, as illustrated by the design accompanying this resolution, and underneath said shield or design in white letters shall be placed the word "Oklahoma," and the same is hereby adopted as the official flag and banner of the State of Oklahoma.[59]

The same section describing the flag also sets out the official salute to the flag: "I salute the flag of the state of Oklahoma: Its symbols of peace unite all people." The salute was adopted in 1982.[60]

In 1957, the legislature approved a governor's flag:

The flag of the Governor of the State of Oklahoma shall be forest green, bearing on each side the following: the Great Seal of the State of Oklahoma, centered, surrounded by five equidistant white stars with one of the stars placed directly above the Great Seal; and the flag to be edged with golden fringe.[61]

Oregon

The Oregon state flag was adopted in 1925, and the official colors were designated in 1959. The law is as follows:

(1) A state flag is adopted to be used on all occasions when the state is officially and publicly represented, with the privilege of use by all citizens upon such occasions as may be fitting and appropriate. It shall bear on one side on a navy blue field the state escutcheon in gold, supported by 33 gold stars and bearing above the escutcheon the words "State of Oregon" in gold and below the escutcheon the figures "1859" in gold, and on the other side on a navy blue field a representation of the beaver in gold.

(2) The official colors of the State of Oregon are navy blue and gold.[62]

Pennsylvania

Pennsylvania's state flag was approved in 1907.

The flag to be known as the official flag of the commonwealth of Pennsylvania shall be of blue, same color as the blue field in the flag of the United States, and of the following dimensions and design; to wit, The length, or height of the staff to be nine feet, including brass spearhead and ferrule; the fly of the said flag to be six feet two inches, and to be four feet six inches on the staff; in the center of the flag there shall be embroidered in silk the same on both sides of the flag the coat of arms of the commonwealth of Pennsylvania, in proportionate size; the edges to be trimmed with knotted fringe of yellow silk, two and one-half inches wide; a cord, with tassels, to be attached to the staff, at the spearhead, to be eight feet six inches long, and composed of white and blue silk strands.[63]

Rhode Island

The original act designating the state flag was passed in 1897. Although amended, the flag remains essentially unchanged.

The flag of the state shall be white, five (5) feet and six (6) inches fly and four (4) feet and ten (10) inches deep on the pike, bearing on each side in the centre a gold anchor, twenty-two (22) inches high, and underneath it a blue ribbon twenty-four (24) inches long and five (5) inches wide, or in these proportions, with the motto "Hope" in golden letters thereon, the whole surrounded by thirteen (13) golden stars in a circle. The flag to be edged with yellow fringe. The pike shall be surmounted by a spearhead and the length of the pike shall be nine (9) feet, not including the spearhead, provided, however, that on the 29th day of August, 1978 the flag of the Rhode Island first regiment shall be flown as the official state flag for that day.[64]

The law also allows for a flag and pennant of the governor.

The flag and pennant of the governor shall be white bearing on each side the following: A gold anchor on a shield with a blue field and gold border; above the shield a gold scroll bearing the words in blue letters "State of Rhode Island"; below the shield a gold scroll bearing in blue letters the word "Hope"; the shield and scrolls to be surrounded by four (4) blue stars; both the flag and pennant to be edged with yellow fringe.[65]

South Carolina

The first state flag was designed by Colonel William Moultrie at the request of the Revolutionary Council of Safety in 1775. It was in truth a flag for the troops. Moultrie chose the blue of the soldiers' uniforms as the color of the field. A crescent in the upper right of the flag reproduced the silver emblem worn by the soldiers on the front of their caps. A palmetto tree was added in the center of the flag after Moultrie's defense of a palmetto-log fort on Sullivan's Island in 1776. In 1861, with South Carolina's secession, this same flag was chosen as the state's national flag. It became the state flag again when South Carolina rejoined the union.[66]

A 1966 act designated the pledge of allegiance to the state flag.

The pledge to the flag of South Carolina shall be as follows: "I salute the flag of South Carolina and pledge to the Palmetto State love, loyalty and faith."[67]

South Dakota

South Dakota has two official state flags. The first flag, adopted in 1909, depicted the sun on the obverse and the seal on the reverse. Because of the expense of manufacturing a flag with two emblems, however, a new flag with a single emblem was designed and approved in 1963.[68] The description of the new flag is as follows:

The state flag or banner shall consist of a field of sky-blue one and two-thirds as long as it is wide. Centered on such field shall be the great seal of South Dakota made in conformity with the terms of the Constitution, which shall be four-ninths the width of the said flag in diameter; such seal shall be on a white background with the seal outlined in dark blue thereon, or, in the alternative shall be on a sky-blue background with the seal outlined in dark blue thereon; surrounding the seal in gold shall be a serrated sun whose extreme width shall be five-ninths the width of the said flag. The words "South Dakota" symmetrically arranged to conform to the circle of the sun and seal shall appear in gold letters one-eighteenth the width of the said field above said sun and seal and the words "The Sunshine State" in like-sized gold letters and in like arrangement shall appear below the said sun and seal. Flags designed of such material as may be provident for outdoor use need have no fringe but flags for indoor and display usage shall have a golden fringe one-eighteenth the width of said flag on the three sides other than the hoist.

All state flags made in conformity with state law prior to March 11, 1963 shall remain official state flags but the creation of a state flag from and after said date, other than in conformity with § 1–6–4, is prohibited.[69]

Tennessee

The Tennessee state flag was designed by LeRoy Reeves and adopted in 1905.[70]

The flag or banner of the state of Tennessee shall be of the following design, colors, and proportions, to wit, an oblong flag or banner in length one and two thirds (1 2/3) times its width, the principal field of same to be of color red, but said flag or banner ending at its free or outer end in a perpendicular bar of blue, of uniform width, running from side to side, that is to say, from top to bottom of said flag or banner, and separated from the red field by a narrow margin or stripe of white of uniform width; the width of the white stripe to be one fifth (1/5) that of the blue bar; and the total width of the bar and stripe together to be equal to one eighth (1/8) of the width of the flag. In the center of the red field shall be a smaller circular field of blue, separated from the surrounding red field by a circular margin or stripe of white of uniform width and of the same width as the straight margin or stripe first mentioned. The breadth or diameter of the circular blue field, exclusive of the white margin, shall be equal to one half (1/2) of the width of the flag. Inside the circular blue field shall be three (3) five-pointed stars of white distributed at equal intervals around a point, the center of the blue field, and of such size and arrangement that one (1) point of each star shall approach as closely as practicable without actually touching one (1) point of each of the other two (2) around the center point of the field; and the two (2) outer points of each star shall approach as nearly as practicable without actually touching the periphery of the blue field. The arrangement of the three (3) stars shall be such that the centers of no two (2) stars shall be in a line parallel to either the side or end of the flag, but intermediate between same; and the highest star shall be the one nearest the upper confined corner of the flag.[71]

Texas

The flag of the Republic of Texas became the official state flag when it was adopted in the 1876 state constitution.

The Texas flag is an emblem of four sides, and four angles of ninety (90) degrees each. It is a rectangle having its width equal to two-thirds of its length. The flag is divided into three equivalent parts, called bars or stripes, one stripe being bloodred, one white, and the other azure blue. These stripes are rectangles, also, and they are exact duplicates of one another in every respect. The width of each stripe is equal to one-half of its length, or one-third of the length of the Flag, while the length of each stripe is equal to the width of the Flag, or two-thirds of the length of the Emblem.

One end of the Flag is blue, and it is called the Flag's "right." This stripe is a perpendicular bar next to the staff or the halyard, and it is attached by means of a heading made of strong and very durable material. The remaining two-thirds of the Flag is made up of two horizontal bars of equal width, one being white and the other red, and this end of the Emblem is called the Flag's "left." Each one of the stripes is perpendicular to the blue stripe, and when the Flag is displayed on a flagpole or staff, or flat on a plane surface, the white stripe should always be at the top of the Flag, with the red stripe directly underneath it. Thus, each stripe on the Texas Flag touches each of the other stripes, which signifies that the three colors are mutually dependent upon one another in imparting the lessons of the Flag: bravery, loyalty, and purity.

Description of the Star

In the center of the blue stripe is a white star of five points. One point of this star is always at the top, and in a vertical line drawn from one end of the blue stripe to the other, and midway between its sides. This line is the vertical axis of the blue stripe, and it is perpendicular to the horizontal axis at the central point of the stripe. The two lowest points of the star are in a line parallel to the horizontal axis, and the distance from the topmost point of the star to the line through these two points is equal to approximately one third of the length of the blue stripe, or one-third of the width of the Flag. The center of the star is at the point of intersection of the horizontal axis with the vertical axis, or at the central point of the blue stripe. The other two points of the star are above the horizontal axis, and near the sides of the blue stripe.

The salute to the Texas flag is:

Honor the Texas Flag; I pledge allegiance to thee, Texas, one and indivisible.[72]

Utah

The Utah state flag was adopted in 1896 and revised in 1933. It was designated the governor's flag in 1911.[73]

The state flag of Utah shall be a flag of blue field, fringed, with gold borders, with the following device worked in natural colors on the center of the blue field:

The center a shield; above the shield and thereon an American eagle with outstretched wings; the top of the shield pierced with six arrows arranged crosswise; upon the shield under the arrows the word "Industry," and below the word "Industry" on the center of the shield, a beehive; on each side of the beehive, growing sego lilies; below the beehive and near the bottom of the shield, the word "Utah," and below the word "Utah" and on the bottom of the shield, the figures "1847"; with the appearance of being back of the shield there shall be two American flags on flagstaffs placed crosswise with the flags so draped that they will project beyond each side of the shield, the heads of the flagstaffs appearing in front of the eagle's wings and the bottom of each staff appearing over the face of the draped flag below the shield; below the shield and flags and upon the blue field, the figures "1896"; around the entire design, a narrow circle in gold.[74]

Vermont

The current state flag of Vermont was adopted in 1923. It replaced the state flags adopted in 1803 and 1837. The 1923 law states simply that "the flag of the state shall be blue with the coat of arms of the state thereon."[75]

Virginia

The flag of the Commonwealth of Virginia was adopted by legislative act in 1930.

The flag of the Commonwealth shall hereafter be made of bunting or merino. It shall be a deep blue field, with a circular white centre of the same material. Upon this circle shall be painted or embroidered, to show on both sides alike, the coat of arms of the State . . . for the obverse of the great seal of the Commonwealth; and there shall be a white silk fringe on the outer edge, furthest from the flagstaff. This shall be known and respected as the flag of Virginia.[76]

Washington

The state flag of Washington was adopted in 1923 and amended slightly in 1925. The law declares

That the official flag of the state of Washington shall be of dark green silk or bunting and shall bear in its center a reproduction of the seal of the state of Washington embroidered, printed, painted or stamped thereon. The edges of the flag may, or may not, be fringed. If a fringe is used the same shall be of gold or yellow color of the same shade as the seal. The dimensions of the flag may vary.[77]

West Virginia

The current state flag of West Virginia was adopted in 1929, after numerous other flags had come into use and become infeasible. The flag is described as follows:

The proportions of the flag of the state of West Virginia shall be the same as those of the United States ensign; the field shall be pure white, upon the center of which shall be emblazoned in proper colors, the coat-of-arms of the state of West Virginia, upon which appears the date of the admission of the state into the Union, also with the motto "Montani Semper Liberi" (Mountaineers Always Freemen) above the coat-of-arms of the state of West Virginia there shall be a ribbon lettered, state of West Virginia, and arranged appropriately around the lower part of the coat-of-arms of the state of West Virginia a wreath of rhododendron maximum in proper colors. The field of pure white shall be bordered by a strip of blue on four sides. The flag of the state of West Virginia when used for parade purposes shall be trimmed with gold colored fringe on three sides and when used on ceremonial occasions with the United States ensign, shall be trimmed and mounted in similar fashion to the United States flag as regards fringe cord, tassels and mounting.[78]

Wisconsin

In 1979, the legislature revised the state flag, which had been adopted in 1913. The 1979 law became effective in 1981 and sets out these requirements:

(1) The Wisconsin state flag consists of the following features:
(a) Relative dimensions of 2 to 3, hoist to fly.
(b) A background of royal blue cloth.
(c) The state coat of arms, as described under s. 1.07, in material of appropriate colors, applied on each side in the center of the field, of such size that, if placed in a circle whose diameter is equal to 50% of the hoist, those portions farthest from the center of the field would meet, but not cross, the boundary of the circle.
(d) The word "WISCONSIN" in white, capital, condensed Gothic letters, one-eighth of the hoist in height, centered above the coat of arms, midway between the uppermost part of the coat of arms and the top edge of the flag.
(e) The year "1848" in white, condensed Gothic numbers, one-eighth of the hoist in height, centered below the coat of arms, midway between the lowermost part of the coat of arms and the bottom edge of the flag.
(f) Optional trim on the edges consisting of yellow knotted fringe.
(2) The department of administration shall ensure that all official state flags that are manufactured on or after May 1, 1981 conform to the requirements of this section. State flags manufactured before May 1, 1981 may continue to be used as state flags.[79]

Wyoming

The state flag of Wyoming, designed by Mrs. A. C. Keyes of Casper, was adopted in 1917. The colors of the flag carry important symbolism: the red border symbolizes the Indian and the blood of the pioneers; the white signifies purity; the blue symbolizes fidelity and justice.[80] The current law reads as follows:

A state flag is adopted to be used on all occasions when the state is officially and publicly represented. All citizens have the privilege of use of the flag upon any occasion they deem appropriate. The width of the flag shall be seven-tenths (7/10) of its length; the outside border shall be in red, the width of which shall be one-twentieth (1/20) of the length of the flag; next to the border shall be a stripe of white on the four (4) sides of the field, which shall be in width one-fortieth (1/40) of the length of the flag. The remainder of the flag shall be a blue field, in the center of which shall be a white silhouetted buffalo, the length of which shall be one-half (1/2) of the length of the blue field; the other measurements of the buffalo shall be in proportion to its length. On the ribs of the buffalo shall be the great seal of the state of Wyoming in blue. The seal shall be in diameter one-fifth (1/5) the length of the flag. Attached to the flag shall be a cord of gold with gold tassels. The same colors shall be used in the flag, red, white and blue, as are used in the flag of the United States of America.[81]

Notes

1. Ala. Code § 1–2–5.
2. Ibid., § 31–2–54.
3. *Alaska Blue Book, 1979*, p. 123.
4. Alaska Stat. § 44.09.020.
5. Ariz. Rev. Stat. Ann § 41–851.
6. *Arkansas Almanac, 1972* (Little Rock: Arkansas Almanac, Inc., 1972), p. 31.
7. Ark. Stat. Ann § 5–107.
8. Ibid., § 5–108.
9. Cal. Gov't. Code § 420 (West).
10. Colo. Rev. Stat. § 24–80–904.
11. Conn. Gen. Stat. Ann. § 3–107 (West).
12. Del. Code Ann. tit. 29, § 306.
13. Ibid., tit. 29 § 307.
14. Fla. Stat. Ann. § 15.012 (West).
15. Ga. Code Ann. § 50–3–1.
16. Ibid., § 50–3–2.
17. *Hawaii, The Aloha State* (Honolulu: State of Hawaii, Hawaii Visitors Bureau, Chamber of Commerce of Hawaii, n.d.).
18. Idaho Code § 46–801.
19. Ill. Ann. Stat. ch. 1, § 3001 (Smith-Hurd).
20. Ind. Code Ann. § 1–2–2–1 (West).
21. *1985–86 Iowa Official Register*, vol. 61, p. 236.
22. Iowa Code Ann. § 31.1 (West).

23. Kan. Stat. Ann. § 73–702.
24. Ibid., § 73–704.
25. Ky. Rev. Stat. Ann. § 2.030 (Baldwin).
26. La. Rev. Stat. Ann. § 9–153 (West).
27. Ibid., § 49–167 (West).
28. Me. Rev. Stat. tit. 1, § 206.
29. Ibid., tit. 1, § 207.
30. *Maryland Manual, 1981–82*, p. 10.
31. Md. Ann. Code § 13–202.
32. Mass. Gen. Laws Ann. ch. 2, § 3 (West).
33. Ibid., ch. 2, § 4 (West).
34. Mich. Comp. Laws Ann. § 2–23.
35. Ibid., § 2.29.
36. Ibid., § 2.24.
37. *Official Minnesota Symbols* (St. Paul: Minnesota Historical Society, Education Division, December 1983).
38. Minn. Stat. Ann. § 1.141 (West).
39. 1894 Miss. Laws 154.
40. Miss. Code Ann. § 37–13–7.
41. *State of Missouri Official Manual, 1975–1976*, p. 1438.
42. Mo. Ann. Stat. § 10.020 (Vernon).
43. Mont. Rev. Codes Ann. § 1–1–502.
44. *Nebraska Blue Book, 1982–83*, p. 12.
45. Neb. Rev. Stat. § 90–102.
46. Nev. Rev. Stat. § 235.020.
47. N.H. Rev. Stat. Ann. § 3:2.
48. N.J. Stat. Ann. § 52:3–1 (West).
49. Ibid., § 52:2A–1 (West).
50. Information provided by the New Mexico State Library.
51. N.M. Stat. Ann. § 12–3–2.
52. Ibid., § 12–3–3.
53. Ibid., § 12–3–7.
54. N.Y. State Law § 70 (McKinney).
55. N.C. Gen. Stat. § 144–1.
56. N.D. Cent. Code § 54–02–02.
57. Ohio Rev. Code Ann. § 5.01 (Baldwin).
58. Ibid., § 5.011 (Baldwin).
59. Okla. Stat. Ann. tit. 25, § 91 (West).
60. Ibid., tit. 25, § 92 (West).
61. Ibid., tit. 25, § 93.1 (West).
62. Or. Rev. Stat. § 186.010.
63. Pa. Stat. Ann. tit. 44, § 45 (Purdon).
64. R.I. Gen. Laws § 42–4–3.
65. Ibid., § 42–7–4.
66. *South Carolina State Symbols and Emblems* (Columbia: House of Representatives, n.d.).
67. S.C. Code § 1–1–670.

68. *History of the South Dakota State Flag* (Pierre: Bureau of Administration, Division of Central Services, The State Flag Account, n.d.).

69. S.D. Codified Laws Ann. § 1–6–4, § 1–6–5.

70. *Tennessee Blue Book, 1985–1986*, pp. 338–39.

71. Tenn. Code Ann. § 4–1–301.

72. Tex. Rev. Civ. Stat. Ann. art. 6142a (Vernon).

73. *Symbols of the Great State of Utah* (n.p., n.d.).

74. Utah Code Ann. § 63–13–5.

75. Vt. Stat. Ann. tit. 1, § 495.

76. Va. Code § 7.1–32.

77. Wash. Rev. Code Ann. § 1.20.010.

78. 1929 W.Va. Acts 495.

79. Wis. Stat. Ann. § 1.08 (West).

80. *Wyoming: Some Historical Facts* (Cheyenne: Wyoming State Archives, Museums and Historical Department, n.d.), p. i.

81. Wyo. Stat. Ann. § 8–3–102.

5 | State Capitols

The history of American state capitols is replete with political intrigue, architectural blunderings, frequent destruction by fire, and occasional destruction by war. This history is also, however, a record of the deep and abiding patriotism of the citizens of each state and their respect for and pride in the functions of their state governments.

Many of today's state capitols were constructed at the end of the nineteenth or beginning of the twentieth century. The architecture of these buildings is clearly informed by the style of the United States Capitol—neoclassical, domed capitols that call to mind ancient democracies. Some states, however, chose contemporary architecture to express their belief in progress. Notable among all the capitols in this regard are the "skyscraper" style capitols of Nebraska and Louisiana, built in the second and third decades of this century. The capitols of Hawaii and New Mexico, completed in the 1960s, are contemporary designs that express the individual history and heritage of those states. But whatever their design, state capitols stand as monuments to the people, to their hard work, and to their belief in the progress of democracy.

Alabama

Montgomery was chosen as the capital city of Alabama during the 1845–1846 legislative session. Since becoming a state in 1817, the legislature had met in Huntsville, Cahaba, and Tuscaloosa before choosing Montgomery as a permanent capital. Because the legislative act designating Montgomery stipulated that the state should bear no expense in purchasing land or building a capitol, the city floated a $75,000 bond issue, which paid for the site known as Goat Hill and the erection of a Greek revival capitol designed by Stephen D. Dutton. Completed in 1847, it was destroyed in December

1849. The legislature appropriated $60,000 in 1850 and employed Bara-chias Holt to design a new building to be erected on the foundation of the destroyed capitol. The new capitol, also in the Greek revival style embellished with Corinthian columns and a towering, white dome, was completed in 1851. In 1885, an east wing was erected at a cost of $25,000. A south wing was added in 1905–1906 for $150,000 and a north wing, in 1911 for $100,000. The wings, constructed of brick with a stucco finish, maintain the box-like, Greek style and are adorned with Ionic columns. Frank Lockwood was the architect for all of the additions.[1]

Alaska

The six-story Alaska State Capitol in Juneau, begun in 1929, was completed in 1931 as the Federal and Territorial Building. When Alaska became a state in 1958, the state was given possession of the building. In fact, the people of Juneau had donated half of the property to the federal government, as Congress had not appropriated enough money to pay for the building site. Construction and site costs approximated $1 million.

The capitol was designed by James A. Wetmore, who was the federal government's supervising architect. It is made of reinforced concrete with a brick facing. Indiana limestone was used for the lower facade and Tokeen marble, native to Alaska, was used for the four Doric columns of the portico as well as the interior trim.[2]

Arizona

The Arizona Capitol, designed by James Riely Gordon, is located in Phoenix. The Victorian four-story structure is made primarily from Arizona materials, as mandated by the legislature. The exterior is made of granite, tuff stone, and malapai. Oak woodwork adorns the interior. The building was completed in 1900 at a cost of $135,744. Today the capitol houses the Arizona State Capitol Museum. Government offices have been moved to nearby or adjacent buildings.[3]

Arkansas

The Arkansas State Capitol was begun in 1899 when the existing building became inadequate with the growth of the government. It was completed after numerous delays in 1916. Final construction costs totalled about $2.5 million, considerably more than the $1 million originally appropriated. The Grecian design of the building, including the dome, which is copied from St. Paul's via the Mississippi Capitol, is essentially that of George R. Mann. Cass Gilbert became the architect toward the end of the project, but he made few changes in the exterior design. The exterior is constructed of

Batesville marble and some Indiana Bedford limestone. The interior is finished in Alabama marble.[4]

California

In 1854, after meeting in San Jose, Vallejo, Sacramento, Vallejo again, and Benicia, the California legislature moved the state capital to Sacramento. Construction of the permanent capitol building, designed by M. F. Butler, began in September 1860, and the cornerstone was laid in May 1861. Although some offices were occupied as early as 1869, the building was not fully completed until 1874. Remodeling work was undertaken from 1906 to 1908 and again in 1928. The capitol was completely restored between 1976 and 1981 at a cost of $68 million.

The "Old Capitol," as it is known today, is a four-story building topped by a copper-clad dome. A cupola extending from the dome is supported by twelve columns. Its roof is covered with gold plate and supports a copper ball, 30 inches in diameter, which is plated with gold coins. The building itself, Roman Corinthian in design, is 219 feet 11½ inches in height, 320 feet in length, and 164 feet wide. The dome rises on a two-story drum. A colonnade of twenty-four Corinthian columns supports the roof, from which a clerestory rises. The first story was constructed from granite out of nearby quarries, and stuccoed brick construction was used for the top three stories.

In 1949 construction of an annex was begun. Completed in January 1952, at a cost of $7.6 million (about three times the cost of the Old Capitol), the annex is 103½ feet high, 210 feet long, and 269 feet wide. This six-story building, designed by the State Division of Architecture, is joined to the Old Capitol and, although it is contemporary in style, blends with the lines of the older building.[5]

Colorado

When Colorado entered the Union in 1876, Denver had been its capital city for nine years. Although a ten-acre site had been donated and accepted for erection of a capitol in 1874, excavation did not begin until 1886. The government continued to operate out of rented quarters until 1894, when offices in the permanent capitol were first used. The building was not completed, however, until twenty-two years after work first began at a cost of almost $3 million.

Colorado's capitol was designed by architect E. E. Myers to resemble the U.S. Capitol. The building measures 383 feet in length and 315 feet in width; its floor plan is in the form of a Greek cross. Gunnison granite was used for the five-foot-thick exterior walls, sandstone from Fort Collins for the foundations, marble from Marble, Colorado for the floors and stairs, and rose onyx unique to Beulah, Colorado for wainscoting. The dome rises

272 feet above the ground. Copper was first used to cover the dome, but, because of the public outcry that copper was not native to Colorado, sheets of gold leaf donated by Colorado miners were applied to the dome. A second coating of gold was applied to the dome in 1950.[6]

Connecticut

The Capitol of Connecticut is located in Hartford, overlooking Bushnell Memorial Park on a site contributed by the city. Funds were appropriated for the building in 1871 and it was completed in 1879 at a cost of $2,532,524. Built by James G. Batterson and designed by Richard M. Upjohn, this Victorian Gothic capitol is constructed of New England marble and granite and is topped by a gold-leaf dome. In 1972, the capitol was declared a national historical landmark.[7]

Delaware

In 1787, the Levy Court of Kent County, in which the capital city of Dover is located, decided that the 1722 courthouse had grown too small for county and state offices. Using bricks from the old building as the foundation for the new, the building was finally opened in April 1792 with the proceeds of a state lottery to overcome financial difficulties. The cost was £2107:7:5. In 1795, the General Assembly appropriated £404:4:4½ to complete the brick, colonial style state house, including a copper roof.

In 1836, when it was necessary to expand the facility, $3,000 was spent on a two-story plus basement addition that measured 40 by 50 feet. Finally, in April 1873, the legislature purchased the statehouse for its exclusive use at a cost of $15,000. After some remodeling, the capitol was ready for use in 1875. Another addition, built during 1895–1897, added 40 feet to the 1836 addition, and a south wing was added in 1910 at a cost of $62,500. In 1925–1926, a three-story annex was erected to the east side of the original building.[8]

Florida

Tallahassee was chosen to be Florida's capital city in 1824. Two years later, a 40 by 26 foot, two-story masonry building was constructed as the capitol. Although this was to be the wing of a larger building, by 1839, no further addition had been made. Instead, the original structure was razed and a new brick capitol was finally completed in 1845. In 1902, a copper dome was added along with four bay wings. Further enlargements were made in 1923, 1936, and 1947.

By 1972 it was clear that the old capitol did not provide enough space to carry on government operations. A capitol complex was authorized by the legislature that included new legislative chambers and offices as well as a 307-foot, twenty-two-story executive office building. The new concrete and steel capitol, completed in 1977 and dedicated in 1978, cost $43,070,741. It was designed jointly by Edward Durell Stone of New York and Reynolds, Smith and Hills of Jacksonville.[9]

Georgia

The people of Georgia voted in 1877 to make the city of Atlanta the state's capital. When Georgia became a state in 1788, Augusta was the capital, and the capital city was subsequently moved to Louisville, Milledgeville, Macon, back to Milledgeville, and, finally, to Atlanta in 1868. In 1883, the legislature appropriated $1 million for the construction of a capitol, to be supervised by a board of five commissioners.

The firm of Edbrooke and Burnham in Chicago was awarded the contract for its Classic Renaissance design. Georgia marble was used for the interior finish and Indiana limestone for the exterior. Construction began in 1884 and was completed within the amount appropriated in 1889. Its largest dimensions are 347 feet, 9 inches in length and 272 feet, 4½ inches in width. A rotunda extends from the second floor to a height of 237 feet, 4 inches. The gilded dome is 75 feet in diameter. The cupola is adorned by a 15-foot statue that represents freedom. The main entrance to the capitol is a four-story portico supported by six Corinthian columns.

Renovation work, which included applying native Georgia gold to the dome, was authorized in 1957. In 1981, it was necessary to apply more gold to the dome. The capitol was dedicated as a national historic landmark in 1977.[10]

Hawaii

The Hawaiian State Capitol in Honolulu is certainly one of the most unique of any of the state capitols. The concrete and steel building rises from an 80,000-square-foot reflecting pool to symbolize the creation of the islands out of the water. The legislative chambers are shaped like the volcanoes that gave birth to the islands. The forty columns that surround the capitol are shaped like royal palms.

The architectural firms of Belt, Lemmon and Lo of Honolulu and John Carl Warnecke and Associates of San Francisco planned and designed the 558,000-square-foot structure. Ground was broken late in 1965 and the capitol was dedicated in 1969. Construction costs came to $21,745,900. Total costs, including construction, equipment, furnishings, design, and fine arts totalled $24,576,900.[11]

Idaho

The Capitol Building in Boise was designed by the local firm of Tourtellette and Hummell in the same style as the U.S. Capitol. Construction began in 1905. By 1911, the central part of the building was completed, and, by 1920, the east and west wings were ready for use by the legislature. Construction costs totalled nearly $2.3 million.

Idaho sandstone, quarried by convicts, was used for exterior facing. Marble from Vermont, Alaska, Georgia, and Italy was used in the interior. The dome, which rises 208 feet, is topped by a solid copper eagle dipped in bronze, itself standing 5 feet, 7 inches tall. Eight massive columns ring the rotunda and support the dome. The columns are scagliola—a mixture of granite, marble dust, glue, and gypsum that is dyed to look like marble. Artisans from Italy were brought to Boise to do the scagliola veneer.[12]

Illinois

Illinois became a state in 1818. Its capital at that time was Kaskaskia. In 1820, the capital was moved to Vandalia and then, in 1839, with the help of Abraham Lincoln, to its permanent location, Springfield. The building used today is the sixth capitol and the second built in Springfield. Its construction was authorized in 1867, the cornerstone was laid in 1868, and it was completed in 1888 at a cost of $4.5 million. Situated on nine acres of land, the building was designed by John C. Cochrane of Chicago in the form of a Latin cross combining classical Greek and Roman styles. Its height from ground to dome is 361 feet. From north to south the capitol measures, at its extreme, 379 feet and from east to west, 268 feet. The walls supporting the dome are made from granular magnesian limestone. The interior walls are constructed of Niagara limestone. The corridors and walls of the rotunda employ decorative mosaics of marble. Bedford blue limestone and Missouri red granite were used to face the interior stone walls.[13]

Indiana

In 1824 the Indiana capital was moved to Indianapolis from Corydon, which had been the capital even before Indiana became a state in 1816. The first statehouse, a Greek revival building occupied in 1835, had been outgrown by 1877. Construction of the new Modern Renaissance capitol, designed by local architect Edwin May, began in 1878 and was completed in 1888 at a cost of approximately $2 million. The four-story capitol, constructed of Indiana limestone, contains over twelve acres of floor space. It is distinguished by the dome, 72 feet in diameter, which reaches a height of 234 feet. The inner dome, rising 108 feet above the main floor, is a 48-foot-wide work of stained glass, which was installed in 1887.[14]

Iowa

When the first General Assembly met in Iowa City after Iowa became a state in 1846, it began the search for a new capital. In 1857, the governor finally declared Des Moines to be the capital city. The government occupied temporary quarters in Des Moines until the new capitol was completed in 1884.

A capitol commission was formed in 1870 to construct a capitol for $1.5 million. The commission named John C. Cochrane and A. H. Piquenard architects, and the cornerstone for the traditional, modified Renaissance building was laid in 1871. The cornerstone had to be laid again in 1873 owing to the deterioration of the stone used. The capitol was finally completed eleven years later at a cost of $2,873,294. A fire in 1904, which occurred during repair and modernization work, resulted in additional expenditures for renovation that brought the total cost of the capitol to $3,296,256.

The steel and stone dome, covered with gold leaf that was replaced in 1964–1965, is surmounted by a lookout lantern and terminates in a filial that reaches 275 feet. The capitol was constructed of Iowa stone for the foundation, Iowa granite, Missouri limestone, and Anamosa from Iowa, Ohio, Minnesota, and Illinois. Interior wood came entirely from Iowa hardwood forests, and twenty-nine different foreign and domestic marbles were used for interior facing.[15]

Kansas

In 1861, the citizens of the new state of Kansas voted to make Topeka their capital city. The next year, the state accepted a donation of twenty acres on which to build a capitol building. In 1866 the cornerstone of the east wing was laid, but it had to be replaced in 1867. By 1870 the building was opened for use by the legislature. In 1879 work started on a west wing with a $60,000 appropriation and a tax increase. The Kansas House of Representatives met in the still unfinished west wing in 1881. Finally, the legislature authorized erection of the central portion, which was completed in 1903. Total costs came to approximately $3.2 million. McDonald Brothers of Louisville were the designing architects.

The classical capitol is 399 feet north to south, 386 feet east to west, and 304 feet to the top of the dome, on which is situated a statue of the goddess Ceres. The central part of the building is five stories high. Each wing is four stories. The interior is decorated with a number of rich marbles, and the rotunda contains eight murals designed by David H. Overmyer. The second floor contains a series of murals by John Stewart Curry.[16]

Kentucky

In 1904 the legislature of Kentucky passed a bill providing for the construction of a capitol in Frankfort, thus ending a long debate as to where the permanent capital should be located. Collection of $1 million of debt left from the Civil and Spanish-American wars owed Kentucky by the United States War Department provided the funding. F. M. Andrews and Company had been retained as architects and work commenced in 1905, with the cornerstone having been laid in 1906. The building was dedicated in 1910.

Kentucky's capitol combines French Renaissance and neoclassical designs in a building that measures 402 feet, 10 inches east to west, 180 feet north to south, and 212 feet from the top of the lantern to the terrace floor, on a thirty-four-acre site. The base of the exterior is Vermont granite, and the face-work on the three-story building is Bedford limestone. The exterior walls are adorned with seventy Ionic columns of limestone. The rotunda, 57 feet in diameter, the dome, and the lantern were copied from the Hôtel des Invalides of Napoléon's tomb in Paris. The State Reception Room is a copy of Marie Antoinette's drawing room in the Grand Trianon Palace. Total construction and furnishing costs totaled $1,820,000.[17]

Louisiana

When Huey Long became governor of Louisiana in 1928, one of his top priorities was to centralize the state's government under one roof. The 100-year-old neo-Gothic capitol in downtown Baton Rouge had grown inadequate. In 1930, the legislature granted Long's wish and appropriated $5 million for a new capitol building. Work commenced in December 1930 and was completed only fourteen months later.

The New Orleans architectural firm of Weiss, Dreyfous, and Seiferth designed a statehouse that replaced the traditional dome and rotunda with a thirty-four-story, 450-foot tower, and a public hall in accordance with the governor's wishes. The capitol became, at the time, the tallest building in the South, and it remains a fine example of the Art Moderne school of American architecture. The 10 percent savings in building costs were used to embellish the capitol with art deco ornamentation.

The capitol is surrounded by twenty-seven acres of formal gardens, which were once occupied by Louisiana State University. In 1935, Huey Long was assassinated in the very building he had envisioned to be a monument to the people of Louisiana. His grave is located at the center of the formal gardens.[18]

Maine

Augusta was selected as Maine's capital in 1827, seven years after Maine became a state. Charles Bulfinch was chosen to design the building for a thirty-four-acre plot that had been chosen. The cornerstone of the Greek and Renaissance influenced capitol was laid in 1829 and was completed in time for the legislative session beginning in January 1832. The completed capitol, made of Hallowell granite, cost $139,000, including furnishings and grounds.

The interior was remodeled in 1852 and again in 1860. A three-story wing was added at the rear in 1890–1891. Major remodeling work was accomplished in 1909 and 1910. The length of the structure was doubled to 300 feet, but the original front was maintained. However, a dome that reaches to 185 feet, surmounted by a statue of Wisdom made of copper covered with gold, replaced the original cupola.[19]

Maryland

The Maryland State House in Annapolis, begun in 1772 and first occupied in 1779, is the oldest state capitol still used for legislative purposes. The roof was refashioned in 1785 and the dome, designed by Joseph Clark, in 1789. The interior height of the cypress-beamed dome is 113 feet, the largest wooden dome in the country. Annexes were added in 1858 and 1886, but they were replaced between 1902 and 1904. This brick colonial building, trimmed in stone, was built originally for £7500. Most of the rooms of the original building have been restored to their eighteenth-century luster, a task that has occupied most of the years of this century.[20]

Massachusetts

The site of the statehouse of Massachusetts in Boston was formerly John Hancock's cow pasture. The building was designed by Charles Bulfinch and completed in 1798 after three years of construction. Bulfinch designed the brick capitol after months of studying Greek and Roman temples. The large wooden dome, now covered with 23 karat gold, was originally covered with copper from Paul Revere. Except for two marble wings on each side added in this century and a yellow brick north annex, the original building still looks much as it did in 1798.[21]

Michigan

In 1847, ten years after becoming a state, Michigan moved its capital from Detroit to Ingham township. A new capital city, temporarily named Michigan, was fashioned out of the woods. After only a few months, the city's name was changed to Lansing.

Having quickly outgrown a temporary statehouse, a permanent brick building was erected in 1854 and added to in 1863 and 1865. These buildings were also outgrown within a few years. In 1871, the legislature set a limit of $1.2 million for the construction of a new capitol. Elijah E. Myers, a self-taught architect from Springfield, Illinois, was named the winner of the architectural contest to build the capitol in 1872. The cornerstone was laid in 1873, and the academic-classical structure was completed in 1879. The capitol building covers more than an acre of land. It is 420 feet long, 274 feet wide, and 267 feet high. It is made of Ohio sandstone, Illinois limestone, Massachusetts granite, and Vermont marble. It has a cruciform floor plan, a high dome in the center, and a two-story portico at the head of the outside stairway above the central entrance. The exterior facade of the top floors is decorated with Corinthian, Tuscan, and Ionic columns.[22]

Minnesota

Ground was broken for the Minnesota Capitol in St. Paul in 1896. The legislature had recognized by 1893 that its Romanesque capitol building had become too small to conduct the state's business. Cass Gilbert won the architectural competition with a familiar domed design in the classical Renaissance style. The capitol was ready for occupancy in 1905 at a cost of $4.5 million, including grounds and furnishings.

The basement of the Michigan Capitol is constructed of St. Cloud granite and the rest of the building, of Georgia marble. It measures 434 feet from east to west and 229 feet from north to south. The white dome reaches a height of 223 feet.[23]

Mississippi

In 1822, Mississippi moved its capital to Jackson from Natchez. Eleven years later, a new capitol, Greek revival in style, was planned. What is now referred to as the "Old Capitol" was completed in 1839 and remained in use as the capitol building until the current capitol was completed in 1903.

The "New Capitol," designed by Theodore C. Link of St. Louis, was constructed at a cost of $1,093,641 from 1901–1903. The exterior of this beaux arts classic masterpiece is Bedford limestone and the base course, Georgia granite. Blue Vermont marble, Italian white marble, Belgian black marble, jet black New York marble, and columns of scagliola adorn the interior. The dome rises to a height of 180 feet. An 8-foot eagle of copper coated in gold leaf stands atop the dome.[24]

Missouri

Having moved its capital from St. Louis and temporarily to St. Charles, the legislature of Missouri chose Jefferson City to be the capital and appropriated $18,373 in 1825 to construct a permanent capitol there. In 1837, this building was destroyed by fire. A new capital was constructed in 1848 and enlarged in 1888. In 1911 this structure was also destroyed by fire. A $3.5 million bond issue was floated to construct a new capitol. The design contest was won by Tracy and Swartwout and construction began in 1913. Ready for occupancy in 1918, it cost $4,215,000, including furnishings and grounds. The Renaissance-classical capitol, constructed of Burlington limestone, is five stories high, 437 feet east to west, 300 feet wide at the center, and 200 feet wide in the wings. It houses 500,000 square feet of floor space. The dome stretches to a height of 238 feet. Above the dome is a bronze statue of Ceres. Extensive renovation and restoration activities have been completed recently.[25]

Montana

Six years after becoming a state in 1889, the Montana legislature authorized $1 million to be spent on a permanent capitol in Helena. Owing to depression and scandal, the original plan was abandoned, and, in 1897, the legislature authorized a less grandiose capitol that would cost, when completed in 1902, only $485,000.

Charles Emlen Bell and John Hackett Kent of Council Bluffs, Iowa were selected as architects. The cornerstone of the Greek Ionic neoclassical capitol was laid in 1899. Sandstone quarried in Columbus, Montana was used for the exterior. The rotunda decoration suggests that of a nineteenth-century opera house. The copper-clad dome above the rotunda was refaced in 1933–1934. East and west wings were added to the original building in 1909–1912. The wings, which maintain the style of the first building, were designed by Frank M. Andrews in association with John G. Link and Charles S. Haire. The facing of the wings is Jefferson County granite, chosen over sandstone for its durability. Some alterations were made in the central and end blocks of the original building during reconstruction in 1963–1965.[26]

Nebraska

The Nebraska Capitol, constructed in Lincoln between 1922 and 1932, is unlike any other state capitol building. Rather than imitating the architecture of the U.S. Capitol or harkening back to classical style, this statehouse is thoroughly modern in inspiration, and it received the Building Stone Institute's Award for architectural excellence in 1982. The Indiana limestone building was designed by Bertram Goodhue who, in turn, chose August Vincent Tack to execute the murals, Hildreth Meiere to design the mosaic and tile decoration, and Lee Lawrie to do the sculpture. The base of the capitol is 437 feet square and two stories high. A 400-foot tower, adorned with a bronze statue of "The Sower," rises from the base. The capitol, including grounds and furnishings, was completed at a cost exceeding $10 million.[27]

Nevada

Early in 1869, the Nevada legislature designated a ten-acre site in Carson City, where it had been using temporary facilities, on which to construct a new capitol for no more than $100,000. The design submitted by Joseph Gosling, which called for a "two-story building in the form of a Grecian Cross, compounded of the Corinthian, Ionic and Doric," was chosen. The plans called for the building to be 148 feet long and 98 feet wide and the cupola to be 30 feet in diameter and 120 feet high.

The cornerstone was laid in 1870, and the capitol was completed on time in 1871. Sandstone from the state prison quarry was used for the facade, and Alaskan marble was used for inlay to the interior arches, floors, and wainscoting. The completed building cost $169,830. An annex was added in 1905, and north and south wings were added in 1913.[28]

New Hampshire

The New Hampshire statehouse in Concord is the oldest state capitol in the country in which the legislature uses its original chambers. The cornerstone for the original building, designed with simple classical lines by Stuart Park, was laid in 1816. The capitol was ready for use in 1819. The two-story New Hampshire granite structure which measures 126 feet wide and 57 feet deep, was completed for $82,000.

In 1864 a project to double the size of the original building was begun using the design of Gridley J. F. Bryant. At this time, a portico was added with Doric and Corinthian columns. A new dome replaced the original, but the gilded eagle that had first been perched on the capitol dome in 1818 was placed on the new dome. In 1909, under the auspices of Peabody and Stearns, the capitol building was again enlarged. The legislature, however, retained its same quarters. The Senate chamber was refurbished in 1974 and the Representatives Hall, in 1976.[29]

New Jersey

The New Jersey statehouse in Trenton is the second oldest in continuous use of all the statehouses in the United States. Traces of the original two-story colonial structure, built in 1792 by Jonathan Doanne, can still be seen. In the mid–1800s, John Notman was employed to do a major restructuring of the capitol, at which time the building attained a Greek revival flavor with the addition of columned porticoes and a rotunda.

When fire destroyed much of the capitol in 1885, repairs and renovation were begun at once under the supervision of architect Lewis Broom. When completed in 1889, the capitol had taken on the French academic classic style popular at the time. Additions were made to the refurbished building in 1891, 1898, 1900, 1903, 1906, 1911–12, and 1917. Major renovations are planned for 1986–1988 to improve the functional aspects of the building and to return it aesthetically to its original design.[30]

New Mexico

Santa Fe, New Mexico's capital city, boasts the oldest capitol building— El Palacio, built in 1610—and one of the newest—the Round House or Bull Pen, completed in 1966. The exterior of the new capitol is modified New Mexico territorial design. The interior is circular and contains four levels. The adobe-colored building with a total area of 232,206 square feet was designed by W. C. Kruger and Associates. Construction costs totaled $4,676,860.

The capitol was designed to include the shape of the Zia, an Indian sun symbol. The Zia, a sign of friendship, is composed of four rays around an inner circle. The entrances to the circular building continue this symbolism. Native marble adorns the interior. The rotunda is 24½ feet in diameter and 60 feet high.[31]

New York

By 1865 the New York legislature had moved to erect a new capitol building, since Philip Hooker's Greek revival capitol, which had first been occupied in 1809, had clearly become inadequate. Late in 1867, the design of an Italian Renaissance capitol by Arthur D. Gilman and Thomas Fuller was accepted, and ground was broken very shortly thereafter. The 1868 legislature set the spending limit at $4 million, but, by 1874, the commissioners overseeing construction knew that at least $10 million would be needed. The cornerstone was laid in 1871, with architect Fuller still in command. Fuller was dismissed in 1876 and replaced by a board of advisors that included Frederick Law Olmstead and architects Leopold Eidlitz and H. H. Richardson. Plans were redrawn by Eidlitz and Richardson that called for completion of the capitol in 1879 and an additional expenditure of only $4.5 million. Finishing touches were still under way, however, in 1898. As a result of changes in architects and the collaboration of two architects whose styles were quite different, the capitol represents an admixture of Gilman's Italian Renaissance, Richardson's romanesque, Eidlitz's Victorian Gothic, and a bit of Moorish-Saracenic finished with French Renaissance. By 1879, the building was ready for occupancy. The granite building was partially destroyed by fire in 1911. Reconstruction costs amounted to $2 million. From 1978 to 1980, renovation work restored some parts of the building to their original splendor. In 1979, the capitol was designated a national historic landmark.[32]

North Carolina

Raleigh was chosen as North Carolina's permanent capital city in 1792, and, by 1796, a two-story brick statehouse had been completed. Between 1820 and 1824, additions were made to this simple building, which was completely destroyed by fire in 1831. The general assembly that met during the 1832–33 session appropriated $50,000 to construct a new capitol, which was to be a larger version of the old statehouse. Architect William Nichols was hired to prepare plans for a building in the shape of a cross with a central, domed rotunda. Nichols was replaced in August 1833 by the New York firm of Ithiel Town and Alexander Jackson Davis. The firm is responsible for giving the capitol its present appearance, although David Paton, who replaced Town and Davis early in 1835, made several changes to the interior.

The cornerstone for the Greek revival capitol was laid in 1833, and soon after construction began another $75,000 had to be appropriated. By the time the building was completed in 1840, its total cost with furnishings came to $532,682. The capitol measures 160 feet by 140 feet. The exterior walls are North Carolina gneiss and the interior walls, stone and brick. The Doric exterior columns are modeled after the Parthenon. The new capitol has been extensively renovated.[33]

North Dakota

The "Skyscraper Capitol of the Plains" in Bismarck was completed in 1934 at a cost of $2 million, after the original capitol had been destroyed by fire in 1930. The nineteen-story Indiana limestone building in modern American style was designed by Holabird and Root of Chicago, Joseph Bell De Remer of Grand Forks, and William F. Kurke of Fargo. A four-story judicial wing and state office building was added to the original capitol in the 1970s. The annex, finished in limestone to match the capitol, provides another 100,000 square feet of space. Between 1971 and 1981, over $10 million was spent on various renovation projects.[34]

Ohio

The Ohio legislature voted in 1817, fourteen years after Ohio became a state, to locate the capital in Columbus, which at the time possessed no name. The capital was first located in Chillicothe, moved to Zanesville in 1809, and moved back to Chillicothe in 1812. The desire of the legislature was to fashion a capital city in the center of the state. In December 1916, the legislature moved into the new capital city, Columbus.

The first statehouse, which was destroyed by fire in 1852, had become inadequate by 1838, when the legislature approved a new capitol. The building commission decided on a composite plan, designed from plans received in a competition. The plan decided on was a Greek revival capitol with Doric columns made of native stone. Henry Walter of Cincinnati was named architect, and construction began in 1839. In 1840, construction stopped as the legislature repealed the authorization, and work was not resumed until 1846. In 1848, William R. West was named architect and work was proceeding rapidly. In 1854, when N. B. Kelly became the architect, all the stonework but the cupola had been finished. By 1856, with the appointment of Thomas U. Walter and Richard Upjohn as consulting architects, the legislative chambers had been completed. In 1858, Isaiah Rogers was appointed the architect to complete the interior designs. Finally, the 184 foot by 304 foot capitol was completed in 1861 at a cost of $1,359,121. From 1899 to 1901, an annex was added at a cost of $450,000.[35]

Oklahoma

The Capitol of Oklahoma, located in Oklahoma City, is unique among state capitol buildings if only for the oil wells that surround the grounds. The structure itself, designed by the firm of Layton-Smith in modern classic style based on Greek and Roman architecture, was begun in 1914 and completed in 1917. The Indiana limestone capitol with a pink and black granite base is six stories high, 480 feet east to west, and 380 feet north to south. There are in fact only five main floors excluding the basement, as the dome and legislative chambers are two stories in height. The exterior facade is ornamented with smooth columns that have Corinthian capitals. The capitol cost approximately $1.5 million. In 1966, a seal was inlaid in the rotunda area at a cost of $4,000.[36]

Oregon

The Oregon statehouse in Salem is the third capitol building in that city; the previous two were destroyed by fire like so many earlier capitols of other states. The first capitol was erected in 1854 at a cost of $40,000. In 1872 another capitol was begun, modeled somewhat after the U.S. Capitol, at a cost of about $325,000. It was destroyed in 1935. Construction began on the present capitol in 1935 and was completed in 1938.

The four-story, modern Greek capitol, designed by Francis Keally of New York, is constructed of white Vermont marble and bronze. It cost approximately $2.5 million. An 8½-ton bronze statue enameled with gold leaf stands atop the capitol tower. The "Golden Pioneer" looks to the west in tribute to Oregon's early settlers. In 1977, wings were added to the capitol, which added 144,000 square feet of usable area to the 131,750 feet in the original building at a cost of $12,025,303.[37]

Pennsylvania

In 1810, the General Assembly passed an act making Harrisburg Pennsylvania's capital city after 1812. Philadelphia was the capital from 1683 to 1799, and Lancaster was the capital from 1799 until the move to Harrisburg. Construction of a capitol was authorized in 1816, and it was occupied in 1821. An addition was authorized in 1864. The main building was destroyed by fire in 1897.

The present capitol was authorized in 1897, supplemented by a 1901 act, and was dedicated by Theodore Roosevelt in 1906. Designed by Joseph M. Houston in the classic style adapted from the Italian Renaissance, the five-story capitol is constructed of Vermont granite. It measures 520 feet in length and 254 feet in width. The dome reaches a height of 272 feet and is surmounted by a figure symbolic of the Commonwealth. The interior is finished in marble, bronze, mahogany, and tiling. Exclusive of furnishings, the building cost $10,073,174.[38]

Rhode Island

In 1895, groundbreaking ceremonies were held in Providence for a new statehouse. Charles Follen McKim designed a capitol in the Greek Renaissance tradition with exterior walls of white Georgia marble. It is 333 feet long and 180 feet wide at the center. The dome, one of four unsupported marble domes in the world, is surmounted by an 11-foot-high, gold-leafed statue of the "Independent Man." Some offices of the capitol were occupied as early as 1900, but the building and grounds were totally completed in 1904 at a cost including furnishings of $3,018,416.[39]

South Carolina

The building of South Carolina's capitol spanned over fifty years owing to war and scandal. In 1851, the legislature began the process of erecting the new capitol. In 1854, the first architect was dismissed and the new architect, Major John R. Niernsee, determined that the workmanship and materials were defective. A new site was chosen and work began, but not according to schedule. Still not completed in 1865, work was suspended when Sherman's army destroyed Columbia. Although the building was not heavily damaged, work did not recommence until 1885. John Niernsee died in the same year. He was succeeded by J. Crawford Neilson and, in 1888, Frank Niernsee replaced Neilson. The younger Niernsee worked primarily on the interior, but work was suspended in 1891. In 1900, Frank P. Milburn was appointed architect. He built the dome and the north and south porticoes. In 1904, Charles C. Wilson became the architect, and the building was finally completed. In the end, the granite capitol was a freely interpreted Roman Corinthian structure that cost $3,540,000.[40]

South Dakota

Pierre had been the temporary capital city since South Dakota became a state in 1889. Not until 1904 did an election determine that Pierre would be the permanent capital. Construction began in 1907 on the capitol building. It was completed in 1910 at a cost of $1 million. C. E. Bell of Minneapolis designed the building, patterning it after Montana's capitol. The exterior is limestone. The rotunda is decorated with marble, scagliola pillars, and mosaic floors. The inner dome rises 96 feet and is made of leaded stained glass. The outer dome rises 159 feet. Its now blackened roof is fashioned from 40,000 pounds of copper. An annex was added to the original building in 1932.[41]

Tennessee

Forty-seven years after joining the Union, a bitter debate was ended when Nashville was designated the permanent capital city in 1843. An area known as Campbell's Hill was purchased by the city in the same year for $30,000 and was given to the state for the capitol site. William Strickland, a strong adherent of the Greek revival style, was chosen as architect. The cornerstone for the Tennessee marble structure was laid in 1845. State convicts and slaves performed much of the labor. Although the building was not entirely completed then, it was first occupied by the General Assembly in 1853. By 1857, building costs had amounted to $711,367.

The capitol is designed after an Ionic temple. Eight fluted Ionic columns adorn the north and south porticoes and six adorn the east and west porticoes. The tower rises 206 feet, 7 inches from the parallelogram-shaped structure, which measures 112 feet by 239 feet. Exterior restoration was performed beginning in 1956 and interior restoration and repair, in 1958. In 1969 and 1970, more restoration work was undertaken in the assembly chambers and in various offices and meeting rooms.[42]

Texas

Austin was chosen as the permanent capital of the Republic of Texas in 1839. It remained the capital city after Texas joined the Union in 1845. The present capitol was begun in 1882 to replace an 1852 structure that burned down in 1881. A temporary building, constructed in 1881, was used until the completion of the new capitol in 1888. The temporary structure burned down in 1889. The classical Renaissance capitol, shaped as a Greek cross, was designed by E. E. Myers of Detroit. The exterior walls are Texas pink granite; the interior and dome walls, Texas limestone. The building measures 585 feet, 10 inches in length and 299 feet, 10 inches in width. It is 309 feet, 8 inches from the basement floor to the top of the sixteen-foot statue of the goddess Liberty that stands atop the dome. The capitol provides 273,799 square feet of usable space. The builders of the capitol accepted 3 million acres of land in the Texas Panhandle as payment for constructing the capitol.[43]

Utah

Utah became a state in 1896, and, although Salt Lake City had long been a capital city, it was not until 1911 that the legislature authorized the construction of a permanent capitol. The Renaissance revival design of Richard K. A. Kletting was chosen for the Utah granite and Georgia marble building. Groundbreaking took place in 1913, and the capitol was completed at a cost of $2,739,528 in 1915.

The capitol is 404 feet in length and 240 feet in width. The ceiling of the copper dome is 165 feet above the floor of the rotunda. The dome itself rises above a pediment and a colonnade of twenty-four Corinthian columns.[44]

Vermont

Vermont entered the Union in 1791. Its legislature designated Montpelier as the permanent capital city in 1805. The first capitol, in use from 1808 to 1836, was torn down and replaced by a new structure designed by Ammi B. Young after the Greek temple of Theseus. This capitol was destroyed by fire in 1857. The present statehouse, occupied since 1859, was modeled after the building that had burned down except for the dome and larger wings.

The exterior is constructed of Barre granite. The building is accented by a six-columned Doric portico and a 57-foot-high wooden dome. The dome is sheathed in copper and is covered with gold leaf. A statue of Ceres surmounts the dome. The original statue of the goddess of agriculture was replaced in 1938. Construction cost approximately $220,000.[45]

Virginia

The Virginia General Assembly, the oldest law-making body in the western hemisphere, held its first session at Jamestown in 1619. The capitol was moved to Williamsburg in 1699 and then to Richmond in 1779. In 1785, Thomas Jefferson was asked to consult an architect for the design of a capitol. Jefferson chose an architect who shared his interest in classical buildings. Charles Louis Clerisseau, with Jefferson's assistance, modeled a

State Capitols | 111

capitol after a Roman temple in France known as "La Maison Carrée." The cornerstone was laid in 1785, and the General Assembly first met in the new capitol in 1788. The two-story brick structure is rectangular with a portico secured by Ionic columns. Between 1904 and 1906, wings were added to each side of the original building. Extensive renovation and re-modeling, begun in 1962, was completed in 1963.[46]

Washington

When Olympia became the territorial capital of Washington in 1855, a wooden capitol was built there. When Washington entered the Union in 1889, a more suitable capitol was desired. In 1893, the design submitted by Ernest Flagg was chosen, and work began in 1894 only to be delayed while the foundation and basement were being constructed. In 1901, what is now known as the "Old Capitol" was purchased by the state and utilized as the statehouse until 1928.

By 1909, the government had decided that the Old Capitol had become inadequate. Ernest Flagg visited Olympia in 1911 and proposed a group concept for the capitol. Architects Walter R. Wilder and Harry K. White of New York were chosen to carry out Flagg's idea. In 1919, work began on an enlarged foundation for Flagg's original building. Construction began in 1922 and continued until completion in 1928.

The Wilkeson sandstone legislative building cost $6,798,596. It is 413 feet long and 179.2 feet wide. The total height is twenty-two stories. The dome, crowned by the "Lantern of Liberty," which rises 287 feet, is the fifth largest in the world. Doric columns adorn the colonnade around the building. Corinthian columns decorate the main north entrance and south portico.[47]

West Virginia

Wheeling was the location of West Virginia's first capital. In 1870, the capital was moved to Charleston and, in 1875, back to Wheeling. In 1877, the capital was moved again to Charleston by vote of the people. A capitol was built in 1885 in downtown Charleston, but it was destroyed by fire in 1921 as was the temporary capitol six years later. The capitol now in use was built in stages—the west wing in 1924–1925, the east wing in 1926–1927, the center in 1930–1932—and was dedicated in 1932. Total construction costs came to $10 million.

The capitol was designed by Cass Gilbert, who also designed the U.S. Supreme Court. This Renaissance building provides over fourteen acres of floor space. Porticoes at the north and south entrances are supported by limestone pillars, each of which weighs 86 tons. The exterior of the capitol is buff Indiana limestone, and an assortment of marbles was used to finish the interior. The dome reaches 293 feet, 5 feet higher than the dome of the U.S. Capitol.[48]

Wisconsin

The state capitol in Madison is Wisconsin's fifth capitol building, the third in Madison. The first Madison capitol was in use from 1838 to 1863. The second building was destroyed by fire in 1904. The current capitol was designed by George B. Post and Sons of New York. Construction began in 1906 and was completed in 1917 at a cost of $7.5 million.

The capitol is situated between Monona and Mendota lakes in a 13.4-acre park. The Roman Renaissance marble and granite structure itself occupies 2.42 acres and rises to a height of 285.9 feet, from the ground to the top of Daniel Chester French's gilded bronze statue "Wisconsin." This capitol boasts the only granite-domed capitol in the nation. The interior is finished in forty-three varieties of stone, glass mosaics, and murals.[49]

Wyoming

Wyoming became a state in 1890. Cheyenne had been the territorial capital, and, in 1886, the first of three separate contracts for a capitol was let, with David W. Gibbs and Company as architect. The cornerstone for the pseudo-Corinthian building, reminiscent of the U.S. Capitol, was laid in 1887, and, by 1888, it was ready for use. The first wings were finished in 1890. New east and west wings were approved in 1915 and completed in 1917. The cost of the original building and its additions totaled $389,569. The sandstone capitol was renovated between 1974 and 1980 at a cost of almost $7 million. The 24-karat gold-leafed dome, 145 feet high, has been leafed four times, most recently in 1980.[50]

Notes

1. *Alabama Capitol Complex* (Montgomery: Bureau of Publicity and Information, n.d.); *Alabama Emblems* (Montgomery: Alabama State Department of Archives and History, n.d.), pp. 1–2.

2. *Alaska Blue Book, 1979*, p. 82.

3. Information provided by Anne Wallace, Museum Educator, Arizona State Capitol Museum, Phoenix, Arizona.

4. Clara B. Eno, "Old and New Capitols of Arkansas," *The Arkansas Historical Quarterly* 4 (Autumn 1945): 246–48; John A. Treon, "Politics and Concrete: The Building of the Arkansas State Capitol, 1899–1917," *The Arkansas Historical Quarterly* 31 (Summer 1972): 127, 132.

5. *California's Legislature, 1984*, pp. 135–48.

6. *Colorado State Capitol* (Denver: Colorado Department of Education, n.d.).

7. *State of Connecticut Register and Manual, 1983*, p. 905.

8. *Official Insignia of Delaware* (Dover: Delaware State Development Department, n.d.).

9. *Florida's Capitol* (Tallahassee: Department of State, 1983); *The State of Florida's Heritage and Emblems* (Tallahassee: Department of State, n.d.); information provided by the Florida Legislative Library.

10. *Georgia's Capitol* (Atlanta: Max Cleland, n.d.).

11. *Hawaii State Capitol Fact Sheet* (Honolulu: State Archives, February 1975), pp. 1–2.

12. *Idaho Blue Book, 1981–1982*, p. 214.

13. *Illinois Blue Book, 1983–1984*, pp. 28–32.

14. *The State House, 1888 to Present* (Indianapolis: Indiana Department of Commerce, n.d.); *A Guide to the Indiana State Capitol*...(Indianapolis: Indiana Sesquicentennial Commission, 1967).

15. *1985–86 Iowa Official Register*, vol. 61, pp. 228–31.

16. *Kansas Directory, 1982*, pp. 104–113.

17. *Kentucky's Capitol* (Frankfort: Kentucky Department of Public Information, n.d.); *75th Birthday Celebration, State Capitol Building, 1910–1985; Commemorative Program, October 26, 1985*, p. 10.

18. *Louisiana Facts* (Baton Rouge: Louisiana Department of State, n.d.); *The Louisiana State Capitol* (n.p., n.d.).

19. *Maine, the Pine State* (n.p., n.d.).

20. *The Maryland State House, Annapolis* (Annapolis: Maryland Commission on Artistic Property of the State Archives and Hall of Records, Commission for the Maryland Heritage Committee, September 1984).

21. "Additions and Corrections to *Massachusetts*"; material provided by the Massachusetts Citizen Information Service.

22. *Michigan History Salutes...The Historic State Capitol Built in 1879* (Lansing: Michigan Department of State, 1980), pp. 3–15.

23. *Minnesota Legislative Manual, 1985*, pp. 2–3.

24. *Souvenir of Mississippi* (Jackson: Dick Molpus, n.d.), pp. 8–16.

25. *Official Manual, State of Missouri, 1975–76*, pp. 1428–30.

26. *The Montana Capitol: A Self-Guiding Tour* (Helena: Montana Historical Society, n.d.), pp. 1–10.

27. *Nebraska Blue Book, 1982–83*, pp. 8–9.

28. *The History of the Capitol Building* (Carson City: Department of Economic Development, n.d.); information supplied by the Nevada State Library.

29. *New Hampshire's State House: A Visitor's Guide* (n.p., n.d.).

30. *New Jersey's Historic State Capitol* (n.p., n.d.); records of the State Capitol Building Commission, 1945–1946 (supplied by John T. Jacobsen, Assistant to the Secretary of State).

31. Information from clippings files provided by Michael Miller, Southwest Librarian, New Mexico State Library, Santa Fe, New Mexico.

32. C. R. Roseberry, *Capitol Story* (Albany: New York State Office of General Services, 1982), pp. 24–25, 45, 126.

33. Information from *North Carolina Manual* provided by Thad Eure, Secretary of State, North Carolina.

34. Lloyd B. Omdahl, *Governing North Dakota, 1981–83* (Grand Forks: Bureau of Governmental Affairs, University of North Dakota, 1981), pp. 72–73; *Facts*

About North Dakota (Bismark: North Dakota Economic Development Commission, revised July 1983), p. i; "History of the State Capitol and Grounds Renovations" (n.p., n.d.), one page.

35. *Ohio's Capitals and the Story of Ohio's Emblems* (Columbus: n.p., n.d.), pp. 5–12.

36. *Directory of Oklahoma, 1981*, pp. 36–38.

37. *Oregon Blue Book, 1977–1978*, pp. 141–142.

38. *1976–77 Pennsylvania Manual*, 103 ed., pp. 848–53.

39. *The State of Rhode Island and Providence Plantations 1983–1984 Manual*, pp. 1–5.

40. *South Carolina State Symbols and Emblems* (Columbia: House of Representatives, n.d.).

41. Jan Clark, *South Dakota State Capitol* (Pierre: South Dakota Department of State Development and G. F. Thomsen and Associates, n.d.); *South Dakota History and Heritage* (n.p., n.d.).

42. *Tennessee Blue Book, 1985–86*, pp. 308–12.

43. *Texas Capitol Guide* (Austin: State Department of Highways and Public Transportation, Travel and Information Division, 1983).

44. *Utah: A Guide to Capitol Hill* (n.p., n.d.).

45. *Vermont Legislative Directory and State Manual, 1979–1980*, pp. 4–5.

46. *The Virginia State Capitol, Richmond, Virginia* (Richmond: Division of Engineering and Buildings, 1974).

47. Shanna Stevenson, *A Guide to Washington's Capitol—Walking Tour* (Olympia: Prepared for Office of the Secretary of State, December 1984), pp. 1–4, 11.

48. *State Capitol* (Charleston: Ken Hechler, n.d.).

49. *Wisconsin State Capitol* (Madison: Department of Administration, n.d.); information provided by Kim Varnell, Capitol Tour Guide, Department of Administration, Madison, Wisconsin.

50. *Wyoming Facts* (Cheyenne: Wyoming Travel Commission, n.d.).

6 | State Flowers

Reasons for selecting a particular state flower are as varied as their colors and varieties. Some flowers have historical significance—the golden poppy caught the attention of early explorers in California who nicknamed the state the Land of Fire upon observing its golden blooms spread across the countryside. The mountain laurel, state flower of Connecticut, was first discovered by the Swedish explorer, Peter Kalm, who sent it to Linnaeus in 1750 for identification. Kansas designated the wild sunflower as a symbolic emblem of early Kansas settlement.

School children and agriculturalists in Delaware lobbied for the peach blossom because the peach was often associated with the state. Florida, of course, named the orange blossom as its state flower in recognition of the orange industry. The apple blossom, named as the state flower of Michigan, pays tribute to their apple industry. Proud of its pine forests, Maine designated the pine cone and tassel as its floral emblem.

A commercial peony grower in Indiana convinced fellow state representatives to name the peony the state flower, in spite of strong opposition. It seems likely, however, that naturalists will try again to see that a flower native to the state will be named the state flower.

Many states seemed to have chosen flowers on the basis of their beauty, such as New York's selection of the rose, Minnesota's pink and white lady slipper, and New Hampshire's purple lilac. Hawaii not only chose a state flower, the hibiscus, but also designated an official flower for each of its eight islands.

Two states selected the apple blossom, Arkansas and Michigan. Nebraska and Kentucky favored the goldenrod, and Louisiana and Mississippi named the magnolia. The mountain laurel was chosen by Connecticut and Pennsylvania. Several states have named varieties of the violet and rose as their state flowers.

Alabama

The camellia was named the official state flower of Alabama by the legislature in 1959,[1] repealing the 1927 act designating the goldenrod as the state flower. Unofficially, the red camellia variety with red and white colors similar to those in the state flag is considered the Alabama state flower.[2]

Alaska

The wild, native forget-me-not, *Myosotis alpestris Schmidt Boraginaceae*, became the state flower and floral emblem of Alaska in 1949 by act of the legislature.[3] Forget-me-nots are sturdy blue perennial flowers, which grow throughout the Arctic region.[4]

Arizona

The flower of the saguaro, *Carnagiea gigantea*, was officially designated the state flower of Arizona by legislative act in 1931.[5] The saguaro is a member of the cactus family, which includes around 40 genera and 1,000 species mostly native to North America.[6]

Arkansas

The apple blossom, *Pyrus malus*, was declared the state floral emblem of Arkansas by act of the legislature in 1901.[7]

California

The golden poppy, *Eschscholtzia californica*, was named the official state flower of California by the legislature in 1903. A 1973 amendment designated April 6 of each year as California Poppy Day.[8] Also called the *Copa de Oro*, or "cup of gold," because of the brilliantly colored golden bloom, they grew so widely that early explorers nicknamed California the Land of Fire. Indians used poppy oil on their hair and boiled and consumed the edible portions. As perennials, they bloom several times a year if treated to an occasional trimming.[9]

Colorado

The white and lavender columbine, *Columbine aquilegia caerulea*, was declared by the legislature to be the state flower of Colorado in 1899.[10] Further provisions of Colorado state law protect the columbine from needless destruction and waste, forbid tearing up the plant by the roots from any public lands, and limit the number of stems, buds, or blossoms that may be picked from public lands to twenty-five.[11] Violation of these provisions is a misdemeanor and is punishable upon conviction by a fine of not less than $5 nor more than $50.[12]

Connecticut

The mountain laurel, *Kalmia latifolia*, was designated by legislative act in 1907 to be the state flower of Connecticut.[13] The Swedish explorer Peter Kalm sent the fragrant white and pink blossomed flower to Linnaeus in 1750 for identification. Linnaeus named it the *Kalmia latifolia*, the first part to honor Kalm and the second to indicate that it had wide leaves. The mountain laurel blooms most brilliantly every two or three years making different sections of the Connecticut countryside host to a beautiful display of blooms depending upon the cycle of a particular growth of plants. Other names for this brightly colored flower are calico bush and spoonwood.[14]

Delaware

The peach blossom was adopted as the floral emblem of Delaware by legislative act in 1895. It was also named the official state flower in 1955.[15] Agriculturalists and school children, fearing that the popular goldenrod would be named the state flower, flooded the state legislators with petitions requesting that the peach blossom be adopted as the official state flower. It was felt that the orchards with over 800,000 peach trees were responsible for the Delaware nickname, the Peach State, and had a significant economic impact on the state. As a consequence, the peach blossom was given its due recognition and named the state flower.[16]

Florida

In 1909, the state legislature of Florida adopted the orange blossom as the state flower.[17] A fragrant reminder of Florida's multibillion dollar orange industry, the white blossoms bloom throughout central and southern Florida.[18]

Georgia

The Cherokee rose was adopted as the floral emblem of Georgia by legislative act in 1916.[19] Although the Georgia Federation of Women's Clubs supported the adoption of the Cherokee rose, *Rosa sinica*, as the official state flower, they were probably under the mistaken notion that the flower was native to the South. Instead, it is believed that the white, thorny shrub hails from China and was first introduced in England before it arrived in the new world in the latter half of the eighteenth century. The common name of the plant emanates from the Cherokee Indians, who were fond of the plant and were responsible for its widespread propagation. This beautiful plant blooms in the early spring and often in the fall. It is a popular hedge in the South.[20]

In 1979, the Georgia legislature also designated a state wild flower, the azalea.[21]

Hawaii

The *Pua Aloala*, the hibiscus, was designated the flower emblem of Hawaii in 1923.[22] The hibiscus grows abundantly in all color shades throughout the Hawaiian Islands. In addition to a state flower, the Hawaii legislature has designated an official flower for each island:

Hawaii Island	Red *Lehua* (*Ohia*)
Maui	*Lokelani* (pink cottage rose)
Molokai	White *Kukui* blossom
Kahoolawe	*Hinahina* (beach heliotrope)
Lanai	*Kaumaoa* (yellow and orange air plant)
Oahu	*Ilima*
Kauai	*Mokihana* (green berry)
Niihau	White *Pupu* shell[23]

Idaho

The syringa, *Philadelphus lewisii*, was designated the official state flower of Idaho by that state's legislature in 1931.[24] The four-petalled syringa blossoms, white and fragrant, cluster at the ends of short branches.[25]

Illinois

The native violet was declared the state flower of Illinois by legislative act in 1908.[26] School children voted in 1907 from among three floral candidates, the violet, wild rose, and goldenrod. The violet won by nearly 4,000 votes.

Indiana

The flower of the peony, *Paeonia*, was designated by legislative act in 1957 as the official state flower of Indiana.[27] The 1957 act repealed a 1931 act that had named the zinnia the state flower. The 1931 act also repealed

Alaska

Alabama

California

Arizona

Arkansas

Delaware

Colorado

Connecticut

Hawaii

Florida

Georgia

Illinois

Idaho

Iowa

Indiana

Louisiana

Kansas

Kentucky

Massachusetts

Maine

Maryland

Mississippi

Michigan

Minnesota

Montana

Missouri

Camellia
Alabama

Forget-Me-Not
Alaska

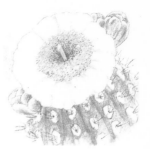

Saguaro
Arizona

Apple Blossom
Arkansas, Michigan

Golden Poppy
California

Columbine
Colorado

Mountain Laurel
Connecticut, Pennsylvania

Peach Blossom
Delaware

Orange Blossom
Florida

Cherokee Rose
Georgia

Hibiscus
Hawaii

Syringa
Idaho

Violet
Illinois, New Jersey, Wisconsin

Peony
Indiana

Wild Rose
Iowa

Wild Native Sunflower
Kansas

Goldenrod
Kentucky, Nebraska

Magnolia
Louisiana, Mississippi

Pine Cone and Tassel
Maine

Black-Eyed Susan
Maryland

Mayflower
Massachusetts

Pink and White Lady Slipper
Minnesota

Red Haw Blossom
Missouri

Bitterroot
Montana

Sagebrush
Nevada

Purple Lilac
New Hampshire

Yucca Flower
New Mexico

Rose
New York

Dogwood
North Carolina, Virginia

Wild Prairie Rose
North Dakota

Scarlet Carnation
Ohio

Mistletoe
Oklahoma

Oregon Grape
Oregon

Wood Violet
Rhode Island

Yellow Jessamine
South Carolina

American Pasque Flower
South Dakota

Iris
Tennessee

Passion Flower
Tennessee

Bluebonnet
Texas

Segolily
Utah

Red Clover
Vermont

Pink Rhododendron
Washington

Rhododendron Maximum
West Virginia

Indian Paintbrush
Wyoming

Southern Pine
Alabama, Arkansas, North Carolina

Sitka Spruce
Alaska

Palo Verde
Arizona

California Redwood
California

Giant Sequoia
California

Blue Spruce
Colorado, Utah

White Oak
Connecticut, Illinois, Iowa,
Maryland

American Holly
Delaware

Sabal Palmetto Palm
Florida, South Carolina

Live Oak
Georgia

Kukui Tree
Hawaii

Western White Pine
Idaho

Tulip Tree
Indiana, Tennessee

Cottonwood
Kansas, Nebraska, Wyoming

Coffeetree
Kentucky

Bald Cypress
Louisiana

Eastern White Pine
Maine, Michigan

American Elm
Massachusetts, North Dakota

Red Pine
Minnesota

Magnolia
Mississippi

Flowering Dogwood
Missouri, Virginia

Ponderosa Pine
Montana

Single-Leaf Pinon
Nevada

White Birch
New Hampshire

Northern Red Oak
New Jersey, Iowa

Nut Pine
New Mexico

Sugar Maple
New York, Vermont, West
Virginia, Wisconsin

Buckeye
Ohio

Redbud Tree
Oklahoma

Douglas Fir
Oregon

Hemlock
Pennsylvania

Red Maple
Rhode Island

Black Hills Spruce
South Dakota

Pecan Tree
Texas

Western Hemlock
Washington

Yellow-Hammer
Alabama

Wild Turkey
Alabama, South Carolina

Willow Ptarmigan
Alaska

Cactus Wren
Arizona

Mockingbird
Arkansas, Florida, Mississippi,
Tennessee, Texas

California Valley Quail
California

Lark Bunting
Colorado

Robin
Connecticut, Michigan, Wisconsin

Blue Hen Chicken
Delaware

Bobwhite Quail
Georgia

Brown Thrasher
Georgia

Nene
Hawaii

Mountain Bluebird
Idaho, Nevada

Cardinal
Illinois, Indiana, Kentucky, North
Carolina, Ohio, Virginia, West
Virginia

Eastern Goldfinch
Iowa, New Jersey

Western Meadowlark
Kansas, Montana, Nebraska,
North Dakota, Oregon, Wyoming

Brown Pelican
Louisiana

Chickadee
Maine, Massachusetts

Baltimore Oriole
Maryland

Loon
Minnesota

Wood Duck
Mississippi

Bluebird
Missouri, New York

Purple Finch
New Hampshire

Chaparral Bird
New Mexico

Scissor-Tailed Flycatcher
Oklahoma

Ruffed Grouse
Pennsylvania

Rhode Island Red
Rhode Island

Carolina Wren
South Carolina

Ring-Neck Pheasant
South Dakota

Sea Gull
Utah

Hermit Thrush
Vermont

Willow Goldfinch
Washington

a 1923 act that had designated the flower of the tulip tree as the state flower, for in 1931 the tulip tree had been designated the official state tree. From 1919 until 1923, the carnation had been Indiana's state flower.[28]

Since the adoption of the first state flower in 1913, there seems to have been much shuffling of floral emblems and discussions concerning the merits of each candidate. In 1957, a House committee changed a Senate-committee-proposed entry, the dogwood blossom, to the peony.

It has been conjectured that a commercial peony grower, also a state representative, had some influence in this decision. Though the peony is not indigenous to Indiana and, for this reason, has been criticized as inappropriately named as the state flower, it nonetheless continues to be the official state flower. If history repeats itself, however, it will not be long before naturalist agitators try again to change the state floral emblem to one that is native to Indiana.

Blooming in late May or early June, the peony sports its apparel in a variety of shades of pink and red, as well as white.[29]

Iowa

The wild rose was designated the official state flower of Iowa by that state's General Assembly in 1897. Specifically, the *Rosa pratincola*, the wild prairie rose, is considered to be the unofficial selection since there are several species and none was singled out for the designation. The wild rose blooms from June throughout the summer. It has large pinkish flowers with yellow centers.[30]

Kansas

The *Helianthus*, or wild native sunflower, was designated the state flower and floral emblem of Kansas in 1903. The laws speak to the symbolism of the sunflower as connoting "frontier days, winding trails, pathless prairies" as well as "the majesty of a golden future."[31]

The law's author, Senator George P. Morehouse, very eloquently expressed his love for the flower as well as the people of the state when he addressed the National Guard at Fort Riley after passage of the law. To quote his heartfelt speech,

This flower has to every Kansan a historic symbolism . . . it is not a blossom lingering a few brief hours, but lasts for a season. It gracefully nods to the caresses of the earliest morning zephyrs. Its bright face greets the rising orb of day and faithfully follows him in his onward course through the blazing noontime, till the pink-tinted afterglow of sunset decorates the western sky and marks the quiet hour of eventide.

It is hard to imagine that the sunflower will ever be dethroned as the state flower.[32]

Kentucky

The goldenrod became the official state flower of Kentucky in 1926 by legislative act.[33] Most of the 125 species of goldenrod have yellow flowers, though a few species sport white flowers instead. This perennial herb is also called the yellow-top or flower-of-gold.[34]

Louisiana

The magnolia was designated the state flower of Louisiana by act of the legislature in 1900.[35] The magnolia family, which includes about ten genera and seventy-five species, is most commonly found throughout eastern North America. The flower from the magnolia tree or shrub is large and extremely fragrant.[36]

Maine

The pine cone and tassel, *Pinus strobus Linnaeus*, was named the floral emblem of the state of Maine by legislative act in 1895.[37] It is obvious from the state seal, the nickname of the state, and the state tree that Maine is proud of its 17 million acres of forestland. It is no surprise that the pine cone and tassel was designated the official state flower of the Pine Tree State.

Maryland

The black-eyed susan, *Rudbeckia hirta*, was proclaimed to be the floral emblem of Maryland by legislative act in 1918.[38] Also called the yellow daisy, this herb is a member of the thistle family, with orange or orange-yellow petals and a purplish brown center.[39]

Massachusetts

The mayflower, *Epigea repens*, was named the flower or floral emblem of the Commonwealth of Massachusetts by legislative act in 1918. A provision was added in 1925 to protect the mayflower, making it unlawful to dig up or injure a mayflower plant, other than to pick the flower, if growing on public lands. A fine of not more than $50 may be levied upon conviction, unless a person violates this law while in disguise or in the secrecy of night, in which case the punishment is increased to a fine of not more than $100.[40]

Large patches of the mayflower, or ground laurel, may be found growing as far north as Newfoundland and as far south as Florida. The pink or white flowers grow in fragrant clusters at the ends of branches.[41]

Michigan

The apple blossom became the state flower of Michigan by joint resolution of the legislature in 1897. The law cites the apple blossom, in particular the *Pyrus coronaria*, which is native to Michigan, as adding to the beauty of the landscape, while Michigan apples have gained a reputation throughout the world.[42]

Minnesota

The pink and white lady slipper, *Cypripedium reginae*, was adopted by the legislature of Minnesota as the official state flower in 1902.[43] The pink and white lady slipper, an orchid, blooms in June and July, thriving in tamarack and spruce marshes. It has been protected by law since 1925.[44]

Mississippi

The flower of the evergreen magnolia, *Magnolia grandiflora*, was designated the state flower of Mississippi by legislative act in 1952. In 1900 the children of the state had selected the magnolia as the state flower, but their selection was not officially acted on until 52 years later.[45]

Missouri

The blossom of the red haw or wild haw, *Crataegus*, was declared the floral emblem of Missouri by the state legislature in 1923. Further, the legislature declared in the same act that the state department of agriculture shall encourage its cultivation because of the beauty of its flower, fruit, and foliage.[46]

The hawthorn's many species are found throughout Missouri and the Ozarks. The most common species are the margaretta, the turkey apple, and the cockspur thorn. A member of the rose family, the shrubby tree ranges from 3 to 30 feet in height with thorns 3 inches long on some trees. Its white blossoms spring forth in April and May.[47]

Montana

The bitterroot, *Lewisia rediviva*, was designated the floral emblem of Montana by legislative act in 1895.[48]

First chosen as the Montana Women's Christian Temperance Union's state flower in 1891, the bitterroot was selected as the official state flower after the Montana Floral Emblem Association held a statewide vote in 1894 and recommended it to the legislature. Of the over 5,800 ballots cast, the bitterroot received 3,621 votes far outdistancing the next runner-up, the evening primrose, which received a mere 787 votes. Early Indians boiled the root of the plant and combined it with meat or berries, making it a nutritious dietary staple.[49]

Nebraska

The late goldenrod, *Solidago serotina*, was declared the floral emblem of Nebraska by the legislature in 1895.[50] A member of the thistle family, it is a perennial herb that grows best in moist soil from Canada south to Georgia, Texas and Utah.[51]

Nevada

The sagebrush, *Artemisia tridentata* or *A. trifida*, was designated the state flower of Nevada by legislative act in 1967. It had been the unofficial state floral emblem since 1917.[52] An odorous silvery-gray member of the thistle family, the sagebrush thrives in the rocky soil or dry plains of the western United States and Canada.[53]

New Hampshire

The purple lilac, *Syringa vulgaris*, was named the state flower of New Hampshire by the legislature in 1919.[54] After months of arguments and committee debates, including an exasperated move by a legislative committee to ask two college botany professors to choose between the Senate preferred purple aster and the House preferred apple blossom, the purple lilac was finally selected. (The two college professors could not agree either, but finally the committee was able to break its deadlock.)[55]

New Jersey

The common meadow violet, *Viola sororia*, was designated the state flower of New Jersey by a legislative act in 1971 that became effective during 1972.[56]

New Mexico

The yucca flower was adopted as the official flower of New Mexico by legislative act in 1927.[57] The yucca flower was selected after a vote by school children and subsequent recommendation by the First Federation of Woman's Clubs. Blooming in early summer, the yucca flowers appear at the ends of long stalks. The base of the yucca consists of sharply pointed leaves making the plant both dastardly and delicate as the lower leaves contrast with the gentle ivory colored flowers. Amole, a soap substitute, can be made from its ground roots, a practice still found in some New Mexican Indian villages.[58]

New York

The rose, in any color or color combination common to it, was designated the official flower of the state of New York by the legislature in 1955.[59]

North Carolina

The dogwood was adopted as the official flower of North Carolina by that state's legislature in 1941.[60]

North Dakota

The wild prairie rose, *Rosa blanda* or *R. arkansana*, was named the floral emblem of North Dakota by legislative act in 1907.[61] An erect shrub, its stems are usually free of prickles, though sometimes they have a few slender thorns. The pink flowers bloom in June or July.[62]

Ohio

The scarlet carnation was adopted by the Ohio General Assembly in 1904 as that state's official flower in memory of William McKinley.[63] The carnation was considered a good luck piece by McKinley because, during an early campaign for a seat in the U.S. House of Representatives, his opponent gave McKinley a red carnation for his buttonhole. After winning the election, he continued to wear a red carnation during later campaigns.[64]

Oklahoma

The mistletoe, *Phoradendron serotinum*, was designated the floral emblem of Oklahoma by legislative act in 1893.[65] A shrub, mistletoe has the dubious distinction of being a tree parasite. There are over 100 American species in the mistletoe family.[66]

Oregon

The Oregon grape, *Berberis aquifolium*, was designated the official flower of Oregon by legislative act in 1899.[67] The Oregon grape, also known as the Rocky Mountain grape or the holly-leaf barberry, is a low trailing shrub. Its spherical berry, about 3 inches in diameter, is blue or purple.[68]

Pennsylvania

The mountain laurel, *Kalmia latifolia*, was adopted as the state flower of Pennsylvania by that state's legislature in 1933.[69] Blooming in June, the laurel's soft pink color is so popular that Tioga County celebrates an annual laurel festival where hundreds attend to soak up its beauty.[70]

Rhode Island

The violet, *Viola palmata*, was designated the state flower of Rhode Island by legislative act in 1968.[71] Also called the early blue violet and Johnny-jump-up, this violet-purple member of the abundant violet family is found from Massachusetts to Minnesota and south to Florida.[72]

South Carolina

In 1924 the General Assembly adopted the yellow jessamine as the official state flower of South Carolina. Reasons given for its selection include its fragrance and resilience. Growing throughout the state, the golden flower's reawakening in the spring has been considered a sign of its constancy and loyalty to the state of South Carolina.[73]

South Dakota

The American pasque flower, *Pulsatilla hirsutissima*, with the motto "I Lead" was made the floral emblem of South Dakota by legislative act in 1903.[74] Also known as the May Day flower, the wild crocus, the April-fools, the rock lily, the badger, and the wind flower, its lavender blooms appear in early spring.[75] It grows best in the arid prairie soil of South Dakota and other midwestern states north to British Columbia.[76]

Tennessee

Tennessee has two state flowers, a wild flower and a cultivated flower. The passion flower, *Passiflora incarnata*, officially became the state wild-flower in 1973 by act of the General Assembly.[77] In 1919 a resolution was passed providing that a vote by the state's school children would determine the state flower, and the passion flower was chosen. In 1933, however, the General Assembly passed another resolution adopting the iris as the state flower without rescinding the earlier resolution. This curious situation was finally rectified by the 1973 act that made the passion flower the state wildflower and the iris the state cultivated flower.[78]

The passion flower, also called the maypop, the wild apricot, and the Indian name *ocoee* grows in southern United States and South America. Early South American Christian missionaries gave the flower its name upon seeing such crucifixion symbols as the crown of thorns and three crosses within the flower.[79]

Texas

The bluebonnet, *Lupinus subcarnosis*, was adopted as the state flower of Texas by legislative act in 1901.[80] A member of the pea family, the bluebonnet is one of the over 100 species in this mostly herbaceous family.[81]

Utah

The sego lily, *Calochortus nuttalli*, was declared to be the state flower of Utah by the legislature in 1911.[82] This slender stemmed member of the lily family has white, lilac, or yellow flowers which bloom in midsummer. It is native from South Dakota to Nebraska and California.[83]

Vermont

The red clover, *Trifolium pratense*, was designated the state flower of Vermont by legislative act in 1894.[84] The red clover, not native to Vermont, was brought to the United States from Europe.[85] A perennial member of the pea family, it grows wild in fields and meadows. It is also called cowgrass, sugar plum, and honeysuckle clover.[86]

Virginia

The American dogwood, *Cornus florida*, was declared the floral emblem of Virginia by legislative act in 1918.[87] The flowering dogwood is known also as boxwood, white cornel, Indian arrowwood, and nature's mistake. The dogwood is a small tree or large shrub, with greenish yellow flowers and scarlet fruit. Found from Maine to Florida and from Minnesota to Texas, it spruces up the landscape in the fall with its red leaves.[88]

Washington

The Pink Rhododendron, *Rhododendron macrophyllum* was designated the state flower of Washington by that state's legislature in 1949.[89]

West Virginia

The *Rhododendron maximum*, or big laurel, was named the state flower of West Virginia by the legislature in 1903, following a vote by school children.[90] Found from Nova Scotia to Alabama, along streams and in low-lying wooded areas, the big laurel often forms dense thickets. It is also called deer-laurel, cow-plant, rose bay, and spoon-hutch. A tall branching shrub, sometimes a tree, its flowers are rose colored or white, lightly spotted in yellow or orange.[91]

Wisconsin

The wood violet, *Viola papilionacea*, was officially adopted as the state flower of Wisconsin by legislative act in 1949.[92] The violet won in an election over the wild rose, the trailing arbutus, and the white water lily. After the Arbor Day vote in 1909, the school children's choice was unofficial until voted into law in 1949.[93]

Wyoming

The Indian paintbrush, *Castilleja linariaefolia*, was made the state flower of Wyoming by legislative act in 1917.[94] Other names for this scarlet-leaved member of the figwort family include prairie fire, bloody warrior, and nose-bleed. Parasitic on plant roots, it can be found in meadows and damp thickets from Maine to Wyoming and Texas.[95]

Notes

1. Ala. Code §1–2–11.
2. *Alabama Official and Statistical Register* (Montgomery: Alabama Department of Archives and History, 1979), p. 24–25.
3. Alaska Stat. §44.09.050.
4. *Alaska Blue Book 1979*, p. 173.
5. Ariz. Rev. Stat. Ann. §41–855.
6. Nathaniel Lord Britton and Addison Brown, *An Illustrated Flora of the Northern United States, Canada and the British Possessions*, 2d ed., rev. and enl. (New York: Scribners, 1913), vol. 2, p. 568.
7. Ark. Stat. Ann. §5–109.
8. Cal. Gov't. Code §421 (West).
9. *California's Legislature 1984*, pp. 202–3.
10. Colo. Rev. Stat. §24–80–905.
11. Ibid., §24–80–906, §24–80–907.
12. Ibid., §24–80–908.
13. Conn. Gen. Stat. Ann. §3–108 (West).
14. *State of Connecticut Register and Manual, 1983*, p. 900.

15. Del. Code Ann. tit. 29, §308.

16. *Delaware State Manual, 1975–1976*, p. 14.

17. 1909 Fla. Laws 688.

18. *The State of Florida's Heritage and Emblems* (Tallahassee: Florida Department of State, 1986).

19. Ga. Code Ann. §50–3–53.

20. *The State of Georgia and Its Capitol* (Atlanta: State Museum of Science and Industry, Department of Archives and History, 1979), p. 16.

21. Ga. Code Ann. §50–3–54.

22. Haw. Rev. Stat. §5–9.

23. *Hawaii, The Aloha State* (Honolulu: State of Hawaii, Hawaii Visitors Bureau, Chamber of Commerce of Hawaii, n.d.).

24. Idaho Code §67–4502.

25. *Idaho Blue Book, 1981–82*, p. 209.

26. Ill. Ann. Stat. ch. 1, §3009 (Smith-Hurd).

27. Ind. Code Ann. §1–2–7–1 (West).

28. George Shankle, *State Names, Flags, Seals, Songs, Birds, Flowers, and Other Symbols*, rev. ed. (Westport, CT: Greenwood Press, 1970, c 1938), pp. 336–37.

29. Information provided by Indiana State Library, Indianapolis, Indiana.

30. *1985–86 Iowa Official Register*, vol. 61, p. 237.

31. Kan. Stat. Ann. §73–1801.

32. *Kansas Directory, 1984*, p. 128.

33. Ky. Rev. Stat. Ann. §2.090 (Baldwin).

34. Britton and Brown, *An Illustrated Flora*, vol. 3, p. 380.

35. La. Rev. Stat. Ann. §49–154 (West).

36. Britton and Brown, *An Illustrated Flora*, vol. 2, pp. 80–83.

37. Me. Rev. Stat. tit. 1, §211.

38. Md. Ann. Code §13–305.

39. Britton and Brown, *An Illustrated Flora*, vol. 3, p. 470.

40. Mass. Gen. Laws Ann. ch. 2, §7 (West).

41. Britton and Brown, *An Illustrated Flora*, vol. 2, p. 692.

42. Mich. Comp. Laws Ann. §2.11.

43. Minn. Stat. Ann. §1.142 (West).

44. Information provided by the Minnesota Historical Society, St. Paul, Minnesota.

45. 1952 Miss. Laws 465.

46. Mo. Ann. Stat. §10.030 (Vernon).

47. *Official Manual, State of Missouri, 1975–1976*, p. 1439.

48. Mont. Rev. Codes Ann. §1–1–503.

49. Rex C. Myers, *Symbols of Montana* (Helena: Montana Historical Society, 1976), p. 12.

50. 1895 Neb. Laws 441.

51. Britton and Brown, *An Illustrated Flora*, vol. 3, p. 394.

52. Nev. Rev. Stat. §235.050.

53. Britton and Brown, *An Illustrated Flora*, vol. 3, p. 530.

54. N.H. Rev. Stat. Ann. §3:5.

55. *Manual for the General Court, 1981*.

56. N.J. Stat. Ann. §52:9 AA–1 (West).

57. N.M. Stat. Ann. §12–3–4.
58. *New Mexico Blue Book 1977–1978*, p. 86.
59. N.Y. State Law §75 (McKinney).
60. N.C. Gen. Stat. §145–1.
61. N.D. Cent. Code §54–02–03.
62. Britton and Brown, *An Illustrated Flora*, vol. 2, p. 283.
63. Ohio Rev. Code Ann. §5.02 (Baldwin).
64. *Ohio Almanac* (Lorain: Lorain Journal Co., 1977), p. 60.
65. Okla. Stat. Ann. tit. 25, §92 (West).
66. Britton and Brown, *An Illustrated Flora*, vol. 1, p. 639.
67. Or. Rev. Stat. §186.
68. Britton and Brown, *An Illustrated Flora*, vol. 2, p. 128.
69. Pa. Stat. Ann. tit. 71, §1006 (Purdon).
70. *Pennsylvania Symbols* (Harrisburg: House of Representatives, n.d.).
71. R.I. Gen. Laws §42–4–9.
72. Britton and Brown, *An Illustrated Flora*, vol. 2, p. 547.
73. *South Carolina State Symbols and Emblems* (Columbia: House of Representatives, n.d.).
74. S.D. Codified Laws Ann. §1–6–10.
75. *South Dakota Legislative Manual, 1981*, p. 145.
76. Britton and Brown, *An Illustrated Flora*, vol. 2, p. 102.
77. Tenn. Code Ann. §4–1–306.
78. Ibid., §4–1–307.
79. *Tennessee Blue Book, 1985–1986*, p. 342.
80. Tex. Rev. Civ. Stat. Ann. art. 6143b (Vernon).
81. Britton and Brown, *An Illustrated Flora*, vol. 2, p. 347.
82. Utah Code Ann. §63–13–6.
83. Britton and Brown, *An Illustrated Flora*, vol. 1, p. 508.
84. Vt. Stat. Ann. tit. 1, §498.
85. *Vermont Legislative Directory and State Manual, 1979–80*, p. 15.
86. Britton and Brown, *An Illustrated Flora*, vol. 2, p. 355.
87. Va. Code §7.1–38.
88. Britton and Brown, *An Illustrated Flora*, vol. 2, p. 664.
89. Wash. Rev. Code Ann. §1.20.030.
90. *West Virginia Blue Book, 1980*, p. 925.
91. Britton and Brown, *An Illustrated Flora*, vol. 2, p. 681.
92. Wis. Stat. Ann. §1.10 (West).
93. *State of Wisconsin, 1983–1984 Blue Book*, p. 948.
94. Wyo. Stat. Ann. §8–3–104.
95. Britton and Brown, *An Illustrated Flora*, vol. 3, p. 214.

7 | State Trees

In 1919, Texas became the first state to select a state tree, the pecan. All of the other states have since chosen state trees, and one state, New Jersey, has named a state tree and a state memorial tree.

Out of the thirty-five trees designated by the states, the white oak and the sugar maple tie for first place. Each was named the state tree for four states. Connecticut, Maryland, Illinois, and Iowa named the white oak their state tree. (Iowa, in fact, designated all species of the oak.) New York, Vermont, West Virginia, and Wisconsin selected the sugar maple. Tying for second place in popularity are the southern pine, designated by Alabama, Arkansas, and North Carolina, and the dogwood, named by Missouri, Virginia, and New Jersey. (New Jersey named the dogwood its state memorial tree.)

Two states chose the American elm (Massachusetts and North Dakota), the white pine (Maine and Michigan), the cottonwood (Kansas and Nebraska), the palmetto (Florida and South Carolina), the blue spruce (Colorado and Utah), and the tulip poplar (Indiana and Tennessee).

Probably the most frequently cited reason for the selection of a particular state tree is the part that tree played in the early history of a state. The palmetto was used to build colonial forts off the coast of South Carolina. The live oak was used to construct homes by early Georgia settlers. In Tennessee, the tulip poplar was used to construct homesteads and barns. The white oak was chosen by Connecticut in remembrance of a famous tree, the Charter Oak, and its role in the American fight for independence. Kansas recognized the cottonwood planted by pioneers.

New Hampshire's white birch, Maine's white pine, and Oregon's Douglas fir, are but a few examples of trees that are strongly identified with a particular state and, therefore, have been made state emblems. Delaware is proud of the many ornamental uses of its state tree, the American holly.

Alabama

The southern pine was designated the official tree of Alabama in 1949.[1]

Scientific name: *Pinus palustris Mill.*

Synonyms: Longleaf yellow pine, pitch pine, hard pine, heart pine, turpentine pine, rosemary pine, brown pine, fat pine, longstraw pine, longleaf pitch pine.

Native to: South Atlantic and Gulf coastal plains.

Physical description: The southern pine is a large tree with coarsely scaly, orange-brown bark and slender dark green needles, three in a cluster and from 10 to 15 inches long. The large cones are from 5 to 10 inches long and are dull brown and prickly.

The bill does not specify which species was intended, even though twelve exist in Alabama. However, the person who introduced the bill, Hugh Kaul of Birmingham, has stated that he meant the longleaf pine.[2]

Alaska

The Sitka spruce, *Picea sitchensis*, became the official tree of Alaska by legislative act in 1962.[3]

Scientific name: *Picea sitchensis (Bong.) Carr.*

Synonyms: Yellow spruce, tideland spruce, western spruce, silver spruce, coast spruce, Menzies' spruce.

Native to: Pacific coast region north to Canada and Alaska.

Physical description: The bark on this large to very large tree is reddish brown and thin with loosely attached scales. The flat, dark green needles are from ⅝ to 1 inch long, and the light orange-brown cones are from 2 to 3½ inches long with long stiff scales.

Arizona

The paloverde, genus *cercidium*, was adopted as the state tree of Arizona in 1954.[4]

Scientific name: *Cercidium torreyanum (Wats.) Sargent.*

Synonym: Green barked Acacia.

Native to: Southern California and Arizona; south into Mexico.

Physical description: The bark of this short, stout tree is yellow to yellow green. Leaves are oblong in shape and paired with two or three leaflets on each side. Soon after the leaves mature in March or April, they fall, making the tree bare of leaves the rest of the year. The brilliant yellow-gold flowers bloom in early spring, and the pod-shaped fruit ripens in July.

Arkansas

The pine tree was designated the state tree of Arkansas in 1939.[5] See the Alabama entry for a description.

California

Two species of the California redwood, *Sequoia sempervirens* and *Sequoia gigantea*, were named the official state trees of California in 1937.[6]

Scientific names: *Sequoia sempervirens* (D. Don) Endl. and *Sequoiadendron giganteum* (Lindl.) Buchholz.

Synonyms: Coast redwood and redwood for the first variety; giant sequoia, bigtree, Sierra redwood, and mammoth tree for the second.

Native to: The coast redwood is native to the Pacific coast of California and southwestern Oregon. The giant sequoia is native to the Sierra Nevada in California.

Physical description: The coast redwood is the world's largest species. Its reddish-brown bark is thick, deeply furrowed, and fibrous. The leaves are scalelike and needlelike, flat, slightly curved, and unequal in length ranging from ¼ to ¾ of an inch. They are dark green, spreading in two rows. The reddish-brown cones are from ¾ to 1 inch long and mature in the first year.

The giant sequoia's bark is reddish brown, thick, deeply furrowed, and fibrous. The tree is swollen at the base. The cones range from 1¾ to 2¾ inches in length, are reddish brown, and mature the second year. The leaves are from ⅛ to ¼ inch long and may grow from leading shoots ½ inch long. The blue-green, sharply pointed leaves grow all around the twig and overlap.

The tallest known *sequoia sempervirens* is 364 feet high. Protected by the state, which matched monies raised by the Save-the-Redwoods League, they are allowed to grow uncut in designated groves.[7]

Located in thirty-two groves on the western slopes of the Sierra Nevada mountains, the *sequoia gigantea* was voted the United States tree by school children across the United States. The largest of these trees, nicknamed "General Sherman" is 36½ feet in diameter, and it is estimated that it could supply enough lumber to build forty houses.[8] It is estimated that this tree is from 3,000 to 4,000 years old.[9]

Colorado

The unofficial state tree of Colorada is the blue spruce, as designated in 1939.[10]

Scientific name: Picea pungens Engelm.

Synonyms: Colorada blue spruce, balsam, Colorado spruce, prickly spruce, white spruce, silver spruce, Parry's spruce.

Native to: Rocky Mountain region.

Physical description: The four-angled needles of the blue spruce are from ¾ to 1⅛ inches long and are dull blue green. This large tree has gray or brown bark that is furrowed into scaly ridges. Cones are from 2½ to 4 inches long and are light brown with long, thin, irregularly toothed scales.

Connecticut

The white oak, *Quercus alba*, was designated the state tree of Connecticut in 1947.[11]

Scientific name: Quercus alba Linn.

Synonym: Stave oak.

Native to: Eastern half of United States and adjacent Canada.

Physical description: The white oak is a large tree with light gray bark, fissured into scaly ridges. The smooth leaves are oblong, from 4 to 9 inches long, and are deeply or shallowly 5 to 9 lobed. They are bright green above, pale or whitish beneath, and turn a deep red in the fall. The acorns are from ¾ to 1 inch long, with shallow cups.

The Charter Oak, a famous oak of the colonial period, was the inspiration for the oak tree's being named the state tree of Connecticut. In 1687 the Charter Oak was a hiding place for a charter earlier given to the General Court of Connecticut by King Charles II that was rescinded twenty-five years later by King James II. The colonists were not eager to return the charter to James' emissary, and, while they were seated at a table holding the charter, the candles went out. When they were re-lit, the charter was gone.[12]

Delaware

The American holly, *Ilex opaca Aiton*, was adopted as the state tree of Delaware in 1939.[13]

Scientific name: Ilex opaca Ait.

Synonyms: Holly, white holly, evergreen holly, boxwood.

Native to: Atlantic and Gulf coasts; Mississippi valley region.

Physical description: A medium-sized to large tree, the American holly's bark is light gray, thin, and smoothish, with wartlike projections. The evergreen elliptical leaves are from 2 to 4 inches long and are coarsely spring toothed, stiff, and leathery. They are green above and yellowish green beneath. The small male and female flowers, which are on different trees, are greenish white. Spherical in shape, the red berrylike fruit is from ¼ to ⅜ of an inch in diameter.

Holly boughs with their colorful red berries make attractive and lucrative Christmas decorations. It is for this reason that the holly tree is considered one of Delaware's most treasured trees.[14]

Florida

The sabal palmetto palm, known also as the cabbage palm, was designated the state tree of Florida in 1953. This act declares further that such designation should not be construed to limit the use of this tree in any way for commercial purposes.[15]

Scientific name: *Sabal palmetto (Walt.) Lodd.*

Synonyms: Cabbage palmetto, palmetto, tree palmetto, Bank's palmetto.

Native to: South Atlantic to Gulf coasts from North Carolina to Florida.

Physical description: The trunk of this medium-sized palm tree is stout and unbranched, grayish brown, roughened or ridged, with a cluster of large leaves at the top. The 4- to 7-foot-long evergreen leaves are coarse, fan-shaped, thick, and leathery, much folded and divided into narrow segments with threadlike fibers hanging between. Leafstalks are from 5 to 8 feet long. Fruits are numerous in a much-branched cluster about 7 feet long and are black, ⅜ to ½ inch in diameter, and one seeded.

Georgia

The live oak was adopted as the official tree emblematic of the state of Georgia in 1937.[16]

Scientific name: *Quercus virginiana Mill.*

Synonyms: Chêne Vert.

Native to: South Atlantic and Gulf coast regions, lower California, southern Mexico, Central America, and Cuba.

Physical description: The live oak is a medium-sized widespreading tree. Its bark is dark brown, furrowed, and slightly scaly. The leaves are evergreen, shiny dark green above and whitish hairy beneath. They are elliptical or oblong, 2 to 5 inches long, and usually rounded at the apex; their edges are usually smooth and rolled under. There are from one to five acorns on stalks ½ to 3 inches long. The narrow acorns are from ¾ to 1 inch long and have deep cups.

The Edmund Burke Chapter of the Daughters of the American Revolution first introduced the native oak as a candidate for state tree. Many of the earlier settlers lived along the coast or on islands where the oak was plentiful. A few of the better known Georgians who seemed appreciative of the tree's beauty were James Oglethorpe, John Wesley, and Sidney Lanier.[17]

Hawaii

The *kukui* tree, *Aleurites moluccana*, which is also known as the candlenut tree, was designated the official tree of Hawaii in 1959.[18]

Scientific name: *Aleurites moluccana (L.) Willd.*

Physical description: The sharply pointed or regularly shaped leaves are greyish green due to a grey fur adorning the surface of the leaf, which is especially pronounced beneath. The five-petalled flowers are small, forming delicate white clusters. The nuts are edible if roasted. The fruits were also once used for torch oil.[19]

Idaho

The white pine, *Pinus monticola*, was declared the state tree of Idaho in 1935.[20]

Scientific name: *Pinus monticola Dougl.*

Synonyms: Western white pine, Idaho white pine, finger-cone pine, mountain pine, little sugar pine, mountain Weymouth pine.

Native to: Northern Rocky Mountain and Pacific coast regions, including southern British Columbia.

Physical description: The bark on this large tree is gray, thin, and smoothish, becoming fissured into rectangular, scaly plates. The blue-green needles are stout, from 2 to 4 inches long, and are five in a cluster. The cones are long stalked, from 5 to 12 inches long, and yellow brown with thin, rounded scales.

Illinois

Following a vote of school children the Illinois legislature, in 1908, declared the native oak to be the official state tree. Since at least two oaks are native to Illinois, however, another selection was held among school children, this time between the northern red oak and the white oak. The white oak won, and, in 1973, the legislature officially designated the white oak as the official tree of Illinois.[21] See the Connecticut entry for a description.

Indiana

The tulip tree, *Liriodendron tulipifera*, was designated the official state tree of Indiana in 1931.[22]

Scientific name: Liriodendron tulipifera L.

Synonyms: Yellow poplar, blue poplar, hickory poplar, basswood, cucumber tree, tulipwood, whitewood, white poplar, poplar, old-wife's-shirt-tree.

Native to: Eastern third of the United States and southern Ontario.

Physical description: The tallest eastern hardwood, the tulip tree's bark is brown, becoming thick and deeply furrowed. The unusually shaped leaves are squarish with a broad, slightly notched or nearly straight apex and two or three lobes on each side. They are from 3 to 6 inches long and are shiny dark green above and pale green beneath. The flowers are large and tulip shaped, from 1½ to 2 inches in diameter, and usually green except in the spring when they are orange. The fruit is conelike, from 2½ to 3 inches long and ½ inch thick.

Iowa

The oak, *Quercus spp.*, was officially designated as the state tree of Iowa in 1961.[23] See the Connecticut and New Jersey entries for descriptions.

Kansas

The cottonwood was designated the official tree of Kansas in 1937.[24]

Scientific name: Populus deltoides Bartr.

Synonyms: Eastern poplar, Carolina poplar, eastern cottonwood, necklace poplar, big cottonwood, Vermont poplar, whitewood, cotton tree, yellow cottonwood.

Native to: Eastern half of the United States and adjacent Canada.

Physical description: A large tree, the cottonwood's bark is at first yellowish green and smooth, becoming gray and deeply furrowed. The leaves are triangular, from 3 to 6 inches long, and wide, long pointed, and coarsely toothed with curved teeth. The smooth leaves are light green and shiny.

The cottonwood has been termed the pioneer tree of Kansas because many homesteaders planted cottonwood. The cottonwood flourished giving the settlers the courage to continue and to lay claim to the land.[25]

Kentucky

The coffee tree was named the Kentucky state tree in 1976.[26]

Scientific name: *Gymnocladus dioicus (Linn.) Koch.*

Synonyms: Kentucky coffee tree, coffeebean tree, coffeenut, mahogany, nickertree, stumptree, virgilia.

Native to: Northeastern United States and southern Ontario; west through Minnesota, Nebraska, and Kansas; southward mainly between the Mississippi River and the Allegheny Mountains to Tennessee.

Physical description: A popular shade tree, the coffee tree grows from 40 to 60 feet in height and lives from 40 to 50 years. Shiny and pale green leaflets turn clear yellow in early autumn. The large seed pods are brown and hang from the tree throughout the winter.

Louisiana

The bald cypress, *Taxodium distichum*, commonly called the cypress tree, was designated the official state tree of Louisiana in 1963.[27]

Scientific name: *Taxodium distichum (L.) Rich.*

Synonyms: Southern cypress, red cypress, yellow cypress, white cypress, black cypress, gulf cypress, swamp cypress, deciduous cypress, tidewater red cypress.

Native to: Swamps and riverbanks of the South Atlantic and Gulf coastal plains and the Mississippi valley.

Physical description: The bald cypress is a large tree with a swollen base and "knees." The bark is reddish brown or gray with long fibrous or scaly ridges. The leaves are light yellow green, whitish beneath, and are crowded featherlike in two rows on slender horizontal twigs. They are flat, from 3/8 to 3/4 of an inch long, and are shed in the fall. The cones are from 3/4 to 1 inch in diameter with hard scales.

Maine

The white pine was named the official tree of Maine in 1959.[28]

Scientific name: *Pinus strobus Linn.*

Synonyms: Eastern white pine, northern white pine, soft pine, Weymouth pine, spruce pine.

Native to: Northeastern United States, adjacent Canada, and the Appalachian Mountain region.

Physical description: The largest northeastern conifer, the white pine's bark is gray or purplish and is deeply fissured into broad ridges. Its slender needles are blue green, from 2½ to 5 inches long, and grow five in a cluster. The cones are long stalked, narrow, from 4 to 8 inches long, and yellow brown with thin, rounded scales.

Maryland

The white oak, *Quercus alba*, was declared the arboreal emblem of Maryland in 1941.[29] See the Connecticut entry for a description.

Massachusetts

The American elm, *Ulmus americana*, was named the state tree of Massachusetts in 1941.[30]

Scientific name: *Ulmus americana Linn.*

Synonyms: White elm, soft elm, water elm, gray elm, swamp elm, rock elm, Orme Maigre.

Native to: Eastern half of the United States and adjacent Canada.

Physical description: The American elm is a large, spreading tree with gray bark that is deeply furrowed with broad, forking, scaly ridges. Twigs are soft and hairy, becoming smooth, not corky winged. Fruits are elliptical and flat, from ⅜ to ½ inch long. Leaves are in two rows, elliptical, from 3 to 6 inches long, and coarsely and doubly toothed with unequal teeth. The two sides of the leaf are unequal. They are dark green and smooth or slightly rough above, and pale and usually soft and hairy beneath.

Michigan

The white pine, *Pinus strobus*, was adopted as the official state tree of Michigan in 1955.[31] See the Maine entry for a description.

Minnesota

The red pine or Norway pine, *Pinus resinosa*, was designated the official state tree of Minnesota in 1953.[32]

Scientific name: *Pinus resinosa Ait.*

Synonyms: Canadian red pine, hard pine.

Native to: Northeastern United States and adjacent Canada.

Physical description: A medium-sized to large tree, the red pine has reddish-brown bark with broad, flat, scaly plates. Needles are two in a cluster, dark green and slender, from 5 to 6 inches long. Cones are 2 inches long and light brown without prickles.

Mississippi

The magnolia or evergreen magnolia, *Magnolia grandiflora*, was designated the state tree of Mississippi in 1938.[33]

Scientific name: Magnolia grandiflora Linn.

Synonyms: Big laurel, bull bay, great laurel magnolia, bat-tree, laurel-leaved magnolia, large-flowered magnolia, laurel bay.

Native to: South Atlantic and Gulf coastal plains.

Physical description: A medium-sized to large tree, the magnolia has gray to light brown bark, broken into small, thin scales. Leaves are evergreen, oblong or elliptical, from 5 to 8 inches long, short pointed, and leathery with smooth edges. They are shiny bright green and smooth above, rusty and hairy beneath. The flowers are cup shaped, from 6 to 8 inches across, white and fragrant during spring and summer. The fruit is conelike, from 3 to 4 inches long, from 1½ to 2½ inches thick, rusty and hairy.

Missouri

The flowering dogwood, *Cornus florida*, was declared the arboreal emblem of Missouri in 1955.[34]

Scientific name: Cornus florida Linn.

Synonyms: Dogwood, boxwood, false box-dogwood, New England boxwood, flowering cornel, cornel.

Native to: Eastern half of the United States and southern Ontario.

Physical description: A small tree, the flowering dogwood's bark is dark reddish brown, broken into small square or rounded blocks. The leaves are paired, elliptical or oval, from 3 to 6 inches long, and short pointed; their edges appear to be smooth but are minutely toothed. They are bright green and nearly smooth above, whitish and slightly hairy beneath; and they turn bright scarlet above in the fall. The greenish-yellow flowers grow in a dense head with four showy, white, petallike bracts from 2¼ to 4 inches in diameter, and bloom in the early spring. The egg-shaped fruits are ⅜ inch long, bright scarlet, shiny, fleshy, and 1 or 2 seeded.

Montana

The ponderosa pine was designated the official state tree of Montana in 1949.[35]

Scientific name: *Pinus ponderosa Laws.*

Synonyms: Western yellow pine, western soft pine, yellow pine, bull pine, foothills yellow pine, red pine, big pine, long-leaved pine, pitch pine, heavy-wooded pine, heavy pine, Sierra brownbark pine, Montana black pine.

Native to: Rocky Mountains and Pacific coast regions, including adjacent Canada; southward to western Texas and Mexico.

Physical description: The ponderosa pine is a large tree with brown or blackish bark, furrowed into ridges. On older trunks, the bark is yellow brown and irregularly fissured into large, flat, scaly plates. The needles are three, or two and three, in a cluster, stout, from 4 to 7 inches long, and dark green. The cones are from 3 to 6 inches long and short stalked with prickly scales, and they are light reddish brown.

Nebraska

The cottonwood was declared the state tree of Nebraska in 1972.[36] See the Kansas entry for a description.

Nevada

The single-leaf piñon, *Pinus monophylla*, was designated the official state tree of Nevada in 1953.[37]

Scientific name: *Pinus monophylla Torr.* and *Frém.*

Synonyms: Nut pine, pinyon, gray pine, Nevada nut pine, singleleaf pinyon pine.

Native to: Great Basin region to California.

Physical description: The single-leaf piñon is a small tree with dark brown bark, furrowed into scaly ridges. The needles are one per sheath, stout, from 1 to 2 inches long, and gray green. The egg-shaped cones are light brown with stout, blunt scales and are from 2 to 2½ inches long. The large, edible seeds, ¾ inch long, are commonly known as pinyon nuts.

New Hampshire

The white birch, *Betula papyrifera*, was named the state tree of New Hampshire in 1947.[38]

Scientific name: *Betula papyrifera Marsh.*

Synonyms: Canoe birch, silver birch, paper birch, large white birch.

Native to: Northeastern United States; across Canada to Alaska; northern Rocky Mountain region.

Physical description: A medium-sized to large tree, the white birch has smooth, thin, white bark, separating into papery strips. Leaves are oval, from 2 to 4 inches long, long pointed and wedge shaped or rounded at the base. They are coarsely and usually doubly toothed, mostly with five to nine main veins on each side, dull dark green and smooth above, and light yellow green and smooth or slightly hairy beneath. The cones are narrow, from 1½ to 2 inches long and ⅜ inch wide, and hang from slender stalks.

The New Hampshire Federation of Garden Clubs recommended that the white birch be designated the state tree for the obvious reason that it is natively so abundant throughout the state. This graceful and beautiful tree had the practical historical use learned by every school child—its bark was used by Indians to construct their canoes.[39]

New Jersey

The northern red oak was designated the official state tree of New Jersey in 1950.[40]

Scientific name: *Quercus rubra Linn.*

Synonyms: Red oak, black oak, Spanish oak.

Native to: Eastern half of the United States except the southern border; adjacent Canada.

Physical description: The northern red oak is a large tree with dark brown bark, fissured into broad, flat ridges. The leaves are from 5 to 9 inches long, oblong, and seven to eleven lobed less than halfway to the middle; the lobes have a few irregular bristle-pointed teeth. The smooth leaves are a dull dark green above and pale yellow green beneath, and they turn red in the fall. Acorns have either a shallow or deep cup and are from ⅝ to 1⅛ inch long.

The dogwood was designated the state memorial tree in 1951 by Assembly Concurrent Resolution No. 12.[41] See the Missouri entry for a description of the dogwood.

New Mexico

The nut pine or piñon, *Pinus edulis*, was adopted as the official state tree of New Mexico in 1948.[42]

Scientific name: *Pinus edulis Engelm.*

Synonyms: Nut pine, pinyon pine, Colorado pinyon pine, New Mexico piñon.

Native to: Southern Rocky Mountain region and adjacent Mexico.

Physical description: A small tree, the nut pine has reddish-brown bark, furrowed into scaly ridges. The needles are two (sometimes three) in a cluster, stout, from ¾ to 1½ inches long, and dark green. The egg-shaped cones are from 1½ to 2 inches long and light brown with stout, blunt scales and large, edible seeds ½ inch long and known as pinyon nuts.

As long ago as the 1500s, when the Spanish first came to New Mexico, they noticed that the piñon nut was a popular food item. People still watch for the periodic overabundant years when there are enough piñons for everyone who is willing to spend some effort to gather them. A close runner-up, the aspen, lost to the piñon after the New Mexico Federation of Women's Clubs selected the piñon for nomination to the state legislature.[43]

New York

The sugar maple, *Acer saccharum*, was designated the official tree of New York in 1956.[44]

Scientific name: *Acer saccharum Marsh.*

Synonyms: Hard maple, rock maple, sugar maple, black maple.

Native to: Eastern half of the United States and adjacent Canada.

Physical description: The sugar maple is a large tree with gray bark, furrowed into irregular ridges or scales. The leaves are paired, heart shaped, with three or five lobes, long pointed and sparingly, coarsely toothed. From 3 to 5½ inches in diameter, they are dark green above and light green and usually smooth beneath, turning yellow, orange, or scarlet in the fall. The fruits, 1 to 1¼ inches long, mature in the fall.

North Carolina

The pine tree was adopted as the official state tree of North Carolina in 1963.[45] See the Alabama entry for a description.

North Dakota

The American elm, *Ulmus americana*, was designated the official tree of North Dakota in 1947.[46] See the Massachusetts entry for a description.

Ohio

The buckeye tree, *Aesculus glabra*, was adopted as the official tree of Ohio in 1953.[47]

Scientific name: Aesculus glabra Willd.

Synonyms: Ohio buckeye, fetid buckeye, stinking buckeye, American horse chestnut.

Native to: Midwestern United States, chiefly Ohio and Mississippi valley regions.

Physical description: The buckeye is a small to medium-sized tree with gray bark, much furrowed and broken into scaly plates. The leaves are paired together with leafstalks from 4 to 6 inches long. Leaflets are five per leafstalk, from 3 to 5 inches long, long pointed, narrowed at the base, and finely toothed. (The shrubby variety of the buckeye tree has from five to seven leaflets.) The showy flowers grow in branched clusters, from 4 to 6 inches long, and are pale greenish yellow with petals nearly as long as the flower, or from ¾ to 1¼ inches long. The one or two poisonous seeds are from 1 to 1½ inches wide and are encased in a prickly fruiting capsule from 1¼ to 2 inches in diameter.

The buckeye got its name because the Indians thought the seed of the tree looked like the "eye of a buck"; in the Indian, the *hetuck*.[48]

Oklahoma

The redbud tree, *Cercis canadensis*, was adopted as the official tree of Oklahoma in 1937.[49]

Scientific name: Cercis canadensis Linn.

Synonyms: Judas tree, red Judas tree, salad-tree, Canadian Judas tree.

Native to: North central and eastern United States.

Physical description: A small tree, the redbud branches at 10 to 15 feet from the ground and forms a narrow and erect or a spreading, flattened, or rounded head. An ornamental tree, it flowers in late February to April in a profusion of small, light pink to purple blossoms.

Oregon

The Douglas fir, *Pseudotsuga menziessii*, was declared the official state tree of Oregon in 1939.[50]

Scientific name: *Pseudotsuga menziesii (Mirb.) Franco.*

Synonyms: Douglas spruce, red fir, yellow fir, Oregon pine, red pine, Puget Sound pine, spruce, fir, Douglas tree, cork-barked Douglas spruce.

Native to: Pacific coast and Rocky Mountain region, including Canada and Mexico.

Physical description: The Douglas fir is a very large tree, next to the giant sequoia and the redwood in size. The bark is reddish brown, thick, and deeply furrowed into broad ridges. The dark yellow-green or blue-green needles are short stalked, flat, and from ¾ to 1¼ inches long. The cones are from 2 to 4 inches long and light brown with thin, rounded scales and long, three-toothed bracts.

The Douglas fir was chosen as the state tree because Oregon is the major supplier of this indispensable lumber tree. Because its wood is relatively lightweight when compared with its strength, it is considered one of the foremost trees in the world for its lumber.[51]

Pennsylvania

The hemlock tree, *Tsuga canadensis*, was adopted as the state tree of Pennsylvania in 1931.[52]

Scientific name: *Tsuga canadensis (Linn.) Carr.*

Synonyms: Eastern hemlock, Canadian hemlock, hemlock spruce, spruce pine, New England hemlock, spruce.

Native to: Northeastern United States, adjacent Canada, and the Appalachian Mountain region to northern Alabama and Georgia.

Physical description: The hemlock tree is a medium-sized to large tree with brown or purplish bark, deeply furrowed into broad, scaly ridges. The needles are short stalked, flat, soft, blunt pointed, and from ⅜ to ⅝ inch long. They are shiny dark green above and lighter beneath, appearing in two rows. The cones are brownish and from ⅝ to ¾ inch long.

Rhode Island

The red maple, *Acer rubrum*, was designated the state tree of Rhode Island in 1964.[53]

Scientific name: *Acer rubrum Linn.*

Synonyms: Soft maple, water maple, scarlet maple, white maple, swamp maple, shoe-peg maple, erable.

Native to: Eastern half of the United States and adjacent Canada; west to the Dakotas, Texas, and Nebraska.

Physical description: A large tree with a large trunk, the red maple's bark is gray, thin, smooth, and broken into long, thin scales. The twigs are reddish, and the leaves are dark green and shiny above, whitish and slightly hairy beneath, turning scarlet or yellow in the fall. The leaves are paired, heart shaped, from 2½ to 4 inches long, and three to five lobed. The lobes are short pointed and are irregularly and sharply toothed. The fruits, ¾ inch long, mature in the spring.

South Carolina

The palmetto tree, *Inodes palmetto*, was adopted as the official tree of South Carolina in 1939.[54] See the Florida entry for a description.

Palmetto logs, used in the construction of the fort on Sullivan's Island, helped withstand the British attack during the American Revolution. For this reason, the palmetto has been memorialized as the state tree and appears on both the flag and the seal.[55]

South Dakota

The Black Hills spruce, *Picea glauca densata*, was named the state tree of South Dakota in 1947.[56]

Scientific name: *Picea glauca (Moench) Voss.*

Synonyms: White spruce, single spruce, bog spruce, skunk spruce, cat spruce, spruce, pine, double spruce.

Native to: Northeastern United States, Black Hills, Canada, Alaska.

Physical description: The Black Hills spruce is a medium-sized tree with thin and scaly gray or brown bark. The blue-green needles are four-angled, from ½ to ¾ inch long, and of disagreeable odor when crushed. The cones are slender, from 1½ to 2 inches long, pale brown, and shiny with scales that are thin, flexible, and rounded with smooth margins.

Tennessee

The tulip poplar, *Liriodendron tulipifera*, was designated the official state tree of Tennessee in 1947.[57] See the Indiana entry for a description.

The tulip poplar is plentiful throughout the state of Tennessee. Early settlers found it particularly useful for dwelling and barn construction.[58]

Texas

The pecan tree was designated the state tree of Texas in 1919. An amendment in 1927 made it the duty of the State Board of Control 69 the State

Parks Board "to give due consideration to the pecan tree when planning beautification of state parks or other public property belonging to the state."[59]

Scientific name: *Carya illinoensis (Wangenh.) K. Koch.*

Synonyms: Pecan nut, pecanier, pecan (hickory).

Native to: Mississippi valley region, Texas, and Mexico.

Physical description: A large tree, the pecan tree has deeply and irregularly furrowed and cracked light brown or gray bark. The compound leaves are from 12 to 20 inches long. The leaflets number from eleven to seventeen and are short stalked, lance shaped, and slightly sickle-shaped. They are from 2 to 7 inches long, long pointed, finely toothed, smooth, and slightly hairy. The nuts are slightly four winged, oblong, and pointed, and they have thin husks. From 1 to 2 inches long, they are sweet and edible.

Utah

The blue spruce was designated the Utah state tree in 1933.[60] See the Colorado entry for a description.

Vermont

The sugar maple was named the state tree of Vermont in 1949.[61] See the New York entry for a description.

Virginia

The flowering dogwood was designated the state tree of Virginia in 1956.[62] See the Missouri entry for a description.

Washington

The western hemlock, *Tsuga heterophylla*, was designated the official tree of the state of Washington in 1947.[63]

Scientific name: *Tsuga heterophylla (Raf.) Sargent.*

Synonyms: West coast hemlock, Pacific hemlock, hemlock spruce, California hemlock spruce, western hemlock fir, Prince Albert's fir, Alaska pine.

Native to: Pacific coast and northern Rocky Mountain regions north to Canada and Alaska.

Physical description: The western hemlock is a large tree with reddish-brown bark, deeply furrowed into broad, flat ridges. The needles are short stalked, flat, from ¼ to ¾ inch long, and shiny dark green above and lighter beneath. The brownish cones are from ¾ to 1 inch long.

West Virginia

The sugar maple, *Acer saccharum Marsh.*, was designated the state tree of West Virginia in 1949.[64] See the New York entry for a description.

Because it is used in furniture building and is enjoyed for its maple syrup, the state's school children and civic clubs voted to recommend the sugar maple as West Virginia's state tree.[65]

Wisconsin

The sugar maple, *Acer saccharum*, was designated the official state tree of Wisconsin in 1949.[66] See the New York entry for a description.

Wisconsin's school children recommended the sugar maple by popular vote in 1948. Though others tried to overrule the 1948 vote by lobbying for the white pine, the legislature followed the recommendation of the Youth Centennial Committee vote.[67]

Wyoming

The cottonwood tree, *Populus sargentii*, was designated the state tree of Wyoming in 1947 and 1961.[68]

Scientific name: *Populus deltoides* var. *occidentalis Ryb.*; *P. sargentii Dode* is the name given in the state law.

Synonyms: Plains cottonwood, plains poplar.

Native to: Great plains and eastern border of Rocky Mountains north into Canada.

Physical description: The plains cottonwood is a large tree with gray, deeply furrowed bark. The leaves are smooth, light green, shiny, and broadly oval. They are often wider than long, from 3 to 4 inches long and wide, long pointed, and coarsely toothed with curved teeth. The leafstalks are flat.

Notes

1. Ala. Code §1–2–12.
2. *Alabama State Emblems* (Montgomery: Alabama State Department of Archives and History, n.d.).
3. Alaska Stat. §44.09.070.
4. Ariz. Rev. Stat. Ann. §41–856.

5. *State Trees and Arbor Days* (Washington, D.C.: Government Printing Office, 1981), p. 4; 1939 Ark. Acts, 1092.

6. Cal. Gov't. Code §422 (West).

7. *State Emblems* (Sacramento: Secretary of State, n.d.).

8. Ibid.

9. *California's Legislature, 1984*, p. 204.

10. *State Trees and Arbor Days*, p. 5.

11. Conn. Gen. Stat. Ann. §3–110 (West).

12. *State of Connecticut Register and Manual, 1983*, p. 907.

13. Del. Code Ann. tit. 29, §305.

14. *Discover Wonderful Delaware!* (Dover: Delaware State Development Department, n.d.).

15. Fla. Stat. Ann. §15.031 (West).

16. Ga. Code Ann. §50–3–55.

17. *The State of Georgia and Its Capitol* (Atlanta: State Museum of Science and Industry, Department of Archives and History, 1979), p. 15.

18. Haw. Rev. Stat. §5–8.

19. Loraine E. Kuck and Richard C. Tongg, *Hawaiian Flowers and Flowering Trees: A Guide to Tropical and Semitropical Flora* (Rutland, VT: Charles E. Tuttle, 1960), p. 12.

20. Idaho Code §67–450.

21. Ill. Ann. Stat. ch. 1, §3009 (Smith-Hurd); *Illinois Blue Book, 1983–1984*, p. 436.

22. Ind. Code Ann. §1–2–7–1 (West).

23. *State Trees and Arbor Days*, p. 8.

24. Kan. Stat. Ann. §73–1001.

25. *Kansas Directory* (Topeka: Secretary of State, 1981), p. 129.

26. Ky. Rev. Stat. Ann. §2.095 (Baldwin).

27. La. Rev. Stat. Ann. §49–160 (West).

28. Me. Rev. Stat. tit. 1, §208.

29. Md. Ann. Code art. 41, §76.

30. Mass. Gen. Laws Ann. ch. 2, §8 (West).

31. Mich. Comp. Laws Ann. §2.31.

32. Minn. Stat. Ann. §1.143 (West).

33. Miss. Code Ann. §3–3–9.

34. Mo. Ann. Stat. §10.040 (Vernon).

35. *State Trees and Arbor Days*, p. 11.

36. Neb. Rev. Stat. §90–113.

37. Nev. Rev. Stat. §235.040.

38. N.H. Rev. Stat. Ann. §3:6.

39. *Manual for the General Court, 1981*.

40. *State Trees and Arbor Days*, p. 12.

41. Edward J. Mullin, ed., *Manual of the Legislature of New Jersey* (Princeton, N.J.: Century Graphics, 1984), p. 11.

42. N.M. Stat. Ann. §12–3–4.

43. *New Mexico Blue Book, 1977–1978*, p. 86.

44. N.Y. State Law §76 (McKinney).

45. N.C. Gen. Stat. §145–3.

46. N.D. Cent. Code §54–02–05.
47. Ohio Rev. Code Ann. §5.05 (Baldwin).
48. *Ohio Almanac* (Lorain, Ohio: Lorain Journal Co., 1977), p. 61.
49. Okla. Stat. Ann. tit. 25, §97 (West).
50. Or. Rev. Stat. §186.
51. *Oregon Blue Book, 1977–1978*, p. 139.
52. Pa. Stat. Ann. tit. 71, §1004 (Purdon).
53. R.I. Gen. Laws §42–4–8.
54. S.C. Code §1–1–660.
55. *1978 South Carolina Legislative Manual*, 59th ed., n.p.
56. S.D. Codified Laws Ann. §1–6–11.
57. Tenn. Code Ann. §4–1–305.
58. *Tennessee Blue Book, 1983–1984*, p. 372.
59. Tex. Rev. Civ. Stat. Ann. art. 6143 (Vernon).
60. Utah Code Ann. §63–13–7.
61. Vt. Stat. Ann. tit. 1, §499.
62. *State Trees and Arbor Days*, p. 16.
63. Wash. Rev. Code Ann. §1.20.020.
64. *State Trees and Arbor Days*, p. 17.
65. *West Virginia Blue Book 1980*, p. 925.
66. Wis. Stat. Ann. §1.10 (West).
67. *Wisconsin Blue Book, 1983–84*, p. 948.
68. Wyo. Stat. Ann. §8–3–106; *State Trees and Arbor Days*, p. 18.

8 | State Birds

Beginning in 1926, when Kentucky officially named the handsome red bird or cardinal as its state bird, campaigns were launched nationwide until each state had selected at least one favorite bird as its avian symbol. Audubon societies and women's clubs from 1926 through the early 1930s were largely responsible for fueling public interest and holding popular votes, many of them among school children. Since then, of course, several states have established or changed state birds.

The cardinal is not only the first to have been proclaimed a state bird, but it also holds the distinction of having been designated by seven states: Illinois, Indiana, Kentucky, North Carolina, Ohio, Virginia, and West Virginia. The western meadow lark holds second place, having been honored by Kansas, Montana, Nebraska, North Dakota, Oregon, and Wyoming. The mockingbird, another favorite, has been named the state bird of Arkansas, Florida, Mississippi, Tennessee, and Texas.

Though the robin is probably the most remembered in idiom and fable, it has surprisingly been selected by only three states: Connecticut, Michigan, and Wisconsin. Maine and Massachusetts concurred that the chickadee was a fine emblem for their states, while Iowa and New Jersey agreed on the Eastern goldfinch.

Both Missouri and New York selected the bluebird in 1927, but New York waited for more than forty years to make it official. Again, over thirty years elapsed between the decisions of Idaho and Nevada to designate the mountain bluebird. Finally, two states, Alabama and South Carolina, chose the wild turkey as the state game bird. Altogether, thirty-two birds have been named as state birds, state game birds, or state waterfowl; four states, Alabama, Georgia, Mississippi, and South Carolina, have designated two birds.

In some cases, it is clear that a state selected a bird for patriotic or economic reasons, but, typically, a bird was selected by sheer popularity based on a number of aesthetic factors. Delaware and Alabama named birds symbolic of Revolutionary and Civil War companies who were nicknamed after the blue hen chicken and the yellowhammer. Utah honored the sea gull for saving farmers' crops in 1848 from pests. On the other hand, the rich blue colors of the mountain bluebird or the bold black and white patterns of Minnesota's loon are reason enough to designate a state symbol.

Alabama

The bird commonly called the yellowhammer, *Colaptes auratus*, was designated the state bird in 1927.[1] Other common names for the yellow-hammer include the yellow-shafted woodpecker and the flicker.

The Ladies' Memorial Association was responsible for encouraging the legislature to adopt this emblem because the gray and yellow plumage resembled the colors of the Confederate Army uniforms.[2] An incident during the Civil War involving a company from Huntsville, Alabama, resulted in the nickname "yellowhammers" being assigned to all Alabama troops. When the Huntsville company rode into camp at Hopkinsville, Kentucky, newly clad in Confederate uniforms trimmed in bright yellow cloth, they were met with the greeting "Yellerhammer, yellerhammer, flicker, flicker!" When the yellowhammer was adopted as the official state bird in 1927, the old soldiers were pleased, noting that the black breast spots were like bullet holes and the red patch on the neck like a bandana.[3]

Size: Total length – 10 to 11 inches; tail length – 4 inches.

Range: North America except treeless Arctic districts; south to Nicaragua and Cuba; mostly found from Florida and Texas to Kansas, Illinois, Indiana, and North Carolina.

Physical description: The back is grayish brown sharply barred in black; the head and hindneck are plain gray with a red crescent-shaped patch at nape; the shafts of the tail feathers (except the middle pair) are bright pure cadmium yellow as are the underwing feathers and the undersurface of the tail. There is a conspicuous black crescent-shaped patch on the chest; the underparts are pale cinnamon or dull buff-pink fading into pale yellow or white and spotted in black. Males have a broad black stripe across the lower side of the head.

Behavior: While on short flights, flickers glide and dip in rhythmic undulations, but at other times they exhibit a strong and steady flight pattern. As they feed on ants, beetles, grasshoppers, grubs, and other harmful insects, they hop from one choice spot to another within a self-prescribed small perimeter. Flickers consume more ants than any other bird, which in turn keeps enemies of ants, such as the destructive aphid, in check as well. Eggs are white and oval in shape and usually average six to eight per set. If the eggs are destroyed, the persistent flicker will lay another set, sometimes laying as many as forty eggs per season.

Alabama also designated an official state game bird, the wild turkey, in 1980.[4]

The wild turkey, *Meleagris gallopavo*, is the largest of the gallinaceous birds; the males measure from 41 to 49 inches in length, and the females are noticeably smaller.

Size: Body weight – 16 to 40 pounds; tail length – 12½ to 15 inches.

Range: Eastern and south central United States; mountains of Mexico; southern Ontario.

Physical description: The bluish head and red upper neck area is nude, warted, and corrugated in the adult male. The female's head and neck are smoother and are covered with short, dusky, downy feathers. The general color is dusky, glossed with brilliant metallic coppery, golden, and greenish hues. Many of the feathers are margined terminally in velvety black. There is a black pectoral tuft or "beard," greenish at the base and wine-tinted brown gloss distally. The female is duller in color with a smaller beard.

Behavior: Perhaps the most distinctive behavioral trait of the wild turkey is his courtship dance in which he gobbles, struts, spreads his fan-shaped tail, and generally makes a spectacle of himself in order to attract the female. During this season, the male's chest becomes a mass of gooey tissue consisting of oil and fat. From this he may draw nutritional sustenance after his frenzied dances. Wild turkeys feed primarily on fruit, berries, and seeds, and they consume large amounts of insects such as grasshoppers and crickets. Though they travel mostly on foot in flocks, they are able to fly to avoid danger and to cross rivers.

Alaska

The Alaska willow ptarmigan (*Lagopus lagopus alascensis Swarth*) became the official state bird in 1955.[5]

Size: Wing length – 7½ inches; tail length – 4 inches.

Range: Alaska; Arctic and subarctic regions of North America, Europe, and Asia.

Physical description: Also known as the willow grouse, the male and female have quite different plumages. The male has a hazel to chestnut forehead, crown, and nape; the back feathers are darker with white tips; the upper tail feathers are hazel; the wings are white; the tail feathers are generally brownish gray tipped with white; the sides of the head, throat, and upper breast are hazel becoming darker on the lower breast, barred with gray or black; the scarlet comb over the eyes swells when the bird is sexually aroused; and the underparts are mostly white. In winter, the male plumage is pure white except for the gray or black median pair of tail feathers. The female is mostly tawny olive above; each feather is barred with black and tipped with pale olive buff; the wings are white; the tail feathers are dark brownish gray tipped with white; the sides of the head, chin, and upper throat are cinnamon buff; the lower throat, abdomen, sides, and flanks are yellow buff to yellow tawny and heavily barred with wavy bands of clove brown; the comb is pale vermilion.

Behavior: Typically, a set of willow ptarmigan eggs are laid one day at a time over a period of from seven to ten days. The eggs are oval and shiny, and upon first being laid are a vivid bright red. As they dry, they turn blackish brown flecked with red to brown spots. During the winter, the bird adapts so completely to its environment, that it grows hairlike feathers on its feet allowing it to glide effortlessly across snow as though clad in snowshoes.

Arizona

The Arizona legislature adopted the cactus wren, known also as Coues' cactus wren or *Heleodytes brunneicapillus couesi (Sharpe)*, as the state bird in 1931.[6]

Size: Total length – 7 to 7½ inches; tail length – 3 inches.

Range: Desert region of southwestern United States and northern Mexico.

Physical description: The top of the head and hindneck are plain deep brown; the back region is pale, grayish brown conspicuously variegated with white; the tail feathers are brownish gray to black and barred with dusky to white; the sides of the head are mostly white except for a brown postocular stripe occupying the upper portion of the auricular region. The underparts are white deepening into cinnamon buff; the whole surface is heavily spotted with black.

Behavior: The wren's disposition is good; the bird rarely becomes embroiled in battle and is insatiably curious. The interested human bystander is often entertained as the playful little bird energetically inspects cracks, crevices, containers, and trash. The cactus wren builds flask-shaped nests from 3 to 9 feet above the ground on thorny shrubs, trees, or cactus. Cactus wrens feed mostly on beetles, ants, wasps, grasshoppers, and other pests. They also consume a significant amount of fruit.

Arkansas

The mockingbird was adopted by the Arkansas legislature as the official state bird in 1929.[7] When it was first introduced to the legislature by the State Federation of Women's Clubs, the legislators thought the issue was a joke. However, they were forthwith presented with rousing speeches enumerating the bird's worth to the farmer. The vote was unanimous, and the issue was settled in favor of the mockingbird.[8]

Size: Total length – 8½ to 9 inches; tail length – 4 to 4½ inches.

Range: Eastern United States and southern Canada; along the Gulf coast to Texas; Bahama Islands.

Physical description: The mockingbird, *Mimus polyglottos*, is mostly plain gray or brownish gray from the top of the head over most of the back region; the lateral tail feathers are white; the wings and tail are dull blackish slate; the middle and greater wing coverts are tipped with dull or grayish white; the primary coverts are white with a subterminal dusky spot or streak; the auricular region is gray; the area beneath the eye and along the side of the head is dull white transversely flecked with gray or dusky; the chin and throat are dull white margined along each side by a distinct dusky streak; the chest is pale smoke gray turning to white on the center of the breast and abdomen; the feathers under the tail are pale buff or buffy white. When the mockingbird is in flight, the broad white spots above can easily be seen against the slate black of the upper wings.

Behavior: Mockingbirds are sturdy creatures which build nests that often last several seasons. From the time when the nest is completed to the time when the fledglings take flight is usually from three to four weeks. Eggs range from bright blue to bluish green or greenish blue spotted with hazel or cinnamon. Both sexes not only build the nests, but also care for the young. Mockingbirds are lively and bellicose, fighting among themselves as well as tormenting cats and dogs. A masterful imitator, the mockingbird is considered one of the most versatile and beautiful songsters, sometimes changing tunes as many as thirty times within a ten-minute period. The diet of the mocking-bird consists equally of insects and wild fruit.

California

The California valley quail, *Lophortyx californica*, was designated the official bird and avifaunal emblem of California by the state's legislature in 1931,[9] winning in a vote involving twenty-four other birds nominated by the California Audubon Society.[10]

Size: Tail length — 3 to 3½ inches; wing length — 4 inches.

Range: Semiarid interior of California as well as the coastal belt south of San Francisco; east to Nevada. (The valley quail has been successfully introduced to other areas.)

Physical description: The adult male is mostly brownish olive on the back and rump; the wings are mostly dark olive brown; the tail feathers are between slate gray and deep mouse gray; the area under the eye, chin, and throat is jet black, the throat bordered by a broad white band extending from each eye to the center throat region in a v-shape; the forehead is pale olive buff with a white line of demarcation across the crown followed by a broader black line. There is a crest on the crown of the head consisting of six forward-drooping, terminally expanded black feathers; a bright design is created by brownish gray feathers of the hindneck speckled with white; the breast is solid deep neutral gray; and the abdomen is warm buff or white with a central bright hazel patch margined in black. The female is the same as the male above but is darker and more brownish; the crest on the crown is smaller and is brownish gray in color; the forehead is a pale buffy brown. There is a light buffy brown speckled pattern on the nape and lower sides of the neck; the chin and throat are grayish white; and the breast is grayish brown.

Behavior: The California valley quail makes little effort to build a safe, sturdy nest for her young. Instead, eggs are found in nests near houses or roads, even in other birds' nests. Traveling in flocks, they feed primarily on seeds, grass, and fruit, consuming minute amounts of flies and insects. Preyed upon by man and animal alike, they make especially easy targets for snakes, raccoons, owls, jays, cats, and dogs. When startled, however, they can make an amazingly quick retreat.

Colorado

The lark bunting, *Calamospiza melancorys stejneger*, was adopted as the Colorado state bird in 1931.[11] A first statewide vote yielded the name of the meadowlark as the most popular bird in the state. A second vote, spearheaded by the *Denver Post*, the Colorado Mountain Club, and the Colorado Federation of Women's Clubs, determined that the mountain bluebird should receive the title. Finally, the Colorado Audubon Society convinced state legislators that since the bluebird and meadowlark were already state birds of other states, the lark bunting was a more appropriate choice.[12]

Size: Total length — 6 inches; tail length — 2½ inches.

Range: Great plains; migrating south through Texas to the Gulf coast and Mexico.

Physical description: In summer, the adult male is black with a grayish cast on his back; the middle and greater wing coverts are mostly white, forming a conspicuous patch; the tertials are edged with white; and the tail coverts (especially the lower) are margined with white. The adult female is grayish above and brown streaked with dusky; the wing is white patched as in the male but smaller, more interrupted, and tinged with buffy; the underparts are white, streaked with dusky. In winter, the female is less grayish brown with paler markings tinged with buff; the adult male in the winter is similar to the adult female, but the feathers of the underparts and the chin are black beneath the surface.

Behavior: A highly sociable bird, the lark bunting is happiest when safely tucked away in a large flock. During courtship, lark buntings perform a dazzling air show commencing with soaring ascents, then drifting back to earth, all the while whistling a lively tune. From this behavior comes the common expression "happy as a lark." The lark's cheerful life can be tragically cut short by such natural enemies as hawks when his song attracts the attention of those for whom it was not intended. Because larks feed on harmful grasshoppers and waste grain, they are held in high regard by farmers.

Connecticut

The American robin, *Turdus migratorius*, became the state bird of Connecticut by action of the state legislature in 1943.[13]

Size: Total length – 8½ to 9 inches; tail length – 4 inches.

Range: Eastern and northern North America; westward to the Rocky Mountains; northwestward to Alaska; winters southward to Florida and along the Gulf coast to Texas.

Physical description: The largest thrush in North America, the male is mostly deep mouse gray or brownish slate gray on the back; the head is black with white spots from the eye to the bill and on both the upper and lower eyelids; the chin is white; the feathers of the neck are black in the center, margined with brownish slate gray or mouse gray; the tail is a dull slate black or sooty black with a large and conspicuous white spot; the chest, flanks, breast, and upper abdomen are a plain, deep cinnamon red color; and the lower abdomen is white. The female is much duller in color with gray of upper parts lighter and chest browner than in the male.

Behavior: Named by the English colonists because of the similarity between this and their robin redbreast, the colonists did not notice the close resemblance to their blackbird or the *Turdus*, a thrush. A bird suggestive of the type-A personality, the robin is jittery and easily upset. However, he sails through the air without faltering, chest out and back straight. It is no wonder that we often think of the robin arising early to catch the first worm. A strong singer, he is up at dawn regaling the neighborhood with lengthy, energetic, and cheerful songs. The pale blue eggs (hence the color "Robin's egg blue") are usually laid in sets of three or four. The male cares for the young almost exclusively while the female prepares for a new brood. Sometimes three separate sets of eggs are laid in a year. Robins subsist mostly on beetles and caterpillars supplemented by an intake of spiders, earthworms, and snails. Since the robin also enjoys fruit, both cultivated and wild, he poses a potential threat to orchards. Fortunately, when the preferred insect or wild fruit is available, the robin leaves the fruit crops alone.

Delaware

The blue hen chicken was adopted as Delaware's state bird in 1939.[14] During the Revolutionary War, a company of soldiers from Kent County in Delaware entertained themselves between battles by staging cockfights between blue hen chickens. The cockfights became so famous that, when the soldiers fought fiercely in battle, they became known as the Blue Hen's Chickens. This nickname was again adopted during the Civil War by a company from the same county.[15]

Physical description: The throat is nude and wattled; there is a median fleshy "comb" on the forehead; the middle tail feathers are strongly hooked; and the feathers of the rump are elongated and linear, or pointed.

Florida

In 1927, the mockingbird was officially designated the state bird of Florida.[16] The Audubon Society of St. Petersburg was responsible for a statewide vote for a state bird. The mockingbird won by a large margin over such other possibilities as the hummingbird, pelican, and buzzard. One can only imagine the chagrin of the Audubon Society when an entire school voted for the buzzard because the students had been studying the bird as part of an airplane building project.[17] See the Arkansas entry for a description.

Georgia

The brown thrasher was designated the state bird of Georgia by the legislature in 1970,[18] even though the governor had officially proclaimed the brown thrasher to be the state bird in 1935.[19]

Size: Total length – 10 inches; tail length – 5 inches.

Range: Eastern United States and southeastern Canada; breeding southward to Florida, Alabama, Mississippi, and Texas and westward to the Rocky Mountains; wintering from North Carolina to Florida and Texas.

Physical description: The plumage above is plain, dull, cinnamon red or tawny red, becoming duller above the eye; the wings are tipped with white or pale buff producing two distinct bands across the wing; the outermost tail feathers are tipped with buff; the auricular region is a light rusty brown, narrowly streaked with dull whitish or pale buffy; the underparts are a pale buff, approaching buffy white on the chin, throat, and abdomen; the chest and sides are streaked with brown or dusky; the throat is margined along each side by a series of blackish streaks forming a distinct stripe along the lower side of the head; the iris is bright lemon or sulphur yellow; and the tail feathers are long.

Behavior: The brown thrasher, *Toxostoma rufum*, is a fickle creature, often changing partners with each new brood during a single mating season. However, both sexes are fiercely protective of their young, launching attacks on any and all creatures, including humans, who dare disturb their nests. Eggs are pale blue, sometimes white, tinged with green, and are evenly spotted in reddish or dull brown. A well-balanced meal consists of the favored beetle, acorns, and wild berries.

Georgia also designated an official state game bird, the bobwhite quail, in 1970.[20] When the thrasher was officially designated the state bird of Georgia, it seemed a proper time to make the bobwhite quail the official state game bird. Known as the "Quail Capital of the World," Georgia was proud to give this designation to a bird so plentiful in Georgia and beloved by sportsmen everywhere.[21]

Size: Wing length – 4½ inches; tail length – 2 to 2½ inches.

Range: Resident of open uplands from Maine through southern New England; westward through Minnesota, North Dakota, and Wyoming; south through northern Florida, the Gulf coast region, northern Texas, and eastern Colorado; southern Ontario.

Physical description: The bobwhite quail, *Colinus virginianus*, is mostly dark amber brown to chestnut above, heavily blotched with fuscous-black and narrowly tipped with pale, warm buff; the lateral feathers of the upper back and the feathers of the lower back and rump are paler, narrowly barred with dusky and crossed by numerous pale warm buffy bands; the tail feathers are gray; the chin, upper throat, and forehead are white with a broad white stripe extending from above the eye to the back of the neck (in the female, the stripe, chin, and throat are pale orange-yellow, and the forehead and crown are between tawny and russet). There is a fairly broad blackish band across the lower throat (auburn in the female), followed by a broader one of cinnamon; the upper abdomen is white washed with pale warm buff; the feathers are crossed by four or five narrow black bars.

Behavior: The bobwhite quail, also commonly referred to as the partridge, feeds on grain left in the field after harvest, as well as locusts, grasshoppers, and potato beetles, making it a popular friend of farmers. The bobwhite quail's plumage makes it possible for the bird to conceal himself quite effectively from hunters and other threats. When it becomes too dangerous to remain stationary, the bobwhite launches himself into sudden flight giving the impression that he is a strong flyer. However, this is not the case, as quail have been known to collapse into the water in failed attempts to cross wide rivers.

Hawaii

The *nene*, *Nesochen sandwicensis* or *Bernicata sandwicensis*, was designated the state bird in 1957.[22]

Physical description: The *nene*, or Hawaiian goose, is a land goose, only recently saved from extinction by being bred in England and returned to Hawaii by Herbert Shipman and Peter Scott with U.S. financial support. The Hawaiian goose has a long, creme-colored neck, streaked vertically in black, with the light coloring extending upward into the malar region. The back of the neck and head are black. There is a black ring around the neck separating the creme color from the variegated pattern of the grayish brown back.[23]

Idaho

The mountain bluebird, *Sialia arctica*, was designated and declared to be the state bird of Idaho in 1931.[24] The Idaho State Federation Conservation chairman initially indicated that the western tanager was the best choice for state bird. However, the state's school children felt differently, and the mountain bluebird received the most votes.[25]

Size: Total length – 6½ inches; tail length – 2½ to 3 inches.

Range: Mountain districts of western North America; winters southward to southern California and northern Mexico.

Physical description: A thrush, the male and female plumage differ as follows: The male is a plain, rich turquoise blue, sky blue, or porcelain blue; the head, throat, chest, and sides are paler in color than the upper parts; the abdomen and lower parts are white; the tail and wing feathers are black with longer undertail feathers a pale turquoise or sky blue tipped with white. The female head and back are plain mouse or smoke gray, sometimes tinged with greenish blue; the chin, throat, breast, and sides are a pale brownish gray passing into dull white on the abdomen; the longer undertail feathers are dusky sometimes tinged with blue; the rump, upper tail feathers, tail, and wings are mostly turquoise blue or light sky blue, sometimes nile blue. The adult male in winter turns a duller blue; the adult female's color deepens, especially the buffy grayish underparts.

Behavior: The *Sialia arctica* is now called the *Sialia currucoides* because, unlike previously thought, it is not native to the Arctic region. (Instead, it only summers there.) Mountain bluebirds feed mostly on ants and beetles with a small dietary component of grapes and berries. Flocks of bluebirds may be identified by their strange way of pausing between their deep swooping movements. They build nests in holes in trees, along river banks, in houses, and even in other birds' nesting holes. Bluebird fledglings sometimes fall prey to flickers who have been known to keep parents from feeding their young by blocking the entrance to the nests.

Illinois

The cardinal, *Cardinalis cardinalis*, was designated the state bird of Illinois by the legislature in 1929,[26] after a vote of Illinois school children. The cardinal received 39,226 votes; the next runner-up was the bluebird which received 30,306 votes.[27]

Size: Total length – 7½ to 8 inches; tail length – 4 inches.

Range: Eastern United States, west to the Great Plains, southern Arizona, and northwestern Mexico, and south through Georgia to the Gulf states.

Physical description: A finch, the cardinal is conspicuously crested and thick-billed with the tail longer than the rather short and rounded wing. Adult males are entirely bright red, except for the black patchy band from the eye to the throat on both sides of the bill. The female has a dull grayish patch on the face and throat, is brownish above and dull tawny or pale buffy below; the crest, wings, and tail are a dull reddish color, and the underwing feathers are pinkish red.

Behavior: The cardinal builds its nest in shrubs and bushes, seemingly oblivious to its proximity to people. Eggs are whitish with brown spots incubating over a twelve- to thirteen-day period. Both parents attend to the young with frequent feedings of insects. As the young mature, they become primarily grain and fruit eaters, though insect pests still make up a third of their diet. Cardinals are beautiful birds, popular not only for their striking plumage, but also for their pleasant songs, which are loud, flutelike whistles. The trills last approximately three seconds.

Indiana

The red bird or cardinal, *Richmondena Cardinalis cardinalis*, was designated the state bird of Indiana by act of legislature in 1933.[28] See the Illinois entry for a description.

Iowa

In 1933, the eastern goldfinch, *Spinus tristis tristis*, was designated the state bird of Iowa by the forty-fifth General Assembly.[29]

Size: Total length – 4½ inches; tail length – 1½ to 2 inches.

Range: United States and southern Canada east of the Rocky Mountains; wintering southward to the Gulf coast.

Physical description: The adult male in the summer is generally pure lemon yellow or canary yellow; the forehead, crown, wings, and tail are black; and white stripes appear near the base of the wings and along the ends of the tail feathers. The adult female and the adult male in the winter are olive brownish or grayish above; the wings and tail are blackish or dusky marked with white; the upper tail feathers are pale grayish or grayish white; and the underparts are dull grayish white tinged with yellow.

Behavior: The eastern goldfinch is a flock bird, often seen in undulating flight, cheerfully singing with his friends. The birds usually sing in choral fashion, whistling their high-pitched tunes which last from two to three seconds. Breeding very late in the season (from July to September), the male and female are constant companions as they build their nests and raise their young. Egg sets average five in number, and the coloration is plain bluish white. Seeds are the mainstay of their diet, supplemented in the winter months by a delicacy, plant lice eggs.

Kansas

The western meadowlark, *Sturnella neglecta (Audubon)*, was designated by the legislature in 1937 as the official state bird of Kansas, as preferred by a vote of school children in the state.[30]

Size: Total length – 8 to 9 inches; tail length – 2½ to 3 inches.

Range: Western United States, southwestern Canada, northwestern Mexico; east to the prairie areas of the Mississippi valley, in Minnesota, Iowa, Missouri, and Texas.

Physical description: The head and back of the neck are a pale dull buffy or white with broad lateral crown stripes of pale grayish brown; the lower sides of the head are largely yellow, topped by a dull grayish white area streaked with gray; mostly buffy or grayish brown above streaked with black; the outermost tail feathers are mostly white; the throat, breast, and abdomen are a deep yellow sometimes with an orangish hue. The yellow area is relieved by a black horseshoe-shaped patch on the chest.

Behavior: An oriole, the western meadowlark feeds mostly on insects with perhaps one third of its diet consisting of grain. Its loud, distinctive song is considered one of its most appealing qualities; the bird sometimes hammers out as many as 200 notes per minute. The young leave their nests early, unable to fly but still under the protection of their parents until they are able to care for themselves. Fledglings are easy prey for weasels, skunks, snakes, owls, and hawks.

Kentucky

The native red bird commonly known as the Kentucky cardinal (*Cardinalis cardinalis*) was designated the official state bird by the legislature in 1926.[31] See the Illinois entry for a description.

Louisiana

The brown pelican, as it appears on the seal of the state, was designated as the official state bird of Louisiana by the legislature in 1966.[32] This amended a 1958 act naming the pelican, with no further designation, as the official state bird.

Physical description: Mostly grayish brown streaked with brown, the pelican feathers are white tipped, and he has a long brown neck (white in the winter), a white head and white stripe that extends under the bill in a straplike fashion, a yellow forehead that turns to white at the crown followed by a rust-colored tuft at the back of the head, a long bill, and a throat pouch.

Behavior: The *Pelecanus occidentalis occidentalis*, or brown pelican, usually lays three dull white eggs after a solemn courtship culminating on the water's surface. As is the case with many newly hatched birds, the young pelican is fed regurgitated food of a parent. However, it has the unique experience as it grows older of selecting meals smorgasbord-style from the parent's pouch, until it is old enough to capture its own meal from the sea. A hunting expedition is carried out when the pelican dives head first into the water at a downwind angle, making a somersault beneath the surface and emerging against the wind. This remarkable spectacle usually results in catching a supply of fresh fish that is stashed in the pouch for digestion later.

Maine

The chickadee, *Penthestes atricapillus*, was adopted as official state bird of Maine in 1927.[33]

Size: Total length – 4½ to 5 inches; tail length – 2 to 2½ inches.

Range: Northern United States and Canada.

Physical description: The entire top and back of the head is black; most of the upper back is plain olive gray, passing into buffy gray on the rump and upper tail feathers; the wings and tail are a dusky or blackish slate color; the chin and throat are black; the sides of the head and most of the underparts are white, the sides tinged with buffy. In autumn and winter, this long-tailed small bird is much more deeply colored, contrasting even more strongly with the white abdomen and white wing edgings.

Behavior: The black-capped chickadee is a member of the titmouse family. Beloved by early colonial settlers, the chickadee is friendly and somewhat tame. It has been known to perch fearlessly on fingers and to feed from the hand. One of its songs is calling its own name— "chicka" followed by "dee dee dee."

Maryland

The Baltimore oriole, *Icterus galbula*, was designated the official state bird of Maryland by the General Assembly in 1947. The assembly has also made special provision for its protection.[34] The first Lord Baltimore chose orange and black as the colors for his coat of arms because of his fondness for the bird, which he saw often on his estate, that was later named the Baltimore Oriole.[35]

Size: Total length – 6½ to 7 inches; tail length – 2½ to 3 inches.

Range: Eastern United States, west to the Rocky Mountains; winters in Mexico and Central America to Colombia and Venezuela.

Physical description: The male's head, back, and upper chest area are black; the rump, upper tail feathers, and underparts range from cadmium yellow to intense orange; the upper wings are black, broadly tipped with white. The female's head and back are saffron olive, with distinct central spots of black or dusky; the rump and tail feathers are olive saffron; the wings are dusky, narrowly tipped with white or gray; the underparts are saffron yellow or dull orange-yellow, duller on the abdomen and tinged with olive on the sides and flanks.

Behavior: The Baltimore oriole is a talented weaver, building a nest from grapevine bark, plant fibers, and milkweed silk. The nest hangs pouchlike from 30 feet above the ground. Fledglings are strangely quiet until a few days prior to leaving the nest, when they then cry for days in a high-pitched monotonous whine. The oriole feeds heavily on caterpillars and other insects and exhibits a taste for green peas and berries.

Massachusetts

The chickadee, *Penthestes atricapillus*, was designated the state bird of the Commonwealth of Massachusetts by legislative act in 1941.[36] See the Maine entry for a description.

Michigan

A 1931 House concurrent resolution made the robin the official state bird of Michigan.[37] See the Connecticut entry for a description.

Minnesota

The loon, *Gavia immer*, was adopted as the official bird of Minnesota by the legislature in 1961.[38]

Size: Total length – 3 feet; wing span – 5 feet.[39]

Physical description: The head is black with black and white stripes around the head in a vertical zebra pattern; the lower neck is coal black; the upper chest and underparts are white. Above there appears a black and white checkerboard pattern and, along the sides, the same colors give an appearance of polka dots. The winter plumage is grayish brown above, with a brownish head and white underparts.

Behavior: The loon mates for life and returns to the same lake in the spring of every year. After laying two or three eggs, one usually infertile, the loon incubates the eggs for nearly a month. Within two days, the young loons are led into the water by their mother where they exhibit great skill in swimming and diving. They remain in the water, relatively safe from attack, until they are able to fly. Fish eaters, loons capture their prey with great alacrity and strength. Trout are often the objects of their underwater escapades; the loons quickly swallow them before resurfacing. Half running and half flying, the loon puts forth a considerable effort in taking flight, sometimes gliding along the surface for quite a distance before ascending.

Mississippi

The mockingbird was designated the state bird of Mississippi by the legislature in 1944.[40] See the Arkansas entry for a description.

The state of Mississippi also designated the wood duck, *Aix sponsa*, as the official state waterfowl in 1974.[41]

Range: United States and southern Canada.

Physical description: The crown of the head is metallic green streaked laterally with two white stripes; two white stripes also appear under the chin area; the breast is russet; metallic green, bronze, blue, and purple appear above and buffy to white below; the back, breast, and side regions are separated by white stripes. In July or August, the adult male begins to molt and takes on brownish shades above and yellowish tones below. The female is similar but duller, mostly brownish gray above, brown on the sides, and white below. There is a white ring around the eye.

Behavior: Also called the summer duck because it breeds and summers regularly throughout the South and a tree duck because it nests in tree trunks or branch cavities, the wood duck lays from ten to fifteen eggs per season. After incubating for nearly a month, the whitish eggs hatch and, from then on, the fledglings know little peace until their mother has managed to acclimate them to the water. Sometimes carrying them on her back or in her bill, the mother coaxes and protects her brood as they learn to manage for themselves. The wood duck feeds primarily on vegetable matter such as nuts, weeds, and seeds retrieved by scavenging under leaves and feeding on aquatic plants. The rest of his diet consists of miscellaneous insects, dragonflies, beetles, and locusts, as well as a few small fish, minnows, and frogs. A good swimmer and flyer, the wood duck is usually hunted as he goes from his sheltered roosting spot to his feeding spot along marshy streams.

Missouri

The bluebird, *Sialia sialis*, native to Missouri, became that state's official bird by legislative act in 1927.[42]

Size: Total length – 6 inches; tail length – 2½ inches.

Range: United States and southern Canada east of the Rockies; breeds south to Texas, along the Gulf coast and Florida.

Physical description: Above, the male is bright blue, the average hue being between ultramarine and deep blue; the shafts of the wing and tail feathers are black; the sides of the head are light or gray blue; the underparts are mostly a dull cinnamon red or cinnamon chestnut except the abdomen and under the tail feathers, which are white. The female is bluish gray above, tinged with grayish brown; the rump and tail feathers are bright blue; the wings are blue, edged with whitish gray; the underparts are mostly dull cinnamon; the chin, abdomen, and under tail feathers are white.

Behavior: Known as the eastern bluebird, this tiny bird was nicknamed the blue robin by early settlers because it reminded them of the English robin redbreast. Though an amorous and flirtatious suitor, the male loses no time in selecting another companion upon the loss of his mate. The courtship is marked by alluring songs from the male, who attentively pays friendly visits to the female. On such visits he may even feed her by placing food in her mouth. Once egg incubation begins, the singing stops until it is time to begin again with a new nesting (and often a new mate). The majority of the bluebird's diet is insect matter, such as harmful beetles, grasshoppers, crickets, and katydids.

Montana

The western meadowlark, *Sturnella neglecta (Audubon)*, was declared to be the official state bird of Montana by the legislature in 1931, following a referendum vote of Montana school children.[43]

In 1805 the famous explorer, Meriwether Lewis, entered into his journal the observance of a lark he found similar to the eastern lark. This is believed to be the first recorded mention of what is now known as the western meadowlark. The most notable difference between the two larks is their song.[44]

See the Kansas entry for a description.

Nebraska

The western meadowlark was designated the state bird of Nebraska by the legislature in 1929.[45] See the Kansas entry for a description.

Nevada

The mountain bluebird, *Sialia currucoides*, was designated the official state bird of Nevada by the legislature in 1967.[46] See the Idaho entry for a description.

New Hampshire

The New Hampshire legislature designated the purple finch, *Carpodacus purpureus*, the official state bird in 1957,[47] the year in which a Dartmouth College forester, Robert S. Monahan, along with the Audubon Society of New Hampshire, the New Hampshire Federation of Garden Clubs, and the State Federation of Women's Clubs recommended the designation of the purple finch. Thereupon, Republican Doris M. Spollett, who had previously tried with no success to name the New Hampshire hen as the state bird, began again to campaign for her personal favorite. She lost when, within three months of its introduction, the bill making the purple finch the state bird was signed into law.[48]

Size: Total length – 5½ inches; tail length – 2 inches; wing length – 3 inches.

Range: Eastern North America; winters south to Gulf coast area.

Physical description: The male's top of head and back of the neck are deep wine purple (more crimson in the summer). There is a dusky brownish red spot near the ear and along the side of the head; the rest of the head is pinkish wine purple; the back is reddish brown or wine purplish with dark streaks; the wings and tail are dusky with light brownish red or light brown edgings; the abdomen and under tail feathers are white. The female is olive or olive grayish above streaked with dusky and white; the wings and tail are dusky with light olive or olive grayish edgings; the upper sides of the head are mostly white streaked with olive; the underparts are white, broadly streaked with olive.

Behavior: The purple finch feeds on seeds in the winter and spring, insects in the late spring, and fruit in the summer. Finches are considered generally beneficial by orchard growers, since they prune rather than destroy fruit trees. They also eat such harmful insects as plant lice, cankerworms, and caterpillars. Courtship consists of a wild dance and song by the male, sometimes followed by an equally eccentric response by the female who first ignores the male and then pecks at him before they fly off together to build a nest. The four or five eggs commonly produced by the happy couple are bluish green or pale blue, with black or brown spots mostly located at the large end of each egg.

New Jersey

The eastern goldfinch was designated the state bird of New Jersey by the legislature in 1935.[49] See the Iowa entry for a description.

New Mexico

The chaparral bird, commonly known as the roadrunner, was adopted as the official bird of New Mexico by the legislature in 1949.[50]

Size: Total length – 20 to 21 inches; tail length – 11½ inches.

Range: Southwestern United States; east to Gulf coast of Texas; northern and central Mexico.

Physical description: The roadrunner is a large, long-tailed, long-billed cuckoo. The feathers of the forehead and front of the crown are black, each with a broad lateral spot of russet or light tawny brown; the occipital bushy crest is glossy black or blue-black broken by edgings of tawny brown or pale buffy; above is mostly black broadly edged with light tawny brown passing into dull buffy white on the edges creating a conspicuous streaked effect; the lower back and wing coverts are glossy bronze or bronze greenish and edged with black; the tail feathers are mostly bronzy olive glossed with purplish and margined with dull white; the sides of the head are dull whitish and tawny brown, barred and spotted with black; the chin and throat are mostly dull white; the rest of the underparts are plain grayish white, the neck and chest streaked with black.

Behavior: Many observers have described the roadrunner in unflattering terms such as odd looking and uniquely entertaining. Perhaps because of the barren habitat in which the roadrunner resides, it has had to adapt for survival by exhibiting stealth, speed, ferocity, and strength. This combination of traits and its outward appearance of awkwardness explains why it has attracted such bemused attention. When hungry, the roadrunner runs quickly in pursuit of lizards, scorpions, snakes, tarantulas, mice, insects, and small birds.

New York

The bluebird, *Sialia sialis*, became the official bird of the state of New York by legislative act in 1970.[51] The robin had been selected initially as the state bird, but, after a vote in 1927 and 1928, the bluebird was determined to be more popular.[52] It was not until 1970, however, that this designation was made official. See the Missouri entry for a description.

North Carolina

The cardinal was declared to be the official state bird of North Carolina by the legislature in 1943.[53] See the Illinois entry for a description.

North Dakota

The meadowlark, *Sturnella neglecta*, was named the official bird of North Dakota by the legislature in 1947.[54] See the Kansas entry for a description.

Ohio

The cardinal, *Cardinalis cardinalis*, was named the official bird of Ohio by the legislature in 1933.[55] See the Illinois entry for a description.

Oklahoma

The scissor-tailed flycatcher, *Muscivora forticata*, was designated the state bird of Oklahoma by joint resolution of the legislature in 1951.[56] The joint resolution notes that the flycatcher's nesting range is centered in Oklahoma, and, because its diet consists of harmful and useless insects, the flycatcher is of great economic value. Furthermore, the scissor-tailed flycatcher has been endorsed as the official state bird by numerous ornithologists, biologists, and wildlife societies.[57]

Size: Total length – 11 to 13 inches; tail length – 6 to 9 inches.

Range: Texas to Kansas, less commonly in Missouri, Arkansas, and Louisiana; migrates to Mexico and Central America.

Physical description: The male's head is clear pale gray with a small concealed orange-red patch on the center of the crown; the back is light gray strongly suffused with a pink wine color; the upper tail feathers are black or dusky, margined with gray; the six middle tail feathers are black; the three outermost tail feathers on each side are white, strongly tinged with salmon pink, terminally black; the tail is deeply forked, especially in the male, the lateral tail feathers more than twice as long as the middle pair and longer than the wing; the cheek, chin, and throat are white, shading into gray on the breast; the sides and flanks are a salmon color to an almost saturn red; there is a large concealed patch of bright orange-red on either side of the breast. The female is similar to the male but duller in color; the breast patches are more restricted and orangish; and the concealed crown spot is often missing.

Behavior: Fondest of open terrain, the flycatcher perches on telephone wires and posts. Its diet is composed mainly of noxious insects such as beetles, wasps, and bees. Favorites are grasshoppers and crickets. Interestingly enough, flycatchers do not seem to care much for flies. An extremely energetic bird when provoked or frightened, it is nonetheless a sloppy nest builder who carelessly leaves strings and twine hanging from the nest. The eggs are a creamy white color spotted with brown and gray.

Oregon

The western meadowlark, *Sturnella neglecta*, was declared the official bird of Oregon by gubernatorial proclamation in 1927, following a vote of the state's school children sponsored by the Oregon Audubon Society.[58] See the Kansas entry for a description.

Pennsylvania

Pennsylvania is the only state that has designated only an official state game bird, the ruffed grouse, *Bonasa umbellus*, which was adopted by the legislature in 1931.[59]

Size: Total length – 15 to 19 inches; tail length – 5 to 6 inches.

Range: Wooded portions of North America.

Physical description: A medium-sized wood grouse, the upperparts are brown and rusty or gray variegated with black; the underparts are buff or whitish, broken by broad bars of brownish; the lower half of the tarsus is nude and scalelike; the tail at approximately 5 inches is nearly as long as the wing and has from eighteen to twenty tail feathers; the tail is gray or rusty with numerous zigzag narrow bars of blackish and a broad subterminal band of black or dark brown; the feathers on the crown are distinctly elongated, forming when erected a conspicuous crest. The male in the summer has a bright orange or red naked space above the eye.

Behavior: The courtship behavior of the ruffed grouse has been the source of much interest throughout the years. The drumming noise made by either the wild flapping of the wings against the sides or by the sheer force of the wings against the air is ear splitting, though no one can seem to agree on the exact noise-making mechanism. The ruffed grouse is primarily a fruit and vegetable eater; insects account for approximately ten percent of his diet. Grouse are remarkably tame by nature and, when allowed, they have become pets. The birds who reside in areas where grouse are hunted are much more wary of humans and take the appropriate evasive actions. A popular game bird, the grouse is called a pheasant in the South and a partridge in the northern states. Its enemies include raccoons, weasels, skunks, and opossum. In addition, disease and parasites take a heavy toll on the grouse population.

Rhode Island

The breed of fowl known commonly as the Rhode Island Red was designated the official state bird of Rhode Island by the legislature in 1954.[60]

Physical description: The Rhode Island Red is a well-known American breed of domesticated fowl. It weighs from 6½ to 8½ pounds, has yellow skin beneath brownish red feathers, and a single rose-colored comb extending from the base of its beak to the upper back of its head. The hen lays brown eggs.

South Carolina

The Carolina wren, a member of the family *Troglodytidae*, was designated the official state bird of South Carolina in 1948 by the state legislature.[61] In 1939, however, the legislature had adopted the mockingbird as the state bird, in spite of the fact that the Carolina wren had been recognized unofficially as the state bird prior to that time. The 1948 act designating the Carolina wren as the official state bird repealed the 1939 act.[62]

Size: Total length – 5 inches; tail length – 2 inches.

Range: Eastern United States.

Physical description: The upperparts of the Carolina wren, *Thryothorus ludovicianus*, are plain rusty brown; the wings and tail are a duller brown than the back, narrowly barred with dusky. There is a sharply defined and conspicuous stripe of white or buffy white on each side from the bill and above the eye to the back of the neck, bordered above in black; beneath the white stripe is a broad area of rufous brown covering the upper half of the auricular region; the underparts are a plain dull buffy white to buff color on the chest, sides, and flanks; the under tail feathers are buffy whitish broadly barred with black. In autumn and winter, the colors are decidedly brighter, and the superciliary stripe is buffy.

Behavior: A sweet and vigorous songster, the wren whistles a variety of loud, cheerful songs. A set of wren eggs usually numbers five, and the eggs are creamy or pinkish white with reddish brown spots encircling the larger end of the egg. The wren is a pest eater; its diet comprises mostly beetles, caterpillars, grasshoppers, crickets, and cockroaches. It is no surprise, then, that the wren is an especially quick and energetic bird able to capture its tiny prey, as well as to escape the perceived danger posed by nosy humans. However, the wren is also a curious creature and will often bravely and swiftly investigate the source of suspicious noises before considering its own safety.

In 1976, the legislature made the South Carolina wild turkey, *Meleagris gallopavo*, the official state wild game bird.[63] See the Alabama entry for a description of the wild turkey.

South Dakota

The ring-necked pheasant, *Phasianus colchicus*, was adopted as the state bird of South Dakota by act of the state legislature in 1943.[64]

Size: Total length – 20 to 27 inches; the tail is proportionally long ranging from 10 inches in the female to 18 inches in the male.

Range: Native to eastern China; now well established in the northern half of the United States, southern Canada, Hawaii, and Europe.

Physical description: The male's head, crown, and neck are of varying shades of glossy green from Roman green to bottle green and dark zinc green; the nape of the neck is tinged with a glossy dark violet-blue that also predominates along the sides of the neck; erectile tufts of iridescent blue-green blackish feathers are located on each side towards the back of the crown. There is a white collar around the neck; the exposed interscapulers are a bright buff yellow with a white triangular space at the base; much of the upperparts are light neutral gray or brown tinged with pale olive buff and broadly edged with russet or black; the lower back region is yellow-green to deep lichen green; the breast is a dark coppery hazel, broadly glossed with magenta purple; the bare skin on the side of the head is bright red; the tail is brown or dark olive buff with black transverse markings. The female is brownish and buffy, variegated with black; the interscapulars are a bright hazel to tawny russet, the central area terminating in a brownish gray or black distally pointed "V"; the scapulars and upper wing feathers are brown to tawny olive, edged and tipped with pale buffy; the back and upper tail feathers are brownish black, broadly edged with pale pinkish buff; the tail feathers are a light pinkish hazel transversely blotched with black; the chin, upper breast, and abdomen are white to buffy.

Behavior: The ring-necked, or Chinese, pheasant was introduced in 1881 in Oregon by Judge O. N. Denny, the American consul general of Shanghai. The muted earth tones of the female's plumage serve as effective camouflage, making it possible for potential intruders to come within a few feet and yet never notice her in her nest. The female has no scent, making her even more secure from attack. The ten to twelve eggs in a set are usually brownish olive. Upon hatching, the newborn chicks follow their mother who helps them scavenge for food and protects them from predators. Though pheasant eat a good many harmful insects, they also attack farm and garden crops such as corn, tomatoes, and beans causing severe damage. Able to escape from danger by a rapid vertical movement if trapped by buildings or trees, the pheasant makes a noisy exit by madly fluttering its wings and croaking loudly in alarm. Very sensitive to earth tremors, caused by explosions or earthquakes, they make their alarm known by crowing loudly.

Tennessee

After a popular vote in April 1933, the mockingbird, *Mimus polyglottos*, was selected over the robin, cardinal, bobwhite, and bluebird, among others. In 1933 the General Assembly adopted Senate Joint Resolution 51 naming the mockingbird the official state bird of Tennessee.[65] See the Arkansas entry for a description.

Texas

The mockingbird, *Mimus polyglottos*, was adopted as the state bird of Texas by legislative act in 1927, following the recommendation of the Texas Federation of Women's Clubs.[66] See the Arkansas entry for a description.

Utah

The sea gull, *Larus californicus*, was selected as the state bird of Utah by an act of the legislature in 1955.[67]

Size: Tail length – 6 inches; wing length – 14½ to 16 inches.

Range: Western North America, inland to Nevada, Utah, Kansas, Texas, and Colorado near large lake areas.

Physical description: The head, neck, upper tail feathers, tail, and all underparts are entirely white; the back, scapulars, and wings are between pale and light neutral gray, the wings tipped with white; the eye ring and rictus are vermillion-red; the subterminal third of the bill is red, immediately preceded by a black spot; the legs and feet are a pale grayish green.

Behavior: A faithful friend of the farmer, the California gull eats crickets, grasshoppers, and even mice. This gratitude of the farmer was the primary rationale behind the designation of the gull as the state bird.

In 1848 the gulls were credited with saving farmers' crops by consuming the insects endangering them.[68] Aeronautic wizards, gulls are gymnasts of the sky, making the seemingly impossible appear effortless. They can appear motionless in midair by catching wind currents with perfect timing and precision while positioning their bodies at just the right angle. They are quiet birds, considered quite beneficial by agriculturalists, and are usually gentle creatures, exhibiting neither antagonism to nor fondness for man.

Vermont

The hermit thrush, *Hylocichla guttata faxoni*, became the state bird of Vermont by an act of the legislature in 1941.[69]

Size: Total length – 6½ inches; tail length – 2½ to 3 inches.

Range: Eastern North America; southern migration to Gulf states.

Physical description: The upper parts are a cinnamon brown; the sides and flanks are buffy brown; there is a conspicuous orbital ring of dull white; the ear region is a grayish brown streaked with dull whitish; the underparts are a dull white tinged with a pale cream buff; the throat is streaked along each side in a sooty color; the chest has large triangular spots of dusky grayish brown, broader and more rounded on the lower chest; the tail is a dull cinnamon brown. Spring and summer plumage is brighter.

Behavior: A hardy bird, the hermit thrush arrives in early spring and departs in late fall for its migration southward. Traveling at night, thrushes sometimes become so tired and cold that they lose all natural shyness and feed from the human hand. Hermit thrushes have been observed performing a curious activity known as "anting." The bird catches ants and places them in its feathers beneath the wings. It is thought that either the formic acid in the ants is effective in combating parasitic attacks or the ants are being horded for later consumption during migration. Talented singers, hermit thrushes sometimes sing in unison to form a harmonious chorus. Other times, they are capable of completely fooling the listener into thinking they are farther away or closer than they actually are by calling upon their extraordinary powers of ventriloquism. Protective of their young, thrushes fight so vigorously against predators that they can often fend off attacks.

Virginia

The cardinal was designated the official state bird of Virginia by legislative act in 1950.[70] See the Illinois entry for a description.

Washington

The willow goldfinch, *Astragalinus tristis salicamans*, was designated the official bird of the state of Washington in 1951 by an act of the legislature.[71]

Size: Total length – 4½ inches; tail length – 1½ to 2 inches.

Range: Pacific coast region.

Physical description: The willow goldfinch is very similar to the eastern goldfinch (see the New Jersey entry), but the wings and tail are shorter and the coloration is darker. The adult male summer plumage of the back is tinged with pale olive green, and the winter adults and the young are decidedly darker or browner than the corresponding eastern goldfinch, with broader markings on the wings.

Behavior: Called the willow goldfinch because of its gravitation to damp areas conducive to the growth of willows, this small bird is a cheery singer and a graceful flyer. Very similar to the eastern goldfinch, this goldfinch begins to nest earlier than its counterparts, usually in April or May. The willow goldfinch is primarily a seed eater, munching mostly on seeds from harmful or neutral plants and occasionally supplementing his diet with harmful insects.

West Virginia

The cardinal, *Richmondena cardinalis*, was designated the official bird of West Virginia by legislative act in 1949.[72] See the Illinois entry for a description.

Wisconsin

The robin, *Turdus migratorius*, was designated the official state bird of Wisconsin by an act of the legislature in 1949.[73] When the school children of Wisconsin voted in 1926–1927 to select a state bird, the robin received twice as many votes as any other bird, but it was not until 1949 that the robin officially became the state bird.[74] See the Connecticut entry for a description.

Wyoming

The meadowlark, genus *Sturnella*, became the state bird of Wyoming by legislative act in 1927.[75] See the Kansas entry for a description.

Notes

1. Ala. Code §1–2–7.
2. Katherine B. Tippetts, "Selecting State Birds," *Nature* 19, no. 4 (1932): 231.

3. *Alabama State Emblems* (Montgomery: Alabama State Department of Archives and History, n.d.), pp. 17–18.

4. Ala. Code §1–2–17.

5. Alaska Stat. §44.09.060.

6. Ariz. Rev. Stat. Ann. §41–854.

7. 1929 Ark. Acts 1536.

8. *Nature* 19, no. 4 (1932): 231.

9. Cal. Gov't. Code §423 (West).

10. *Nature* 19, no. 4 (1932): 231.

11. Colo. Rev. Stat. §24–80–910.

12. *Nature* 19, no. 4 (1932): 231, 234.

13. Conn. Gen. Stat. Ann. §3–109 (West).

14. Del. Code Ann. tit. 29, §304.

15. *Discover Wonderful Delaware: Official Insignia of Delaware* (Dover: Delaware State Development Department, n.d.).

16. 1907 Fla. Laws 1612.

17. *Nature* 19, no. 4 (1932): 234.

18. Ga. Code Ann. §50–3–50.

19. *Georgia's Official State Symbols* (Atlanta: Office of the Secretary of State, n.d.).

20. Ga. Code Ann. §50–3–51.

21. *The State of Georgia and Its Capitol* (Atlanta: State Museum of Science and Industry, Department of Archives and History, n.d.), p. 18.

22. Haw. Rev. Stat. §5–9.

23. *Grzimek's Animal Life* (New York: Van Nostrand Reinhold, 1975), vol. 7, pp. 284, 299.

24. Idaho Code §67–4501.

25. *Nature* 19, no. 4 (1932): 234.

26. Ill. Ann. Stat. ch. 1, §3003 (Smith-Hurd).

27. *Illinois Blue Book, 1983–84*, p. 436.

28. Ind. Code Ann. §1–2–8–1 (West).

29. *1985–1986 Iowa Official Register*, p. 241.

30. Kan. Stat. Ann. §73–901.

31. Ky. Rev. Stat. Ann. §2.080 (Baldwin).

32. La. Rev. Stat. Ann. §49–159 (West).

33. Me. Rev. Stat. tit. 1, §209.

34. Md. Ann. Code §13–302.

35. *Nature* 19, no. 4 (1932): 235.

36. Mass. Gen. Laws ch. 2, §9 (West).

37. Information supplied by the Michigan Department of State.

38. Minn. Stat. Ann. §1.145 (West).

39. *Minnesota Legislative Manual, 1985*, p. 12.

40. Miss. Code Ann. §3–3–11.

41. Ibid., §3–3–25.

42. Mo. Ann. Stat. §10.010 (Vernon).

43. Mont. Rev. Codes Ann. §1–1–504.

44. Rex C. Myers, *Symbols of Montana* (Helena: Montana Historical Society, 1976), p. 16.

45. Neb. Rev. Stat. §90–107.
46. Nev. Rev. Stat. §235.060.
47. N.H. Rev. Stat. Ann. §3:10.
48. *Manual for the General Court, 1981.*
49. N.J. Stat. Ann. §52:9A–1 (West).
50. N.M. Stat. Ann. §12–3–4.
51. N.Y. State Law §78 (McKinney).
52. *Nature* 19, no. 4 (1932): 235.
53. N.C. Gen. Stat. §145–2.
54. N.D. Cent. Code §54–02–06.
55. Ohio Rev. Code Ann. §5.03 (Baldwin).
56. Okla. Stat. Ann. tit. 25, §98.
57. 1951 Okla. Sess. Laws 356.
58. Or. Rev. Stat. §186; *Oregon State Blue Book, 1977–78*, p. 139.
59. Pa. Stat. Ann. tit. 71, §1005 (Purdon).
60. R.I. Gen. Laws §42–4–5.
61. S.C. Code §1–1–630.
62. *1978 South Carolina Legislative Manual*, 59th ed.
63. S.C. Code §1–1–635.
64. S.D. Codified Laws Ann. §1–6–9.
65. *Tennessee Blue Book, 1983–84*, p. 373.
66. Tex. Rev. Civ. Stat. Ann. art. 6143c (Vernon).
67. Utah Code Ann. §63–13–9.
68. *Nature* 19, no. 4 (1932): 235.
69. Vt. Stat. Ann. tit. 1, §497.
70. Va. Code §7.1–39.
71. Wash. Rev. Code Ann. §1.20.040.
72. Information supplied by the West Virginia Department of Culture and History.
73. Wis. Stat. Ann. §1.10 (West).
74. *Wisconsin Blue Book, 1983–84*, p. 948.
75. Wyo. Stat. Ann. §8–3–105.

9 | State Songs

State songs may celebrate a state's natural beauty and resources, its history and progress, or the hard work of its citizens. Some are quite familiar: "You Are My Sunshine" (Louisiana), "Home On The Range" (Kansas), and "Yankee Doodle" (Connecticut). Although others may be less familiar, forty-seven states have designated songs that express the unique character of the state. Only New Jersey, New York, and Pennsylvania have never proclaimed state songs. On the other hand, Tennessee has five official songs and West Virginia has three. Furthermore, Georgia also has a state waltz; Kansas and North Dakota, a state march; Massachusetts, a state folk song; New Mexico, a Spanish language song; and Texas, a state flower song.

Alabama

The poem "Alabama" was adopted as the state song of Alabama in 1931. The poem was written by Julia S. Tutwiler and gifted to the state. Edna Gockel Gussen put the poem to music.[1] By the time the legislature officially adopted the song, it had already been in use for ten years as the state song. In 1917 the Alabama Federation of Music Clubs endorsed the song and gave it an award at its annual convention.[2]

Alaska

"Alaska's Flag," composed by Elinor Dusenbury with words by Marie Drake, was adopted as the state song of Alaska in 1955.[3] The poem entitled "Alaska's Flag" first appeared in the October 1935 *School Bulletin*, published by the state's Department of Education. Marie Drake was an employee of that department for twenty-eight years, having become assistant commissioner of education in 1934 and remaining in that post until her retirement in 1945.[4]

Arizona

The Arizona state song or anthem, adopted by the Fourth State Legislature, is entitled "Arizona March Song." The words were written by Margaret Rowe Clifford; the music, by Maurice Blumenthal.[5]

Arkansas

"Arkansas" is the title of the state song of Arkansas. Adopted by the legislature in 1917, the words and music are by Eva Ware Barnett.[6]

California

"I Love You, California," words by F. B. Silverwood and music by A. F. Frankenstein, was first introduced to the public in 1913 by Mary Garden. In 1915, it became the official song of the San Francisco and San Diego Expositions. In 1951 "I Love You, California" was adopted as the official state song by the legislature.[7]

Colorado

The song "Where The Columbines Grow," words and music by A. J. Flynn, was declared the official state song of Colorado by the legislature in 1915.[8]

Connecticut

"Yankee Doodle" was adopted as the state song of Connecticut in 1978. The composer is unknown.[9]

Delaware

In 1925 "Our Delaware" was adopted as Delaware's state song. The words were written by George B. Hynson and the music, by Will M. S. Brown.[10]

Florida

Stephen Foster's well-known song "Old Folks at Home," also known as "The Swanee River," was adopted as Florida's state song in 1935. The song was originally published in 1851.[11]

Georgia

"Georgia on My Mind" was designated the official state song of Georgia in 1979. The lyrics were written by Stuart Gorrell, and the music was composed by Hoagy Carmichael.[12] The 1979 act repealed a 1922 resolution designating "Georgia," words by Lottie Bell Wylie and music by Robert Loveman, as the official state song.[13]

Georgia also adopted an official state waltz, "Our Georgia," in 1951. Composed by James B. Burch to depict the glory of the state, this waltz was first played at the Georgia Democratic Convention in 1950.[14]

Hawaii

The song "Hawaii Ponoi" was adopted as the state song of Hawaii in 1967.[15]

Idaho

In 1931 the Idaho legislature adopted "Here We Have Idaho" as the state song. The music, composed by Sallie Hume Douglas, had been copyrighted under the title "Garden of Paradise" in 1915. In 1930, the state obtained use of the melody forever from the composer. In 1917, McKinley Helm wrote the chorus, and, later, Albert J. Tompkins wrote additional verses to the song. Although other verses to the song had been written for use as an alma mater, the law cites the verses written by Helm and Tompkins as the official text for the state song.[16]

Illinois

The song "Illinois," words by C. H. Chamberlain and music by Archibald Johnston, was established as the Illinois state song in 1925.[17]

Indiana

In 1913 the song "On the Banks of the Wabash, Far Away" became the state song of Indiana. Paul Dresser wrote both the words and the music.[18]

Iowa

In 1911 the Iowa legislature adopted "The Song of Iowa" as the official state song. Although inspired to write the song while in a Confederate prison in Richmond, Virginia, S. H. M. Byers did not do so until 1897. Byers chose the melody of "O Tannenbaum," the same melody used for "My Maryland," for the song. He thus put "loyal words" to the confederate song "My Maryland," which he had heard in prison.[19]

Although it is not officially designated, the "Iowa Corn Song" is recognized by popular approval as another Iowa song. This marching tune was written by George Hamilton and popularized as early as 1912.[20]

Kansas

The Kansas legislature designated "Home on the Range," words by Dr. Brewster Higley and music by Dan Kelly, as the official state song in 1947.[21] This was originally titled "My Western Home" when it was penned by Dr. Higley, a pioneer physician in Kansas, in 1871 or 1872.[22]

Kansas also has designated an official state march. In 1935 the legislature named "The Kansas March" by Duff E. Middleton the state's official march.[23]

Kentucky

"My Old Kentucky Home" by Stephen Collins Foster was designated the official state song of Kentucky in 1928.[24]

Louisiana

Louisiana has two officially designated songs. The first song, "Give Me Louisiana," was written and composed by Doralice Fontane and arranged by John W. Schaum. In 1977 the legislature also designated "You Are My Sunshine" as an official state song. The words and music are by Jimmy H. Davis and Charles Mitchell.[25]

Maine

"State of Maine Song" is the title of the state's official song. The music and lyrics were written by Roger Vinton Snow.[26]

Maryland

"Maryland! My Maryland!" was designated the official state song in 1939. The song, a poem written in 1861 by James Ryder Randall, is sung to the tune of "Lauriger Horatius."[27] Randall, a Marylander who lived in the Confederacy during the Civil War, wrote the poem after Union troops went through Baltimore in 1861.[28]

Massachusetts

In 1981 Massachusetts designated both an official commonwealth song and a folk song. The official commonwealth song is "All Hail to Massachusetts," words and music by Arthur J. Marsh. "Massachusetts," words and music by Arlo Guthrie, is the official commonwealth folk song.[29]

Michigan

"My Michigan," words by Giles Kavanagh and music by H. O'Reilly Clint, was designated an official state song of Michigan in 1937. In 1936 Governor Fitzgerald had designated this song as the official state song, but senate amendments changed a house resolution from designating "My Michigan" as the official song, to designating it as an official state song.[30]

Minnesota

"Hail! Minnesota," written in 1904–1905, was adopted as the state song of Minnesota in 1945. The music and the first verse were written by Truman E. Rickard. Arthur E. Upson wrote the words to the second verse. The song had first been used as the song of the University of Minnesota. Thus, the law adopting the song included a change from the original phrase "Hail to thee our college dear" to "Hail to thee our state so dear."[31]

Mississippi

The Board of Realtors of Jackson, Mississippi, set up an advisory committee to select an appropriate state song. The committee recommended the song "Go, Mississippi," words and music by Houston Davis, to the legislature for adoption. In 1962, the legislature acted positively on this recommendation.[32]

Missouri

"Missouri Waltz," arrangement by Frederick Knight Logan, melody by John Valentine Eppel, and lyrics by J. R. Shannon, was designated the Missouri state song in 1949. The song was first published in 1914.[33]

Montana

In 1945 the Montana legislature declared the song "Montana," words by Charles C. Cohan and music by Joseph E. Howard, to be the official state song. The legislature had also designated an official state ballad, "Montana Melody," written by Carleen and LeGrande Harvey.[34]

Nebraska

"Beautiful Nebraska," words and music by Jim Fras, was adopted as Nebraska's official state song in 1967. The song was copyrighted in 1965.[35]

Nevada

"Home Means Nevada" was adopted as the official state song of Nevada in 1933. It was written by Mrs. Bertha Raffeto of Reno.[36]

New Hampshire

New Hampshire has designated a state song as well as a second state song. In 1949 the legislature declared "Old New Hampshire," words by Dr. John F. Holmes and music by Maurice Hoffmann, to be the state song. In 1963 "New Hampshire, My New Hampshire," music by Walter P. Smith and words by Julius Richelson, was declared the second state song.[37]

New Jersey

The state of New Jersey does not have a state song. Attempts to make such a designation in 1940, 1954, and 1970 failed. Even an attempt in 1980 to designate "Born to Run" as the state's unofficial rock song failed for lack of legislative action.[38]

New Mexico

In 1917 New Mexico adopted "O, Fair New Mexico," words and music by Elizabeth Garrett, as its official state song.[39] In 1971 the legislature declared "Asi Es Nuevo Mejico," written by Amadeo Lucero, to be the Spanish language state song.[40] Thus New Mexico has both an English language and a Spanish language official song.

New York

New York has no state songs. All bills to adopt a state song have thus far failed to pass the legislature.[41]

North Carolina

The song "The Old North State" was declared the official state song of North Carolina in 1927. Another song, "A Toast" to North Carolina, was declared the official toast in 1957.[42]

North Dakota

North Dakota has an official state song and a state march. The state song, "North Dakota Hymn," was written by James W. Foley and composed by Doctor C. S. Putnam. It was declared the state song in 1947.[43] In 1975 the legislature adopted "Spirit of the Land" by James D. Ployhar as the state march. The state march is to be played at appropriate state functions.[44]

Ohio

"Beautiful Ohio" was designated the official state song of Ohio in 1969. It was written by Ballard MacDonald and composed by Mary Earl.[45] Curiously, this 1918 waltz refers not to the state of Ohio, but to the Ohio River.[46]

Oklahoma

"Oklahoma," composed and written by Richard Rogers and Oscar Hammerstein, was declared the Oklahoma state song in 1953.[47] The 1953 act repealed a 1935 act designating "Oklahoma (A Toast)" by Harriet Parker Camden as the state song.

Oregon

"Oregon, My Oregon," words by J. A. Buchanan and music by Henry B. Murtagh, was adopted as the Oregon state song in 1927.[48]

Pennsylvania

The state of Pennsylvania has no state song.[49]

Rhode Island

"Rhode Island," music and words by T. Clarke Brown, was declared to be the state song of Rhode Island in 1946.[50]

South Carolina

The song "Carolina," words by Henry Timrod and music by Anne Custis Burgess, was declared to be the state song of South Carolina in 1911, when the legislature acted on the memorial of the South Carolina Daughters of the American Revolution. There is, however, another state song. "South Carolina On My Mind" was designated as an official state song in 1984 to promote the image of South Carolina beyond its borders "by further developing tourism and industry through the attraction of vacationers, prospective investors, and new residents."[51]

South Dakota

"Hail! South Dakota," music and words by Deecort Hammitt, was adopted as the official state song of South Dakota in 1943.[52]

Tennessee

Tennessee has five official state songs. In designating new official songs, the legislature has not repealed formerly designated songs. The first official song, "My Homeland, Tennessee" by Nell Grayson Taylor and Roy Lamont Smith was adopted in 1925. In 1935 "When It's Iris Time in Tennessee" by Willa Mae Waid became Tennessee's second official song. "My Tennessee" by Francis Hannah Tranum was adopted as the third song in 1955, and "The Tennessee Waltz" by Redd Stewart and Pee Wee King, was designated the fourth in 1965. The fifth official state song, "Rocky Top," by Boudleaux and Felice Bryant, was adopted in 1982.[53]

Texas

In 1928 the Texas legislature adopted "Texas, Our Texas" by William J. Marsh and Gladys Yoakum Wright as the official state song. This song was chosen following contests in each senatorial district and a final contest in Dallas, after which a legislative committee chose it twice.[54]

In 1933 the legislature designated a state flower song: "Bluebonnets," words by Julia D. Booth and music by Lora C. Crockett.[55]

Utah

"Utah We Love Thee" was designated Utah's state song in 1937. It was written by Evan Stephens.[56]

Vermont

In 1937 a committee was empowered to select an official state song. "Hail, Vermont!" was selected from over 100 songs in 1938, and the governor was informed of the selection. The song was written by Josephine Hovey Perry.[57]

Virginia

"Carry Me Back To Old Virginia" by James B. Bland was declared by the General Assembly to be the official Commonwealth of Virginia song in 1940.[58]

Washington

"Washington My Home" by Helen Davis was designated the official state song of Washington in 1959.[59]

West Virginia

West Virginia has adopted three state songs. "This Is My West Virginia" was written and composed by Mrs. Iris Bell of Charleston. "West Virginia My Home Sweet Home," words and music by Colonel Julian G. Hearne, Jr., was designated the official state song in 1947. The third song, "The West Virginia Hills," was written in 1879 by the Reverend David King as a poem for his wife, Ellen King. Mrs. King's name may be found on the music, as this was the request of the poet. H. E. Engle put the poem to music in 1885, and it was designated an official state song in 1961.[60]

Wisconsin

"On, Wisconsin" was designated the state song of Wisconsin in 1959.[61] The song was composed in 1909 by William T. Purdy as a football fight song. While the song was recognized unofficially as the state song, several lyrics had come into existence in the fifty years before it was officially designated the state song. The 1959 law therefore actually prescribes the words to be used.[62]

Wyoming

In 1955 the march song "Wyoming," words by Charles E. Winter and music by George E. Knapp, was designated Wyoming's official state song.[63]

Notes

1. Ala. Code §1–2–16; *Alabama State Emblems* (Montgomery: Alabama State Department of Archives and History, n.d.), pp. 20–21.
2. 1931 Ala. Acts 190.
3. Alaska Stat. §44.09.040.
4. *Alaska Blue Book 1979*, p. 123.
5. *Welcome to Arizona* (Phoenix: Arizona Office of Tourism, n.d.).

6. *Journal of the Senate of Arkansas, Forty-First Regular Session, 1917*, p. 76.
7. *California's Legislature, 1984*, p. 203.
8. Colo. Rev. Stat. §24–80–909.
9. Conn. Gen. Stat. Ann. §3–110c (West).
10. *Official Insignia of Delaware* (Dover: Delaware State Development Department, n.d.).
11. 1935 Fla. Laws 1540.
12. Ga. Code Ann. §50–3–60.
13. *The State of Georgia and Its Capitol* (Atlanta: State Museum of Science and Industry, Department of Archives and History, 1979), p. 11.
14. 1951 Ga. Laws 842.
15. Haw. Rev. Stat. §5–10.
16. "Idaho State Song," Idaho Historical Society Reference Series no. 125 (Boise: Idaho Historical Society, December 1984), p. 1.
17. Ill. Ann. Stat. ch. 1, §3008 (Smith-Hurd).
18. Ind. Code Ann. §1–2–6–1 (West).
19. *1985–86 Iowa Official Register*, vol. 61, p. 238.
20. Ibid., p. 239.
21. Kan. Stat. Ann. §73–1301.
22. *Kansas Directory, 1982*, p. 128.
23. Kan. Stat. Ann. §73–801.
24. Ky. Rev. Stat. Ann. §2.100 (Baldwin).
25. *Louisiana Facts* (Baton Rouge: Louisiana Department of State, n.d.).
26. Me. Rev. Stat. tit. 1, §210.
27. Md. Ann. Code §13–307.
28. *Maryland Manual, 1981–1982*, p. 10.
29. Mass. Gen. Laws ch. 2, §19, §20 (West).
30. *Journal of the Michigan House of Representatives, 1937*, pp. 171, 1183.
31. *Minnesota Legislative Manual, 1958*, pp. 16–17; *Official Minnesota Symbols* (St. Paul: Minnesota Historical Society, December 1983), p. 1.
32. *Souvenir of Mississippi* (Jackson: Dick Molpus, n.d.), p. 28.
33. Mo. Ann. Stat. §10.050 (Vernon).
34. Mont. Rev. Codes Ann. §1–1–511; Rex C. Myers, *Symbols of Montana* (Helena: Montana Historical Society, 1976), p. 14.
35. Neb. Rev. Stat. §90–111.
36. Nev. Rev. Stat. §235.030.
37. N.H. Rev. Stat. Ann. §3:7, §3:7-a.
38. *Manual of the Legislature of New Jersey, 1984*, pp. 11–12.
39. N.M. Stat. Ann. §12–3–5.
40. Ibid., §12–3–6.
41. Information supplied by Maureen Bigness, Director of Information Services, Department of State, Albany, New York.
42. N.C. Gen Stat. §149–1, §149–2.
43. N.D. Cent. Code §54–02–04.
44. Ibid., §54–02–09.
45. Ohio Rev. Code Ann. §5.09 (Baldwin).
46. *Ohio Almanac* (Lorain: Lorain Journal Co., 1977), pp. 46, 60.
47. Okla. Stat. Ann. tit. 25, §94.1, §94.3 (West).

48. *Journals of the Oregon Senate and House of the 34th Legislative Assembly, Regular Session, 1927*, p. 35.

49. Information supplied by Barbara Murphy, Administrative Assistant, Commonwealth of Pennsylvania, Department of State.

50. R.I. Gen. Laws §42–4–4.

51. S.C. Code §1–1–685; *South Carolina State Symbols and Emblems* (Columbia: House of Representatives, n.d.).

52. *South Dakota Signs and Symbols* (n.p., n.d.).

53. Tenn. Code Ann. §4–1–302.

54. Tex. Rev. Civ. Stat. Ann. art. 6143b (Vernon).

55. Ibid., art. 6143bb (Vernon).

56. Utah Code Ann. §63–13–8.

57. 1937 Vt. Acts 350; *Vermont Legislative Directory and State Manual, 1979–80*, p. 19.

58. Va. Code §7.1–37.

59. Wash. Rev. Code Ann. §1.20.070.

60. *West Virginia Blue Book, 1980*, p. 924.

61. Wis. Stat. Ann. §1.10 (West).

62. *State of Wisconsin 1983–84 Blue Book*, p. 948.

63. Wyo. Stat. Ann. §8–3–108.

10 | Miscellaneous Official State Designations

Every state in the union has found it desirable to recognize officially some special symbols that have a unique importance. These legislative actions have largely been phenomena of the past thirty years. Often such official designations recognize the importance of an industry to a particular state. Florida, for example, designated orange juice as its official beverage. Tomato juice is Ohio's state beverage and cranberry juice, Massachusetts'. Wisconsin's official domestic animal is the dairy cow. On the other hand, an official designation may also bring with it special protection for an endangered species. Georgia's and Massachusetts' right whale, California's gray whale, Alaska's bowhead whale, and Florida's manatee received protection as officially designated state marine mammals.

Some designated symbols recall the early history of a state. Gold is the state mineral of California and Alaska. Dog mushing is Alaska's state sport. The American buffalo is the state animal of Kansas, and Plymouth Rock is Massachusetts' historical rock. Other symbols cannot be considered without recalling the state with which they have become identified: Alaskan king salmon, the California grizzly bear, Indiana limestone, Louisiana's crawfish, and Maine's moose.

Whether animals, vegetables, or minerals or even reptiles, mammals, or neckwear, each state expresses its unique character through the symbols it chooses.

Alabama

Dance (1981)   Square dance
Fossil (1984)   Species *Basilosaurus cetoides*

Fresh water fish (1975)	Largemouth Bass, *Micropterus punctulatus*
Horse (1975)	Rocking horse
Mineral (1967)	Hematite
Nut (1982)	Pecan
Rock (1969)	Marble
Salt water fish (1955)	Tarpon[1]

Alaska

Fish (1963)	King salmon, *Oncorhynchus tshawytscha*
Gem (1968)	Jade
Marine mammal (1983)	Bowhead whale
Mineral (1968)	Gold
Sport (1972)	Dog mushing[2]

Arizona

Gem (1974)	Turquoise
Neckwear (1973)	Bola tie[3]

Arkansas

Beverage (1985)	Milk
Gem (1967)	Diamond
Insect (1973)	Honeybee
Mineral (1967)	Quartz crystal
Musical instrument (1985)	Fiddle
Rock (1967)	Bauxite[4]

California

Animal (1953)	California grizzly bear, *Ursus californicus*[5]
Fish (1947)	Golden trout, *Salmo aqua-bonita*[6]
Fossil (1973)	Saber-toothed cat, *Smilodon Californicus*
Insect (1972)	California dog-face butterfly, *Zerene eurydice*

Marine mammal (1975)	California gray whale, *Eschrichtius robustus*
Mineral (1965)	Native gold
Reptile (1972)	California desert tortoise, *Gopherus agassizi*
Rock (1965)	Serpentine[7]

Colorado

Animal (1961)	Rocky Mountain bighorn sheep, *Ovis canadensis*
Gem (1971)	Aquamarine[8]

Connecticut

Animal (1975)	Sperm whale, *Physeter catadon*
Insect (1977)	Praying mantis, *Mantis religiosa*
Mineral (1977)	Garnet[9]
Ship (1983)	*U.S.S. Nautilus*[10]

Delaware

Beverage (1983)	Milk
Bug (1973)	Lady bug
Fish (1981)	Weakfish, genus *Cynoscion*
Mineral (1975)	Sillimanite[11]

Florida

Air fair (1976)	Central Florida Air Fair
Animal (1982)	Florida panther
Beverage (1967)	Juice from the mature oranges of the species *Citrus sinensis* and hybrids of that species
Festival (1980)	"Calle Ocho—Open House 8," historical festival held each year in Dade County
Freshwater fish (1975)	Florida largemouth bass, *Micropterus salmoides floridanus*
Gem (1970)	Moonstone

Litter Control Symbol (1978)	"Glenn Glitter," the litter control trademark of the Florida Federation of Garden Clubs, Inc.
Marine mammal (1975)	Manatee, commonly called the sea cow
Pageant (1979)	"Indian River," historical pageant presented each year in Brevard County
Play (1973)	"Cross and Sword," historical pageant by Paul Green presented each year by the city of St. Augustine
Saltwater fish (1975)	Atlantic sailfish, *Istiophorus platypterus*
Saltwater mammal (1975)	Porpoise, commonly called the dolphin
Shell (1969)	Horse conch, *Pleuroploca gigantea*, also known as the giant band shell
Stone (1979)	Agatized coral[12]

Georgia

Atlas (1985)	*The Atlas of Georgia*[13]
Fish (1970)	Largemouth bass
Fossil (1976)	Shark tooth
Gem (1976)	Quartz
Insect (1975)	Honeybee[14]
Marine mammal (1985)	Right whale[15]
Mineral (1976)	Staurolite[16]

Hawaii

The Hawaiian legislature has established official colors for each island:

Hawaii	Red
Maui	Pink
Molokai	Green
Kahoolawe	Gray
Lanai	Yellow
Oahu	Yellow

Kauai	Purple
Niihau	White[17]

Idaho

Gem (1967)	Star garnet
Horse (1975)	Appaloosa[18]

Illinois

Animal (1982)	White-tailed deer
Insect (1975)	Monarch butterfly, *Danaus plexippus*
Language (1969)	English
Mineral (1965)	Fluorite[19]

Indiana

Language (1984)	English
Poem (1963)	"Indiana" by Arthur Franklin Mapes
Stone (1971)	Limestone[20]

Iowa

Rock (1967)	Geode[21]

Kansas

Animal (1955)	American buffalo, *Bison americanus*
Insect (1976)	Honeybee[22]

Kentucky

Language (1984)	English
Shakespeare festival (1984)	Shakespeare in Central Park of Louisville

Tug-of-war championship (1984)	Nelson County Fair Tug-of-War Championship Contest
Wild animal game species (1968)	Gray squirrel[23]

Louisiana

Crustacean (1983)	Crawfish
Dog (1979)	Louisiana Catahoula leopard dog
Drink (1983)	Milk
Fossil (1976)	Petrified palmwood
Fruit (1980)	The 1980 act designating a state fruit made a different fruit the official fruit for each of the years 1980 through 1987: peach, 1980; watermelon, 1981; fig, 1982; strawberry, 1983; peach, 1984; orange, 1985; tomato, 1986; cantaloupe, 1987
Gem (1976)	Agate
Insect (1977)	Honeybee
Reptile (1983)	Alligator[24]

Maine

Animal (1979)	Moose
Cat (1985)	Maine coon cat
Fish (1969)	Landlocked salmon, *Salmo salar sebago*
Fossil (1985)	*Pertica quadrifaria*
Insect (1975)	Honeybee
Mineral (1971)	Tourmaline[25]

Maryland

Dog (1964)	Chesapeake Bay retriever
Fish (1965)	Striped bass
Fossil shell (1984)	*Ecphora quadricostata*
Insect (1973'	Baltimore checkerspot butterfly, *Euphydryas phaeton*
Sport (1962	Jousting

Summer theater (1978)	Olney Theatre in Montgomery County
Theater (1978)	Center Stage in Baltimore[26]

Massachusetts

Beverage (1970)	Cranberry juice
Building and monument stone (1983)	Granite
Dog (1979)	Boston terrier
Explorer rock (1983)	Dighton Rock
Fish (1974)	Cod
Fossil (1980)	Dinosaur track
Gem (1979)	Rhodonite
Heroine (1983)	Deborah Samson
Historical rock (1983)	Plymouth Rock
Horse (1970)	Morgan horse
Insect (1974)	Lady bug
Marine mammal (1980)	Right whale, *Eubalaena glacialis*
Mineral (1981)	*Babingtonite*
Poem (1981)	"Blue Hills of Massachusetts" by Katherine E. Mullen
Rock (1983)	Roxbury pudding stone[27]

Michigan

Fish (1966)	Trout
Gem (1973)	Chlorastrolite, or greenstone
Stone (1966)	Petoskey Stone[28]

Minnesota

Drink (1984)	Milk
Fish (1965)	Walleye, *Stizostedion v. vitreum*
Gem (1969)	Lake Superior agate

| Grain (1977) | Wild rice, *Zizania aquatica* |
| Mushroom (1984) | Morel[29] |

Mississippi

Beverage (1984)	Milk
Fish (1974)	Largemouth bass, *Micropterus salmoides*[30]
Fossil (1981)	Prehistoric whale[31]
Insect (1980)	Honeybee
Land mammal (1974)	White-tailed deer, *Odocoileus virginianus*
Shell (1974)	Oyster shell
Water mammal (1974)	Bottlenosed dolphin, *Tursiops truncatus*[32]

Missouri

| Mineral (1967) | Galena |
| Rock (1967) | Mozarkite[33] |

Montana

Animal (1983)	Grizzly bear, *Ursus arctos horribilis*
Fish (1977)	Blackspotted cutthroat trout, *Salmo clarki*
Gem (1969)	Sapphire and Montana agate
Grass (1973)	Bluebunch grass, *Agropyron spicatum (pursh)*[34]

Nebraska

Fossil (1967)	Mammoth
Gem (1967)	Blue agate
Grass (1969)	Little blue stem grass
Insect (1975)	Honeybee[35]

| Mammal (1981) | White-tailed deer[36] |
| Rock (1967) | Prairie agate[37] |

Nevada

Animal (1973)	Desert bighorn sheep, *Ovis canadensis nelsoni*
Colors (1983)	Silver and blue
Fish (1981)	Lohonton cutthroat trout, *Salmo clarki henshawi*
Fossil (1977)	Ichthyosaur
Grass (1977)	Indian rice grass, *Oryzopsis hymenoides*
Metal (1977)	Silver[38]

New Hampshire

| Animal (1983) | White-tailed deer |
| Insect (1977) | Lady bug[39] |

New Jersey

| Animal (1977) | Horse |
| Insect (1974) | Honeybee[40] |

New Mexico

Animal (1963)	New Mexico black bear
Fish (1955)	New Mexico cutthroat trout
Fossil (1981)	Coelophysis
Gem (1967)	Turquoise
Grass (1973)	Blue grama grass, *Bouteloua gracillis*
Vegetable (1965)	Pinto bean and the chili[41]

New York

Animal (1975)	American beaver, *Castor canadensis*
Beverage (1981)	Milk
Fish (1975)	Brook or speckled trout, *Salvelinus fontinalis*
Fossil (1984)	Eurypterus remipes

Fruit (1976)   Apple
Gem (1969)   Garnet[42]

North Carolina

Colors (1945)   Red and blue
Insect (1973)   Honeybee
Mammal (1969)   Gray squirrel, *Sciurus carolinensis*
Reptile (1979)   Turtle (the eastern box turtle is the
                                      emblem representing turtles that
                                      inhabit North Carolina)
Rock (1979)   Granite
Saltwater fish (1971)   Channel bass or red drum
Shell (1965)   Scotch bonnet
Stone (1973)   Emerald[43]

North Dakota

Art gallery (1981)   University of North Dakota Art Gallery
                                      on the campus in Grand Forks
Beverage (1983)   Milk
Fossil (1967)   Teredo petrified wood
Grass (1977)   Western wheat grass, *Agropyron
                                      smithii*[44]

Ohio

Beverage (1965)   Tomato juice
Gem (1965)   Ohio flint[45]

Oklahoma

Animal (1972)   American buffalo[46]
Colors (1915)   Green and white
Fish (1974)   White bass, *Morone chrysops*[47]
Grass (1972)   Indian Grass, *Sorghastrum nutans*
Poem (1973)   "Howdy Folks" by David Randolph
                                      Milsten[48]

Reptile (1969)	Collared lizard, *Crotophytus*[49]
Rock (1968)	Barite rose[50]

Oregon

Animal (1969)	Beaver
Fish (1961)	Chinook salmon
Hostess (1969)	Miss Oregon
Insect (1979)	Swallowtail butterfly
Rock (1965)	Thunderegg[51]

Pennsylvania

Animal (1959)	Whitetail deer
Beautification and conservation plant (1982)	Penngift crownvetch, *Coronilla varia L. penngift*
Beverage (1982)	Milk
Dog (1965)	Great dane
Fish (1970)	Brook trout, *Salvelinus fontinalis*
Insect (1974)	Firefly, *Lampyridae*[52]

Rhode Island

American Folk Art Symbol (1985)	Charles I. D. Looff Carousel[53]
Mineral (1966)	Bowenite
Rock (1966)	Cumberlandite[54]

South Carolina

Animal (1972)	White-tailed deer, *Odocoileus virginianus*
Beverage (1984)	Milk
Dance (1984)	The shag
Fish (1972)	Striped bass or rockfish
Fruit (1984)	Peach
Gem (1969)	Amethyst

Shell (1984)   Lettered olive
Stone (1969)   Blue granite[55]

South Dakota

Animal (1949)   Coyote
Fish (1982)   Walleye, *Stizostedion vitreum*
Gem (1966)   Fairburn agate
Grass (1970)   Western wheat grass, *Agropyron smithii*
Insect (1978)   Honeybee
Mineral (1966)   Rose quartz[56]

Tennessee

Fine art (1981)   Porcelain painting
Folk dance (1980)   Square dance
Gem (1979)   Tennessee pearl
Insect (1975)   Firefly and lady bug
Language (1984)   English
Poem (1973)   "Oh Tennessee, My Tennessee" by
                            Admiral William Lawrence
Railroad museum (1978)   Tennessee Valley Railroad Museum in
                            Hamilton County
Rock (1979)   Limestone[57]
Wild animal (1972)   Raccoon[58]

Texas

Plays (1979)   "The Lone Star," presented in Galveston
                            Island State Park; "Texas," presented
                            in Palo Duro Canyon State Park;
                            "Beyond the Sundown," presented at
                            the Alabama-Coushatta Indian
                            Reservation; and "Fandangle,"
                            presented in Shackleford County.[59]

Utah

Animal (1971)   Elk
Emblem (1959)   Beehive

Fish (1971)   Rainbow trout
Gem (1969)   Topaz
Insect (1983)   Honeybee[60]

Vermont

Animal (1961)   Morgan horse
Beverage (1983)   Milk
Insect (1977)   Honeybee
Soil (1985)   Tunbridge soil series[61]

Virginia

Beverage (1982)   Milk
Dog (1966)   American foxhound
Shell (1974)   Oyster shell, *Crassoostraea virginica*[62]

Washington

Dance (1979)   Square dance
Fish (1969)   Steelhead trout, *Salmo gairdnerii*
Gem (1975)   Petrified wood[63]

West Virginia

Animal (1973)   Black bear, *Euarctos americanus*
Fish (1973)   Brook trout
Fruit (1972)   Apple[64]

Wisconsin

Animal (1957)   Badger, *Taxidea taxus*
Domestic animal (1971)   Dairy cow
Fish (1955)   Muskellunge, *Esox masquinongy
                                   masquinongy* Mitchell
Insect (1977)   Honeybee
Mineral (1971)   Galena
Rock (1971)   Red granite
Soil (1983)   Antigo silt loam

Symbol of peace (1971)　　　　Mourning dove

Wild life animal (1957)　　　　White-tailed deer, *Odocoileus*
　　　　　　　　　　　　　　　　virginianus[65]

Wyoming

Gem (1967)　　　　　　　　　Jade[66]

Notes

1. Ala. Code §1–2–18; §1–2–20; §1–2–9; §1–2–10; §1–2–13; §1–2–19; §1–2–14; §1–2–8.
2. Alaska Stat. §44.09.080; §44.09.100; §44.09.075; §44.09.110; §44.09.085.
3. Ariz. Rev. Stat. Ann. §41–858; §41–857.
4. Ark. Stat. Ann. §5–127; §5–115; §5–118; §5–116; §5–119; §5–117.
5. Cal. Gov't. Code §425 (West).
6. *California's Legislature 1984*, p. 201.
7. Cal. Gov't. Code §425.7; §424.5; §425.5; §425.1; §422.5; §425.2 (West).
8. Colo. Rev. Stat. §24–80–911; §24–80–912.
9. Conn. Gen. Stat. Ann. §3–109a; §3–109b; §3–110b.
10. *State of Connecticut Register and Manual 1983*, p. 904.
11. Del. Code Ann. tit. 29, §312; §309; §311; §310.
12. Fla. Stat. Ann. §15.039; §15.0353; §15.032; §15.0395; §15.036; §15.034; §15.041; §15.038; §15.043; §15.035; §15.037; §15.038; §15.033; §15.0336 (West).
13. 1985 Ga. Laws, 562.
14. Ga. Code Ann. §50–3–52; §50–3–56; §50–3–57; §50–3–58.
15. 1985 Ga. Laws. 747.
16. Ga. Code Ann. §50–3–59.
17. *Hawaii, the Aloha State* (Honolulu: State of Hawaii, Hawaii Visitors Bureau, Chamber of Commerce of Hawaii, n.d.).
18. Idaho Code §67–4505; §67–4506.
19. Ill. Stat. Ann. ch. 1, §3020, §3004, §3005, §3006 (Smith-Hurd).
20. Ind. Code Ann. §1–2–10–1; §1–2–5–1; §1–2–9–1 (West).
21. *1985–86 Iowa Official Register*, vol. 61, p. 244.
22. Kan. Stat. Ann. §73–1401; §73–1601.
23. Ky. Rev. Stat. Ann. §2.013; §2.210; §2.260; §2.085 (Baldwin).
24. La. Rev. Stat. Ann. §49–168; §49–165; §49–170; §49–162; §49–166; §49–163; §49–164; §49–169 (West).
25. Me. Rev. Stat. tit. 1, §215, §216, §212, §216, §214, §213.
26. Md. Ann. Code §13–303; §13–304; §13–311; §13–301; §13–308; §13–309.
27. Mass. Gen. Laws Ann. ch. 2, §10, §25, §14, §24, §13, §17, §15, §26, §23, §11, §12, §16, §18, §21, §22 (West).
28. Mich. Comp Laws Ann. §2.15; §2.17; §2.16.
29. Minn. Stat. Ann. §1.1495; §1.146; §1.147; §1.148; §1.149 (West).

30. Miss. Code Ann. §3–3–29; §3–3–21.
31. *Souvenir of Mississippi* (Jackson: Dick Molpus, n.d.), p. 27.
32. Miss. Code Ann. §3–3–27; §3–3–17; §3–3–23; §3–3–19.
33. Mo. Ann. Stat. §10.047; §10.045 (Vernon).
34. Mont. Rev. Codes Ann. §1–1–508; §1–1–507; §1–1–505; §1–1–506.
35. Neb. Rev. Stat. §90–109; §90–108; §90–112; §90–114.
36. *Nebraska Blue Book, 1982–1983*, p. 14.
37. Neb. Rev. Stat. §90–110.
38. Nev. Rev. Stat. §235.070; §235.025; §235.075; §235.080; §235.055; §235.090.
39. N.H. Rev. Stat. Ann. §3:12; §3:11
40. N.J. Stat. Ann. §52:9AAAA–1; §52:9AAA–1 (West).
41. N.M. Stat. Ann. §12–3–4.
42. N.Y. State Law §79; §82; §80; §83; §81; §77 (McKinney).
43. N.C. Gen. Stat. §144–6; §145–7; §145–5; §145–9; §145–10; §145–6; §145–4; §145–8.
44. N.D. Cent. Code §54–02–11; §54–02–12; §54–02–08; §54–02–10.
45. Ohio Rev. Code Ann. §5.08; §5.07 (Baldwin).
46. *Directory of Oklahoma 1981*, p. 20.
47. Okla. Stat. Ann. tit. 25, §93, §98.2.
48. *Directory of Oklahoma 1981*, pp. 18, 19.
49. Ibid., p. 20.
50. Okla. Stat. Ann. tit. 25, §98.1.
51. Or. Rev. Stat. §186.
52. Pa. Stat. Ann. tit. 71, §1007, §1010.2; §1010.1, §1008, §1009, §1010 (Purdon).
53. R.I. Gen. Laws §42–4–11.
54. *The State of Rhode Island and Providence Plantations, 1983–84 Manual.*
55. S.C. Code §1–1–650; §1–1–690; §1–1–665; §1–1–640; §1–1–680; §1–1–610; §1–1–695; §1–1–620.
56. S.D. Codified Laws Ann. §1–6–8; §1–6–15; §1–6–12; §1–6–13; §1–6–14; §1–6–12.
57. Tenn. Code Ann. §4–1–133; §4–1–312; §4–1–310; §4–1–308; §4–1–404; §4–1–303; §4–1–311; §4–1–309.
58. *Tennessee Blue Book, 1983–84*, pp. 373–74.
59. Tex. Rev. Civ. Stat. Ann. art. 6143d (Vernon).
60. Utah Code Ann. §63–13–7.2; §63–13–10; §63–13–7.3; §63–13–7.1; §63–13–11.5.
61. Vt. Stat. Ann. tit. 1, §500, §503, §502, §504.
62. Va. Code §7.1–40; §7.1–39; §7.1–40.
63. Wash. Rev. Code Ann. §1.20.075; §1.20.045; §1.20.090.
64. *West Virginia Blue Book, 1980*, p. 925.
65. Wis. Stat. Ann. §1.10.
66. Wyo. Stat. Ann. §8–3–109.

Selected Bibliography of State Histories

Alabama

Du Bose, Joel C. *Alabama History*. Richmond: B. F. Johnson, 1908.
Griffith, Lucille B. *Alabama: A Documentary History*. Rev. and enl. ed. University: University of Alabama Press, 1972.
Hamilton, Virginia V. *Alabama, A History*. New York: Norton; Nashville: American Association for State and Local History, 1984.
Moore, Albert B. *History of Alabama and Her People*. 3 vols. Chicago: American Historical Society, 1927.
Owen, Marie B. *The Story of Alabama; A History of the State*. 5 vols. New York: Lewis Historical Publishing Company, 1949.
Owen, Thomas M. *History of Alabama and Dictionary of Alabama Biography*. 4 vols. Chicago: S. J. Clarke, 1921.

Alaska

Andrews, Clarence L. *The Story of Alaska*. Seattle: Lowman & Hanford, 1931.
Gruening, Ernest H. *The State of Alaska*. New York: Random House, 1968.
Nichols, Jeannette P. *Alaska*. New York: Russell & Russell, 1963.

Arizona

Farish, Thomas E. *History of Arizona*. 8 vols. Phoenix: State of Arizona, 1915–1918.
Miller, Joseph. *Arizona; The Grand Canyon State; A State Guide*. 4th completely rev. ed. New York: Hastings House, 1966.
Peplow, Edward H. *History of Arizona*. 3 vols. New York: Lewis Historical Publishing Company, 1958.

Sloan, Richard E., and Ward R. Adams. *History of Arizona*. 4 vols. Phoenix: Record Publishing Company, 1930.

Wyllys, Rufus K. *Arizona: The History of a Frontier State*. Phoenix: Hobson & Herr, 1950.

Arkansas

Ashmore, Harry S. *Arkansas, A History*. New York: Norton; Nashville: American Association for State and Local History, 1984.

Fletcher, John G. *Arkansas*. Chapel Hill: University of North Carolina Press, 1947.

Herndon, Dallas T. *Centennial History of Arkansas*. Easley, S.C.: Southern Historical Press, 1984; originally published in 1922.

McNutt, Walter S., et al. *A History of Arkansas*. Little Rock: Democrat Printing and Lithographing, 1932.

Thomas, David Y. *Arkansas and Its People, A History, 1541–1930*. 4 vols. New York: American Historical Society, 1930.

California

Bancroft, Hubert H. *California*. 7 vols. San Francisco: A. L. Bancroft, 1884–1890.

Bean, Walton, and James J. Rawls. *California, An Interpretive History*. 4th ed. New York: McGraw-Hill, 1983.

Chapman, Charles E. *A History of California: The Spanish Period*. New York: Macmillan, 1921.

Cleland, Robert G. *A History of California: The American Period*. Westport, Conn.: Greenwood Press, 1975; reprint of 1922 edition.

Fehrenbacher, Don E. *A Basic History of California*. Princeton, N.J.: Van Nostrand, 1964.

Hutchinson, William H. *California; Two Centuries of Man, Land, and Growth in the Golden State*. Palo Alto: American West Publishing Company, 1969.

Lavender, David S. *California, a History*. New York: Norton; Nashville: American Association for State and Local History, 1985.

Rolle, Andrew F. *California: A History*. 3d ed. Arlington Heights, Ill.: AHM, 1978.

Colorado

Hafen, LeRoy R., ed. *Colorado and Its People; A Narrative and Topical History of the Centennial State*. 4 vols. New York: Lewis Historical Publishing Company, 1948.

Hall, Frank. *History of the State of Colorado...* 4 vols. Chicago: Blakely Printing Company, 1889–1895.

Schmidt, Cynthia. *Colorado: Grassroots*. Phoenix: Cloud Publishing, 1984.

Sprague, Marshall. *Colorado, A History*. New York: Norton; Nashville: American Association for State and Local History, 1984.

Stone, Wilbur F. *History of Colorado*. 6 vols. Chicago: S. J. Clarke, 1918–1919.

Ubbelohde, Carl W., et al. *A Colorado History*. rev., 5th ed. Boulder: Pruett, 1982.

Connecticut

Bingham, Harold J. *History of Connecticut.* 4 vols. New York: Lewis Historical Publishing Company, 1962.

Morgan, Forrest, ed. *Connecticut As a Colony and As a State, or One of the Original Thirteen.* 4 vols. Hartford: Publishing Society of Connecticut, 1904.

Osborn, Norris G. *History of Connecticut in Monographic Form.* 5 vols. New York: The States History Company, 1925.

Roth, David M. *Connecticut, a History.* New York: Norton; Nashville: American Association for State and Local History, 1985.

Trumbull, Benjamin. *A Complete History of Connecticut.* New York: Arno Press, 1972; reprint of 1818 edition.

Delaware

Conrad, Henry C. *History of the State of Delaware.* 3 vols. Wilmington: The Author, 1908.

Eckman, Jeannette, et al., eds. *Delaware: A Guide to the First State.* New and rev. ed. St. Clair Shores, Mich.: Scholarly Press, 1976; reprint of 1955 edition.

Munroe, John A. *History of Delaware.* 2d ed. Newark: University of Delaware Press, 1984.

Reed, H. C. Roy, ed. *Delaware: A History of the First State.* 3 vols. New York: Lewis Historical Publishing Company, 1947.

Scharf, John T. *History of Delaware, 1609–1888.* 2 vols. Philadelphia: L. J. Richards, 1888.

Florida

Brevard, Caroline M., and James A. Robertson. *A History of Florida from the Treaty of 1763 to Our Own Times.* 2 vols. Deland, Fla.: Florida State Historical Society, 1924–1925.

Dovell, Junius E. *Florida: Historic, Dramatic, Contemporary.* 4 vols. New York: Lewis Historical Publishing Company, 1952.

Jahoda, Gloria. *Florida, a History.* New York: Norton; Nashville: American Association for State and Local History, 1984.

Patrick, Rembert W., and Allen Morris. *Florida under Five Flags.* 4th ed. Gainesville: University of Florida Press, 1967.

Georgia

Bonner, James C., and Lucien E. Roberts. *Georgia History and Government.* Spartanburg, S.C.: Reprint Company, 1974; reprint of 1940 edition.

Coulter, E. Merton. *Georgia; A Short History.* Chapel Hill: University of North Carolina Press, 1947.

Jones, Charles C. *The History of Georgia.* 2 vols. Boston: Houghton, Mifflin, 1883.

Hawaii

Day, A. Grove. *Hawaii and Its People*. Rev. ed. New York: Meredith Press, 1968.
Kuykendall, Ralph S. *The Hawaiian Kingdom*. 3 vols. Honolulu: University of Hawaii, 1966–1968.
Kuykendall, Ralph S., and A. Grove Day. *Hawaii: A History, From Polynesian Kingdom to American State*. Rev. ed. Englewood Cliffs, N.J.: Prentice-Hall, 1961.
Tabrah, Ruth M. *Hawaii, a History*. New York: Norton; Nashville: American Association for State and Local History, 1984.

Idaho

Beal, Merrill D., and Merle W. Wells. *History of Idaho*. 3 vols. New York: Lewis Historical Publishing Company, 1959.
Hailey, John. *The History of Idaho*. Boise: Press of Syms-York Company, 1910.
Hawley, James H. *History of Idaho, The Gem of the Mountains*. 4 vols. Chicago: S. J. Clarke, 1920.
Wells, Merle W., and Arthur A. Hart. *Idaho, Gem of the Mountains*. Northridge, Calif.: Windsor Publications, 1985.

Illinois

Alvord, Clarence W., ed. *Centennial History of Illinois*. 5 vols. Chicago: A. C. McClurg, 1922, c 1918–1920.
Bridges, Roger D., and Rodney O. Davis. *Illinois, Its History and Legacy*. St. Louis: River City Publishers, 1984.
Pease, Theodore C. *The Story of Illinois*. 3d ed., rev. by Marguerite J. Pease. Chicago: University of Chicago Press, 1965.

Indiana

Barnhart, John D., and Donald Carmony. *Indiana from Frontier to Industrial Commonwealth*. 4 vols. New York: Lewis Historical Publishing Company, 1954.
Esarey, Logan. *A History of Indiana*. 2 vols. in one. Indianapolis: Hoosier Heritage Press, 1970; reprint of 1915 and 1918 editions.
Wilson, William E. *Indiana: A History*. Bloomington: Indiana University Press, 1966.

Iowa

Brigham, Johnson. *Iowa: Its History and Its Foremost Citizens*. 3 vols. Chicago: S. J. Clarke, 1915.
Cole, Cyrenus. *A History of the People of Iowa*. Cedar Rapids: Torch Press, 1921.
———. *Iowa through the Years*. Iowa City: State Historical Society of Iowa, 1940.
Gue, Benjamin T. *History of Iowa from the Earliest Times to the Beginning of the Twentieth Century*. 4 vols. New York: Century History Company, 1903.

Harlan, Edgar R. *A Narrative History of the People of Iowa.* 5 vols. Chicago: American Historical Society, 1931.
Sabin, Henry, and Edwin L. Sabin. *The Making of Iowa.* Chicago: A. Flanagan, 1916.

Kansas

Blackmar, Frank W., ed. *Kansas: A Cyclopedia of State History* . . . 3 vols. in four. Chicago: Standard Publishing Company, 1912.
Bright, John D., ed. *Kansas: The First Century.* 4 vols. New York: Lewis Publishing Company, 1956.
Connelley, William E. *History of Kansas, State and People.* 5 vols. Chicago: American Historical Society, 1928.
Davis, Kenneth S. *Kansas, a History.* New York: Norton; Nashville: American Association for State and Local History, 1984.

Kentucky

Clark, Thoms D. *A History of Kentucky.* Revised edition, 6th printing. Lexington: John Bradford Press, 1977.
Connelley, William E., and E. Merton Coulter. *History of Kentucky.* 5 vols. Chicago: American Historical Society, 1922.
Smith, Zachariah F. *History of Kentucky, From its Earliest Discovery and Settlement, to the Present Date.* Louisville: Prentice Press, 1895.
Wallis, Frederick A., and Hambleton Tapp. *A Sesqui-Centennial History of Kentucky.* 4 vols. Hopkinsville: Historical Record Association, 1945.

Louisiana

Chambers, Henry E. *A History of Louisiana, Wilderness-Colony-Province-Territory-State-People.* 3 vols. Chicago: American Historical Society, 1925.
Davis, Edwin A. *The Story of Louisiana.* 4 vols. New Orleans: Hyer, 1960–1963.
Davis, Edwin A., et al. *Louisiana, the Pelican State.* Rev. ed. Baton Rouge: Louisiana State University Press, 1985.
Fortier, Alcee. *Louisiana.* 2 vols. Atlanta: Southern Historical Association, 1933.
Gayarre, Charles. *History of Louisiana.* 4 vols. 4th ed. New Orleans: Pelican, 1965; reprint of 1903 edition.
Giraud, Marcel. *A History of French Louisiana.* Trans. Joseph C. Lambert. Baton Rouge: Louisiana State University Press, 1974– .
Taylor, Joe Gray. *Louisiana, a History.* New York: Norton; Nashville: American Association for State and Local History, 1984.
Wall, Bennett H., and Charles E. O'Neill. *Louisiana, a History.* Arlington Heights, Ill.: Forum Press, 1984.

Maine

Abbott, John S. *The History of Maine*. Boston: B. B. Russell, 1875.

Clark, Charles E. *Maine, a History*. New York: Norton; Nashville: American Association for State and Local History, 1985.

Hatch, Louis C. *Maine: A History*. 5 vols. New York: American Historical Society, 1919.

Smith, David C., and Edward O. Schriver. *Maine: A History through Selected Readings*. Dubuque: Kendall/Hunt, 1985.

Smith, Marion J. *A History of Maine from Wilderness to Statehood*. Portland: Falmouth Publishing House, 1949.

Williamson, William D. *The History of the State of Maine*. 2 vols. Freeport, Maine: Cumberland Press, 1966; reprint of 1832 edition.

Maryland

Andrews, Matthew P. *History of Maryland: Province and State*. Hatboro, Pa.: Tradition Press, 1965; reprint of 1929 edition.

Richardson, Hester D. *Side-lights on Maryland History, with Sketches of Early Maryland Families*. 2 vols. in one. Cambridge, Md.: Tidewater Publishers, 1967; reprint of 1913 edition.

Scharf, John T. *History of Maryland from the Earliest Period to the Present Day*. 3 vols. Hatboro, Pa.: Tradition Press, 1967; reprint of 1879 edition.

Walsh, Richard, and William L. Fox. *Maryland, a History*. Annapolis: Hall of Records Commission, Department of General Services, 1983.

Massachusetts

Hart, Albert B., ed., *Commonwealth History of Massachusetts*. 5 vols. New York: Russell & Russell, 1966; reprint of 1930 edition.

Marsh, Daniel L., and William H. Clark. *The Story of Massachusetts*. 4 vols. New York: American Historical Society, 1938.

Michigan

Bald, F. Clever. *Michigan in Four Centuries*. rev. and enl. ed. New York: Harper & Row, 1961.

Catton, Bruce. *Michigan, a History*. New York: Norton; Nashville: American Association for State and Local History, 1984.

Dunbar, Willis F. *Michigan, a History of the Wolverine State*. Rev. ed. by George S. May. Grand Rapids: Eerdman, 1980.

Fuller, George N. *Michigan: A Centennial History of the State and Its People... 5 vols. Chicago: Lewis Publishing Company, 1939.

Quaife, Milo M., and Sidney Glazer. *Michigan: From Primitive Wilderness to Industrial Commonwealth*. New York: Prentice-Hall, 1948.

Utley, Henry M., and Byron M. Cutcheon. *Michigan As a Province, Territory and State*. 4 vols. New York: Publishing Society of Michigan, 1906.

Minnesota

Blegen, Theodore C. *Minnesota: A History of the State*. Minneapolis: University of Minnesota Press, 1975.

Folwell, William W. *A History of Minnesota*. 4 vols. St. Paul: Minnesota Historical Society, 1921–1930.

Hubbard, Lucius F., et al. *Minnesota in Three Centuries, 1655–1908*. 4 vols. New York: Publishing Society of Minnesota, 1908.

Lass, William E. *Minnesota, a History*. New York: Norton; Nashville: American Association for State and Local History, 1983.

Mississippi

Lowry, Robert, and W. H. McCardle. *A History of Mississippi*. Spartanburg, S.C.: Reprint Company, 1978; reprint of 1891 edition.

Rowland, Dunbar. *Encyclopedia of Mississippi History*. 2 vols. Madison, Wis.: S. A. Brant, 1907.

———. *History of Mississippi, the Heart of the South*. 2 vols. Spartanburg, S.C.: Reprint Company, 1978; reprint of Chicago: S. J. Clarke, 1925.

Skates, John R. *Mississippi, a History*. New York: Norton; Nashville: American Association for State and Local History, 1985.

Missouri

Conard, Howard L. *Encyclopedia of the History of Missouri*. 6 vols. New York: Southern History Company, 1901.

Culmer, Frederic A. *A New History of Missouri*. Mexico, Mo.: McIntyre Publishing Company, 1938.

Foley, William E. *History of Missouri, Volume 1: 1673 to 1820*. (The Missouri Sesquicentennial Edition). Columbia: University of Missouri Press, 1971.

Houck, Lewis. *A History of Missouri, from the Earliest Explorations and Settlements Until the Admission of the State into the Union*. 3 vols. Chicago: R. R. Donnelley, 1908.

McCandless, Perry. *A History of Missouri, Volume 2: 1820 to 1860*. (The Missouri Sesquicentennial Edition.) Columbia: University of Missouri Press, 1972.

March, David D. *The History of Missouri*. 4 vols. New York: Lewis Historical Publishing Company, 1967.

Meyer, Duane G. *The Heritage of Missouri*. 3rd ed. St. Louis: River City Publishers, 1982.

Parrish, William E., ed. *A History of Missouri*. (The Missouri Sesquicentennial Edition). Columbia: University of Missouri Press, 1971– .

Shoemaker, Floyd C. *Missouri and Missourians: Land of Contrasts and People of Achievements*. 5 vols. Chicago: Lewis Publishing Company, 1943.

Stevens, Walter B. *Centennial History of Missouri: One Hundred Years in the Union, 1820–1921*. 5 vols. St. Louis: S. J. Clarke, 1921.

Violette, Eugene M., and Forrest Wolverton. *A History of Missouri*. Cape Girardeau: Ramfre Press, 1960; reprint of 1918 edition.

Williams, Walter, and Floyd C. Shoemaker. *Missouri, Mother of the West.* 5 vols. Chicago: American Historical Society, 1930.

Montana

Burlingame, Merrill G., and K. Ross Toole. *History of Montana.* 3 vols. New York: Lewis Historical Publishing Company, 1957.
Hamilton, James M. *History of Montana, From Wilderness to Statehood.* 2d ed. Ed. Merrill G. Burlingame. Portland, Oreg.: Binfords & Mort, 1970.
Leeson, Michael A. *History of Montana, 1739–1885.* Chicago: Warner, Beers & Company, 1885.
Raymer, Robert G. *Montana, the Land and the People.* 3 vols. Chicago: Lewis Publishing Company, 1930.
Sanders, Helen F. *A History of Montana.* 3 vols. Chicago: Lewis Publishing Company, 1913.
Stout, Tom. *Montana: Its Story and Biography.* 2 vols. Chicago: American Historical Society, 1921.
Toole, K. Ross. *Montana: An Uncommon Land.* Norman: University of Oklahoma Press, 1959.

Nebraska

History of the State of Nebraska. Chicago: Western Historical Company (A. T. Andreas, proprietor), 1882.
Morton, Julius S., et al. *Illustrated History of Nebraska.* 3 vols. Lincoln: J. North, 1905–1913.
Olson, James C. *History of Nebraska.* 2d ed. Lincoln: University of Nebraska Press, 1966.
Sheldon, Addison E. *Nebraska: The Land and the People.* 3 vols. Chicago: Lewis Publishing Company, 1931.

Nevada

Angel, Myron, ed. *History of Nevada.* New York: Arno Press, 1973; reprint of 1881 edition.
Davis, Samuel P. *The History of Nevada.* 2 vols. Las Vegas: Nevada Publications, 1984; reprint of 1913 edition.
Mack, Effie M. *Nevada: A History of the State from the Earliest Times through the Civil War.* Glendale, Calif.: Arthur H. Clark Company, 1936.

New Hampshire

Belknap, Jeremy. *The History of New Hampshire.* 3 vols. New York: Arno Press, 1972; reprint of 1791–92 edition.
Jager, Ronald, and Grace Jager. *New Hampshire, an Illustrated History of the Granite State.* Woodland Hills, Calif.: Windsor Publications, 1983.

McClintock, John N. *Colony, Province, State, 1623–1888: History of New Hampshire.* Boston: B. B. Russell, 1889.

Morison, Elizabeth F., and Elting E. Morison. *New Hampshire, a History.* New York: Norton; Nashville: American Association for State and Local History, 1985.

Pillsbury, Hobart. *New Hampshire; Resources, Attractions, and Its People; a History.* 5 vols. New York: Lewis Historical Publishing Company, 1927.

Sanborn, Edwin D. *History of New Hampshire*... Manchester, N.H.: J. B. Clarke, 1875.

Squires, James D. *The Granite State of the United States.* 4 vols. New York: American Historical Company, 1956.

Stackpole, Everett S. *History of New Hampshire.* 4 vols. New York: American Historical Society, 1916.

New Jersey

Fleming, Thomas J. *New Jersey, a History.* New York: Norton; Nashville: American Association for State and Local History, 1984.

Kull, Irving S., ed. *New Jersey, a History.* 6 vols. New York: American Historical Society, 1930–32.

Lee, Francis B. *New Jersey As a Colony and a State; One of the Original Thirteen.* 4 vols. New York: Publishing Society of New Jersey, 1902.

McCormick, Richard P. *New Jersey from Colony to State, 1609–1789.* Rev. ed. Newark: New Jersey Historical Society, 1981.

Myers, William S., ed. *The Story of New Jersey.* 5 vols. New York: Lewis Historical Publishing Company, 1945.

New Mexico

Beck, Warren A. *New Mexico; A History of Four Centuries.* Norman: University of Oklahoma Press, 1962.

Murphy, Dan. *New Mexico, the Distant Land; An Illustrated History.* Northbridge, Calif.: Windsor Publications, 1985.

Twitchell, Ralph E. *The Leading Facts of New Mexican History.* 5 vols. Cedar Rapids, Iowa: Torch Press, 1911–1917.

New York

Brodhead, John R. *History of the State of New York.* 2 vols. New York: Harper, 1853–1871.

Ellis, David M. *A History of New York State.* Ithaca, N.Y.: Cornell University Press, 1967.

Flick, Alexander C., ed. *History of the State of New York.* 10 vols. New York: Columbia University Press, 1933–1937.

North Carolina

Ashe, Samuel A. *History of North Carolina.* 2 vols. Spartanburg, S.C.: Reprint Company, 1971; reprint of 1908–1925 edition.
Henderson, Archibald. *North Carolina: The Old North State and the New.* 5 vols. Chicago: Lewis Publishing Company, 1941.
Lefler, Hugh T., and Albert R. Newsome. *North Carolina.* Rev. ed. Chapel Hill: University of North Carolina Press, 1963.
Powell, William S. *North Carolina, a History.* New York: Norton; Nashville: American Association for State and Local History, 1985.
Williamson, Hugh. *The History of North Carolina.* 2 vols. Spartanburg, S.C.: Reprint Company, 1973; reprint of 1812 edition.

North Dakota

Compendium of History and Biography of North Dakota. Chicago: George A. Ogle and Company, 1900.
Crawford, Lewis F. *History of North Dakota.* 3 vols. Chicago: American Historical Society, 1931.
Hennessy, William B. *History of North Dakota . . . Including the Biographies of the Builders of the Commonwealth.* Bismarck: Bismarck Tribune Company, 1910.
Lounsberry, Clement A. *Early History of North Dakota: Essential Outlines of American History.* Washington: Liberty Press, 1919.
Robinson, Elwyn B. *History of North Dakota.* Lincoln: University of Nebraska Press, 1966.
Schlasinger, Ethel, ed. *North Dakota: A Guide to the Northern Prairie State.* 2d ed. New York: Oxford University Press, 1950.

Ohio

Randall, E. O., and Daniel J. Ryan. *History of Ohio; the Rise and Progress of an American State.* 5 vols. New York: Century History Company, 1912.
Roseboom, Eugene H., and Francis P. Weisenburger. *A History of Ohio.* 2d ed. Columbus: Ohio Historical Society, 1984; originally published in 1967.
Wittke, Carl F., ed. *The History of the State of Ohio.* 6 vols. Columbus: printed under the auspices of the Ohio State Archaeological and Historical Society, 1941–1944.

Oklahoma

Dale, Edward E., and Morris L. Wardell. *History of Oklahoma.* New York: Prentice-Hall, 1948.
Foreman, Grant. *A History of Oklahoma.* Norman: University of Oklahoma Press, 1942.
Gibson, Arrell M. *Oklahoma, a History of Five Centuries.* 2d ed. Norman: University of Oklahoma Press, 1981.

Gibson, Arrell M., and Victor E. Harlow. *The History of Oklahoma*. New ed. Norman: University of Oklahoma Press, 1984.
Morgan, Howard W., and Anne H. Morgan. *Oklahoma, a History*. New York: Norton; Nashville: American Association for State and Local History, 1984.
Thoburn, Joseph B., and Muriel H. Wright. *Oklahoma; A History of the State and Its People*. 4 vols. New York: Lewis Historical Publishing Company, 1929.

Oregon

Bancroft, Hubert H. *History of Oregon*. 2 vols. New York: Arno, 1967; reprint of 1886 edition.
Carey, Charles H. *A General History of Oregon Prior to 1861*. 2 vols. Portland: Metropolitan Press, 1935.
———. *History of Oregon*. Chicago: Pioneer Historical Publishing Company, 1922.
Lyman, Horace S. *History of Oregon: The Growth of an American State*. 4 vols. New York: North Pacific Publishing Society, 1903.
Scott, Harvey W. *History of the Oregon Country*. Comp. Leslie M. Scott. 6 vols. Cambridge: Riverside Press, 1924.

Pennsylvania

Donehoo, George P., ed. *Pennsylvania, a History*. 7 vols. New York: Lewis Historical Publishing Company, 1926.
Dunaway, Wayland F. *A History of Pennsylvania*. 2d ed. New York: Prentice-Hall, 1961.
Jenkins, Howard M. *Pennsylvania, Colonial and Federal; A History, 1608–1903*. 3 vols. Philadelphia: Pennsylvania Historical Publishing Association, 1903.
Stevens, Sylvester K. *Pennsylvania, Birthplace of a Nation*. New York: Random House, 1964.
———. *Pennsylvania: Keystone State*. 2 vols. New York: American Historical Company, 1956.

Rhode Island

Arnold, Samuel G. *History of the State of Rhode Island and Providence Plantations*. 2 vols. New York: Appleton, 1859–60.
Bicknell, Thomas W. *The History of the State of Rhode Island and Providence Plantations* 5 vols. New York: American Historical Society, 1920.
Carroll, Charles. *Rhode Island: Three Centuries of Democracy*. 4 vols. New York: Lewis Historical Publishing Company, 1932.
Field, Edward. *State of Rhode Island and Providence Plantations and the End of the Century: A History*. 3 vols. Boston: Mason, 1902.
McLoughlin, William G. *Rhode Island, a History*. New York: Norton; Nashville: American Association for State and Local History, 1985.
Tanner, Earl C. *Rhode Island: A Brief History*. Providence: Rhode Island State Board of Education, 1954.

South Carolina

Lander, Ernest M. *A History of South Carolina, 1865–1960.* 2d ed. Columbia: University of South Carolina Press, 1970.

McCrady, Edward. *The History of South Carolina.* 4 vols. New York: Paladin Press, 1969; reprint of 1897–1902 editions.

Wallace, David D. *South Carolina, a Short History, 1520–1948.* Columbia: University of South Carolina Press, 1966; reprint of 1951 edition.

South Dakota

Robinson, Doane. *History of South Dakota.* 2 vols. Logansport, Ind.: B. F. Bowen, 1904.

Schell, Herbert S. *History of South Dakota.* 3d ed., rev. Lincoln: University of Nebraska Press, 1975.

Smith, George M. *South Dakota: Its History and Its People.* 5 vols. Chicago: S. J. Clarke, 1914.

Tennessee

Dykeman, Wilma. *Tennessee, a History.* New York: Norton; Nashville: American Association for State and Local History, 1984.

Folmsbee, Stanley J., et al. *History of Tennessee.* 4 vols. New York: Lewis Publishing Company, 1960.

Hale, William T., and Dixon L. Merritt. *History of Tennessee and Tennesseans.* 8 vols. Chicago: Lewis Publishing Company, 1913.

Hamer, Philip M., ed. *Tennessee: A History, 1673–1932.* 4 vols. New York: American Historical Society, 1933.

Moore, John T., and A. P. Foster. *Tennessee: The Volunteer State, 1769–1923.* 5 vols. Chicago: S. J. Clarke, 1923.

Texas

Frantz, Joe B. *Texas, A History.* New York: Norton; Nashville: American Association for State and Local History, 1984.

Johnson, Francis W. *A History of Texas and Texans.* 5 vols. Chicago: American Historical Society, 1916.

Richardson, Rupert N., et al. *Texas: The Lone Star State.* 4th ed. Englewood Cliffs, N.J.: Prentice-Hall, 1981.

Webb, Walter P., et al., eds. *The Handbook of Texas.* 3 vols. Austin: Texas State Historical Association, 1952–1976.

Wooten, Dudley G., ed. *A Comprehensive History of Texas, 1685–1897.* 2 vols. Dallas: W. G. Scarff, 1898.

Utah

Alter, J. Cecil. *Utah, the Storied Domain.* 3 vols. Chicago: American Historical Society, 1932.

Hunter, Milton R. *Utah: The Story of Her People, 1540–1947; A Centennial History of Utah*. Salt Lake City: Deseret News Press, 1946.

Neff, Andrew L. *History of Utah, 1847 to 1869*. Ed. and annot. Leland H. Creer. Salt Lake City: Deseret News Press, 1940.

Peterson, Charles S. *Utah, a History*. New York: Norton; Nashville: American Association for State and Local History, 1984.

Warrum, Noble, ed. *Utah Since Statehood, Historical and Biographical*. 4 vols. Chicago: S. J. Clarke, 1919.

Whitney, Orson F. *History of Utah* . . . 4 vols. Salt Lake City: Cannon, 1892–1904.

Vermont

Crockett, Walter H. *Vermont, the Green Mountain State*. 4 vols. New York: Century History Company, 1921.

Hall, Hiland. *The History of Vermont, From Its Discovery to Its Admission into the Union in 1791*. Albany, N.Y.: Munsell, 1868.

Morissey, Charles T. *Vermont, a History*. New York: Norton; Nashville: American Association for State and Local History, 1984.

Newton, Earle W. *The Vermont Story: A History of the People of the Green Mountain State*. Montpelier: Vermont Historical Society, 1983– .

Virginia

Beverley, Robert. *The History and Present State of Virginia*. Ed. Louis B. Wright. Published for the Institute of Early American History and Culture at Williamsburg, Va. Chapel Hill: University of North Carolina Press, 1947.

Rubin, Louis D. *Virginia, a History*. New York: Norton; Nashville: American Association for State and Local History, 1984.

Washington

Avery, Mary W. *Washington: A History of the Evergreen State*. Seattle: University of Washington Press, 1965.

Barto, Harold E., and Catharine Bullard. *History of the State of Washington*. 2d ed. Boston: Heath, 1953.

Beckett, Paul L. *From Wilderness to Enabling Act: Evolution of the State of Washington*. Pullman: Washington State University Press, 1968.

Meany, Edmond S. *History of the State of Washington*. New York: Macmillan, 1924.

Pollard, Lancaster. *A History of the State of Washington*. New ed., rev. 1951. Portland, Oreg.: Binfords & Mort, 1954.

Snowden, Clinton A. *History of Washington; the Rise and Progress of an American State*. 4 vols. New York: Century History Company, 1909.

West Virginia

Ambler, Charles H., and Festus P. Summers. *West Virginia, the Mountain State*. 2d ed. Englewood Cliffs, N.J.: Prentice-Hall, 1958.

Callahan, James M. *History of West Virginia, Old and New.* 3 vols. Chicago: American Historical Society, 1923.
Conley, Philip, and Boyd B. Stutler. *West Virginia, Yesterday and Today.* 4th ed., Rev. and rewritten. Charleston, W.V.: Education Foundation, 1966.
Miller, Thomas C., and Hu Maxwell. *West Virginia and Its People.* 3 vols. New York: Lewis Historical Publishing Company, 1913.
Myers, Sylvester. *Myer's History of West Virginia.* 2 vols. Wheeling: The Wheeling News Lithograph Company, 1915.
Rice, Otis K. *West Virginia, a History.* Lexington: University of Kentucky, 1985.
Shawkey, Morris P. *West Virginia in History, Life, Literature and Industry.* 5 vols. Chicago: Lewis Publishing Company, 1928.
Williams, John A. *West Virginia, a History.* New York: Norton; Nashville: American Association for State and Local History, 1984.

Wisconsin

Austin, H. Russell. *The Wisconsin Story: The Building of a Vanguard State.* 3d ed. Milwaukee: Milwaukee Journal, 1964.
Campbell, Henry C., ed. *Wisconsin in Three Centuries, 1634–1905.* 4 vols. New York: Century History Company, 1906.
Gara, Larry. *A Short History of Wisconsin.* Madison: State Historical Society of Wisconsin, 1962.
Raney, William F. *Wisconsin, a Story of Progress.* Appleton: Perin Press, 1963.

Wyoming

Bartlett, Ichabod S. *History of Wyoming.* 3 vols. Chicago: S. J. Clarke, 1918.
Beard, Frances B., ed. *Wyoming from Territorial Days to the Present.* 3 vols. Chicago: American Historical Society, 1933.
Coutant, Charles G. *History of Wyoming and the Far West.* Published for University Microfilms. New York: Argonaut Press, 1966; reprint of 1899 edition.
Larson, Taft A. *History of Wyoming.* Lincoln: University of Nebraska Press, 1965.
———. *Wyoming, a History.* New York: Norton; Nashville: American Association for State and Local History, 1984.

Index

Rosa blanda, 123
Rosa sinica, 117–18
Rose, 123
Rose bay, 126
Rose quartz, 200
Rosemary pine, 130
Round House, 105
Roxbury puddingstone, 195
Rudbeckia hirta, 120
Ruffed grouse, 169–70
Russian America, 2

Sabal palmetto palm, 133
Saber-toothed cat, 190
Sacramento, California, 95
Saffold, W. B., 22
Sage State (Nevada), 11
Sagebrush, 122
Saguaro, 116
St. Charles, Missouri, 102
St. Louis, Missouri, 102
St. Paul, Minnesota, 102
St. Paul's Cathedral, 94
Salad-tree, 142
Salem, Oregon, 107
Salmo aqua-bonita, 190
Salmo clarki, 196–97
Salmo gairdnerii, 201
Salmo salar sebago, 194
Salt Lake City, Utah, 110
Salt Lake State (Utah), 16
"Salus populi suprema lex esto" (Motto), 27
Salvelinus fontinalis, 197, 199
Samson, Deborah, 195
San Francisco, Fray Jacinto de, 12
San Jose, California, 95
Sandwich Islands, 5
Santa Fe, New Mexico, 105
Sapphire, 196
Sarpi, Pietro, 24
Scarlet carnation, 123
Scarlet maple, 143–44
Schaum, John W., 180
Scissor-tailed flycatcher, 168–69
Sciurus carolinensis, 198
Scotch bonnet, 198
Scott, Peter, 158

"Scuto bonae voluntatis tuae coronasti nos" (Motto), 25
Sea cow, 192
Sea gull, 172–73
Seals, 35–64
Sego lilly, 125
Sequoia sempervirens (D. Don) Endl., 131
Sequoiadendron giganteum (Lindl.) Buchholz., 131
Serpentine, 191
Seward, William, 2
Seward's Folly (Alaska), 2
Seward's Ice Box (Alaska), 2
The Shag, 199
Shakespeare in Central Park of Louisville (Shakespeare festival), 193
Shannon, J. R., 181
Shark tooth, 192
Shipman, Herbert, 158
Shoe-peg maple, 143–44
Show Me State (Missouri), 10
"Si quaeris peninsulam amoenam circumspice" (Motto), 26
Sialia arctica, 158–59
Sialia currocoides, 158–59, 166
Sialia sialis, 164–65, 167
"Sic Semper Tyrannis" (Motto), 30
Sierra brownbark pine, 139
Sierra Nevada Mountains, 11
Sierra redwood, 131
Sillimanite, 191
Silver, 197
Silver birch, 139–40
Silver spruce, 130, 132
Silver State (Nevada), 11
Silverwood, F. B., 178
Single spruce, 144
Singleleaf pinyon pine, 139
Sioux State (North Dakota), 13
Sitka spruce, 130
Skunk spruce, 144
Smallest State (Rhode Island), 14
Smilodon californicus, 190
Smith, Roy Lamont, 184
Smith, Walter, P., 182
Snow, Roger Vinton, 180
Soft elm, 137

About the Authors

BENJAMIN F. SHEARER is Dean of Student Services, Spring Hill College, Mobile, Alabama. His earlier books include *Communications and Society: A Bibliography on Communications Technologies and Their Social Impact* (compiled with Marilyn Huxford, Greenwood Press, 1984), *Periodical Literature on United States Cities: A Bibliography and Subject Guide* (compiled with Barbara S. Shearer, Greenwood Press, 1983), and *Finding the Source: A Thesaurus-Index to the Reference Collection* (compiled with Barbara S. Shearer, Greenwood Press, 1981).

BARBARA S. SHEARER is Online Services Coordinator and Assistant Professor of Information Science at the University of South Alabama College of Medicine. Her earlier books include *Finding the Source of Medical Information: A Thesaurus-Index to the Reference Collection* (compiled with Geneva L. Bush, Greenwood Press, 1985), *Periodical Literature on United States Cities: a Bibliography and Subject Guide* (compiled with Benjamin F. Shearer, Greenwood Press, 1983), and *Finding the Source: A Thesaurus-Index to the Reference Collection* (compiled with Benjamin F. Shearer, Greenwood Press, 1981).